JOHN CARPENTER'S

TALES FOR A

HALLOWEENIGHT

VOL
1

STORM KING
PRODUCTIONS

JOHN CARPENTER'S
TALES FOR A HALLOWEENIGHT
VOLUME ONE
AN ANTHOLOGY

THE GROUNDSCREEPER (interstitials)
Character created by STEVE NILES & STEVEN HOVEKE   Written by STEVEN HOVEKE
Art by JON BOGDANOVE   Colors by RAY DILLON   Lettering by JOHN J. HILL

THE GHOST MAKER
Written by JOHN CARPENTER   Art by FEDERICO DE LUCA

AT SEA
Written by TRENT OLSEN   Art by TONE RODRIGUEZ
Colors by SIAN MANDRAKE

BUNNY DIDN'T TELL US
Written by DAVID J. SCHOW   Pencils by DARICK ROBERTSON
Inks by RICHARD P. CLARK   Colors by DIEGO RODRIGUEZ

SOME GRUB
Written by JAMES NINNESS   Art by BRETT SIMMONS
Colors and lettering by BEN GLIBERT

NOTICE TO QUIT
Written by DUANE SWIERCZYNSKI   Art by RICHARD P. CLARK

A breeze whistles softly through the immense iron gates that guard the entrance to the old cemetery. The nearly cloudless sky loses her grip on the sun as it slips below the horizon once again. Another night begins at the old place.

All the old places.

A shadowy figure moves among the stones. He moves with smooth purpose, although it appears that even just walking seems to be real work for him. His short, thick legs carry the weight, but they lend a strange gait with a marked check in his step.

Someone once said, 'The journey of a thousand miles begins with a single step', he thinks to himself, 'or something like that.'

The man approaches a large toolshed, produces a small ring of keys and unlocks the door. Swinging the doors wide, he enters.

Then out of the darkness, the roar of a small engine belches forth. Seconds later an aged John Deere tractor bursts out into the twilight, pulling a trailer filled with the tools of the keeper's trade behind it. The driver grins wildly as he exits the shed and heads out in to field of markers. He's been on this journey so long, he thinks, he prefers to drive!

He travels past row upon row of grave markers in this immense old site.

Hello there. WELCOME!

What's that? Oh, well, I keep an eye on the cemetery. All of the cemeteries, as a matter of fact. All of them ever, truth be told.

I look after these folks once they've moved on, and in trade, they give me their stories.

He pulls up to a row of stones, and stops in front of one particularly fancy headstone.

Oh, you say ya' like stories, eh? Scary stories? I suppose I got time to pass along a couple a' stories, I guess.

He gestures towards the elaborate marker in front of him.

Take this gentleman for example. He found himself caught up in a philosophical discussion 'bout life an' death. Now, in my experience, that usually doesn't end well...for somebody involved. Especially if that discussion is with...

THE GHOST MAKER

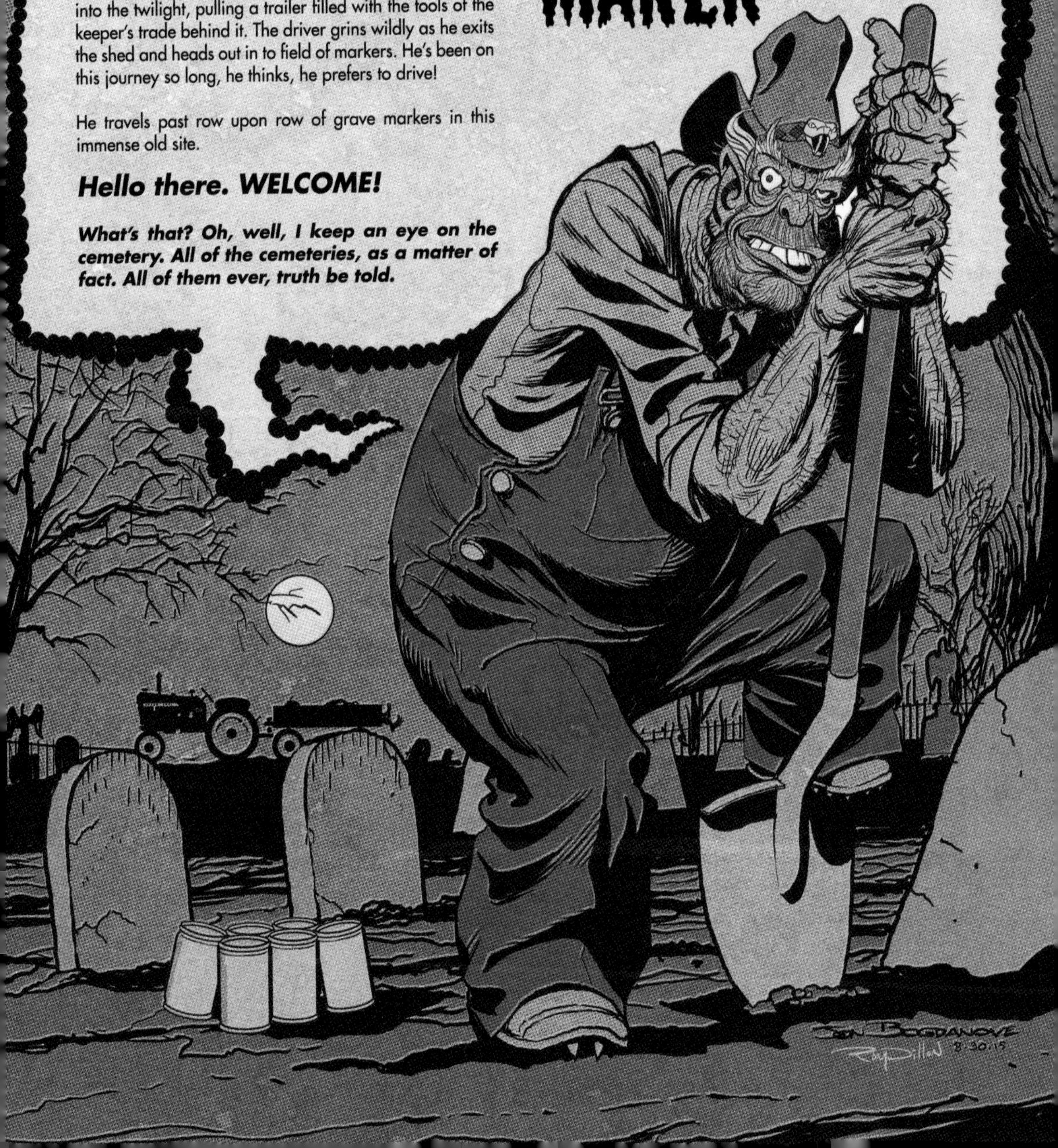

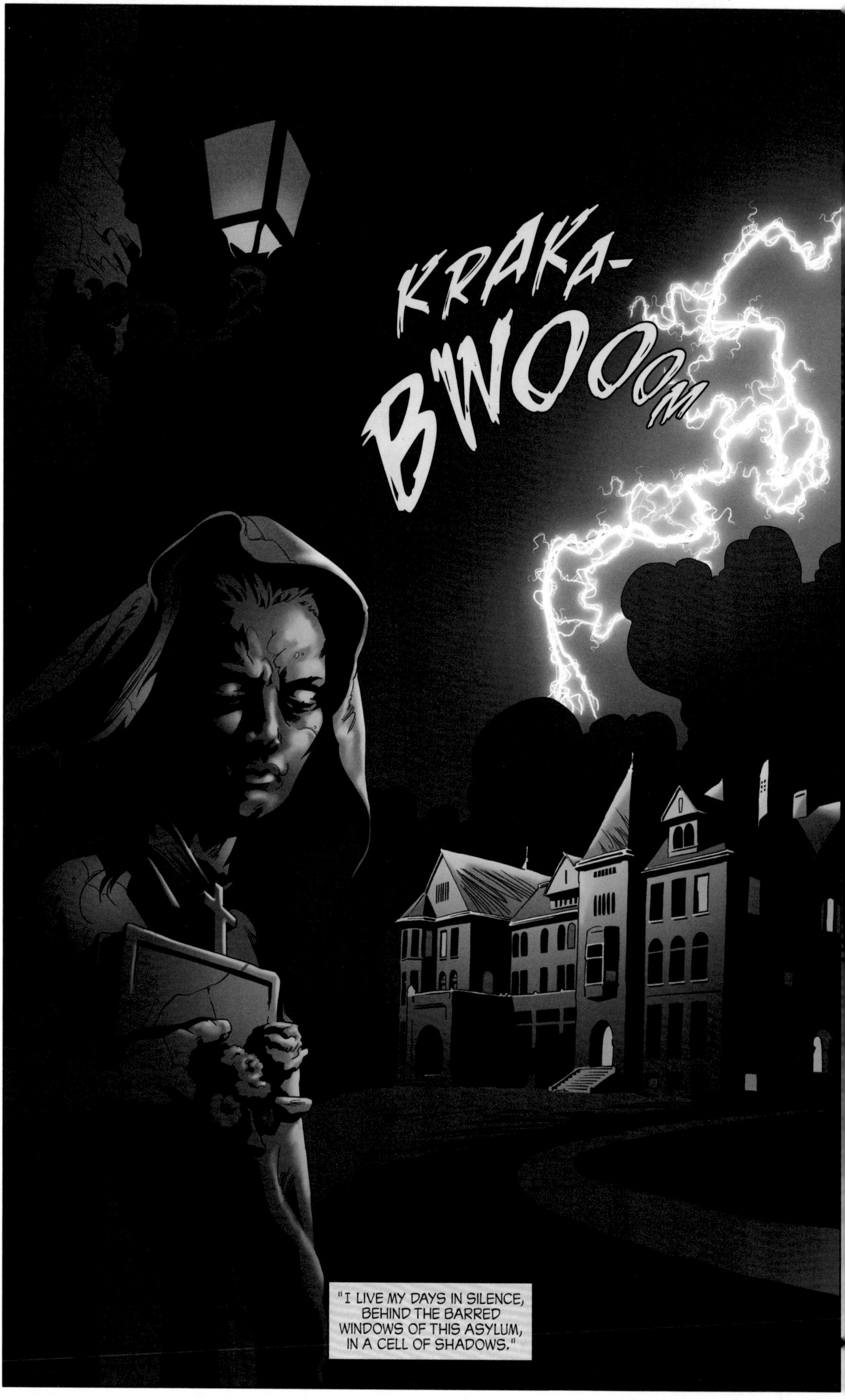
KRAKA-
B'WOOOM
"I LIVE MY DAYS IN SILENCE, BEHIND THE BARRED WINDOWS OF THIS ASYLUM, IN A CELL OF SHADOWS."

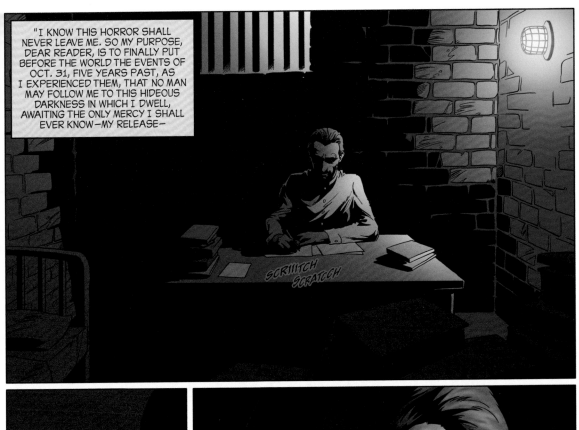

"I KNOW THIS HORROR SHALL NEVER LEAVE ME. SO MY PURPOSE, DEAR READER, IS TO FINALLY PUT BEFORE THE WORLD THE EVENTS OF OCT. 31, FIVE YEARS PAST, AS I EXPERIENCED THEM, THAT NO MAN MAY FOLLOW ME TO THIS HIDEOUS DARKNESS IN WHICH I DWELL, AWAITING THE ONLY MERCY I SHALL EVER KNOW—MY RELEASE—

SCRIIITCH SCRATCCH

"—THE MOMENT OF DEATH."

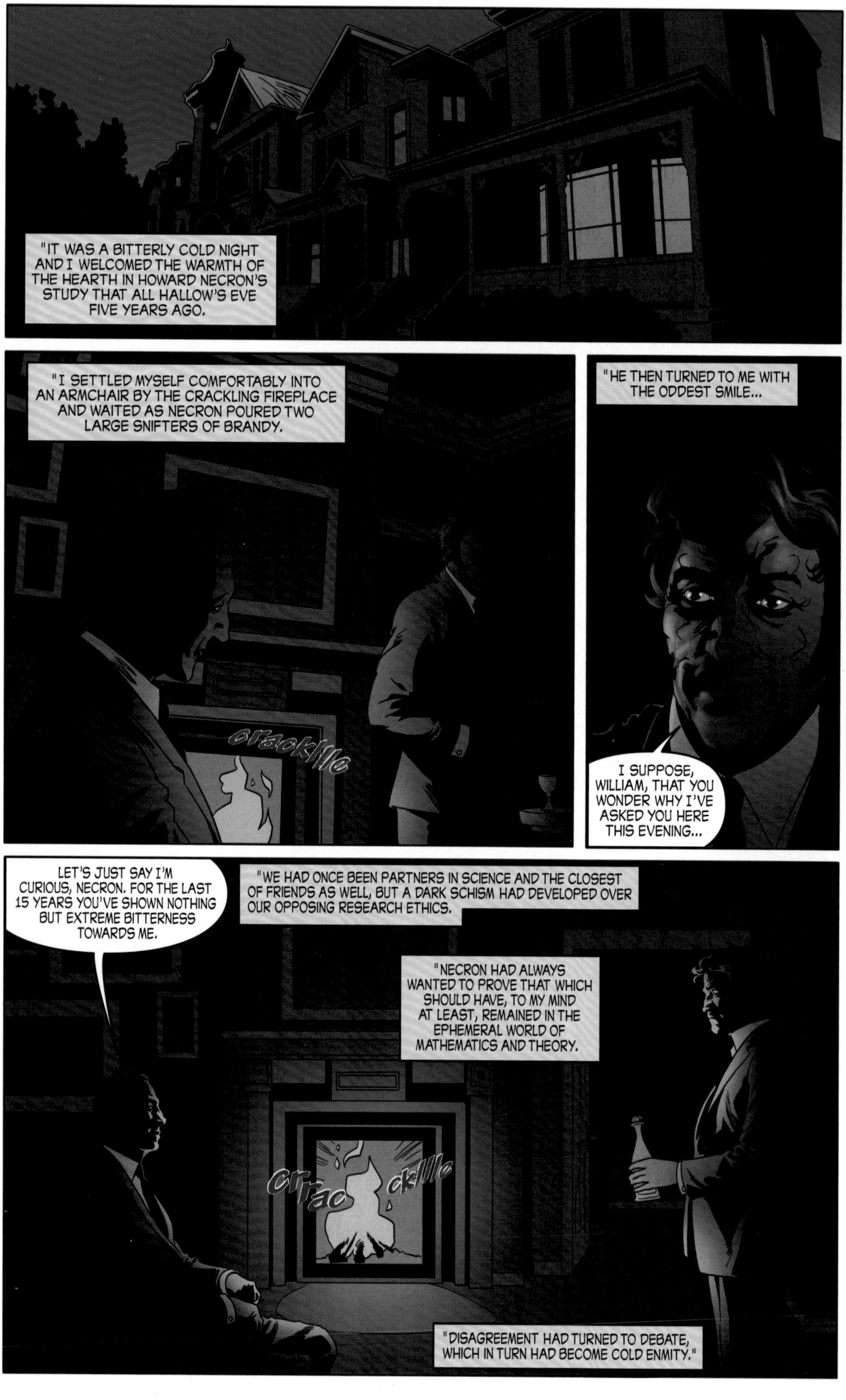
"IT WAS A BITTERLY COLD NIGHT AND I WELCOMED THE WARMTH OF THE HEARTH IN HOWARD NECRON'S STUDY THAT ALL HALLOW'S EVE FIVE YEARS AGO.
"I SETTLED MYSELF COMFORTABLY INTO AN ARMCHAIR BY THE CRACKLING FIREPLACE AND WAITED AS NECRON POURED TWO LARGE SNIFTERS OF BRANDY.
crackllle
"HE THEN TURNED TO ME WITH THE ODDEST SMILE...
I SUPPOSE, WILLIAM, THAT YOU WONDER WHY I'VE ASKED YOU HERE THIS EVENING...
LET'S JUST SAY I'M CURIOUS, NECRON. FOR THE LAST 15 YEARS YOU'VE SHOWN NOTHING BUT EXTREME BITTERNESS TOWARDS ME.
"WE HAD ONCE BEEN PARTNERS IN SCIENCE AND THE CLOSEST OF FRIENDS AS WELL, BUT A DARK SCHISM HAD DEVELOPED OVER OUR OPPOSING RESEARCH ETHICS.
"NECRON HAD ALWAYS WANTED TO PROVE THAT WHICH SHOULD HAVE, TO MY MIND AT LEAST, REMAINED IN THE EPHEMERAL WORLD OF MATHEMATICS AND THEORY.
crrrac ckllle
"DISAGREEMENT HAD TURNED TO DEBATE, WHICH IN TURN HAD BECOME COLD ENMITY."

WHAT WOULD YOU SAY, WILLIAM, IF I TOLD YOU THAT USING UNIVERSALLY ACCEPTED SCIENTIFIC PRINCIPLES, I COULD CREATE A GHOST?

I WOULD SAY, NECRON, THAT YOU WERE AS MAD AS A MARCH HARE.

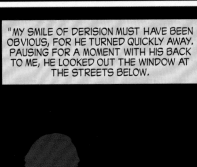

"MY SMILE OF DERISION MUST HAVE BEEN OBVIOUS, FOR HE TURNED QUICKLY AWAY. PAUSING FOR A MOMENT WITH HIS BACK TO ME, HE LOOKED OUT THE WINDOW AT THE STREETS BELOW.

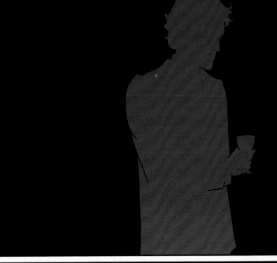

AH, WELL, THEN... SOME THINGS NEVER CHANGE, EH?

"AND THEN HE SLOWLY, ALMOST RESIGNEDLY, CROSSED THE STUDY TO HAND ME THE BRANDY SNIFTER."

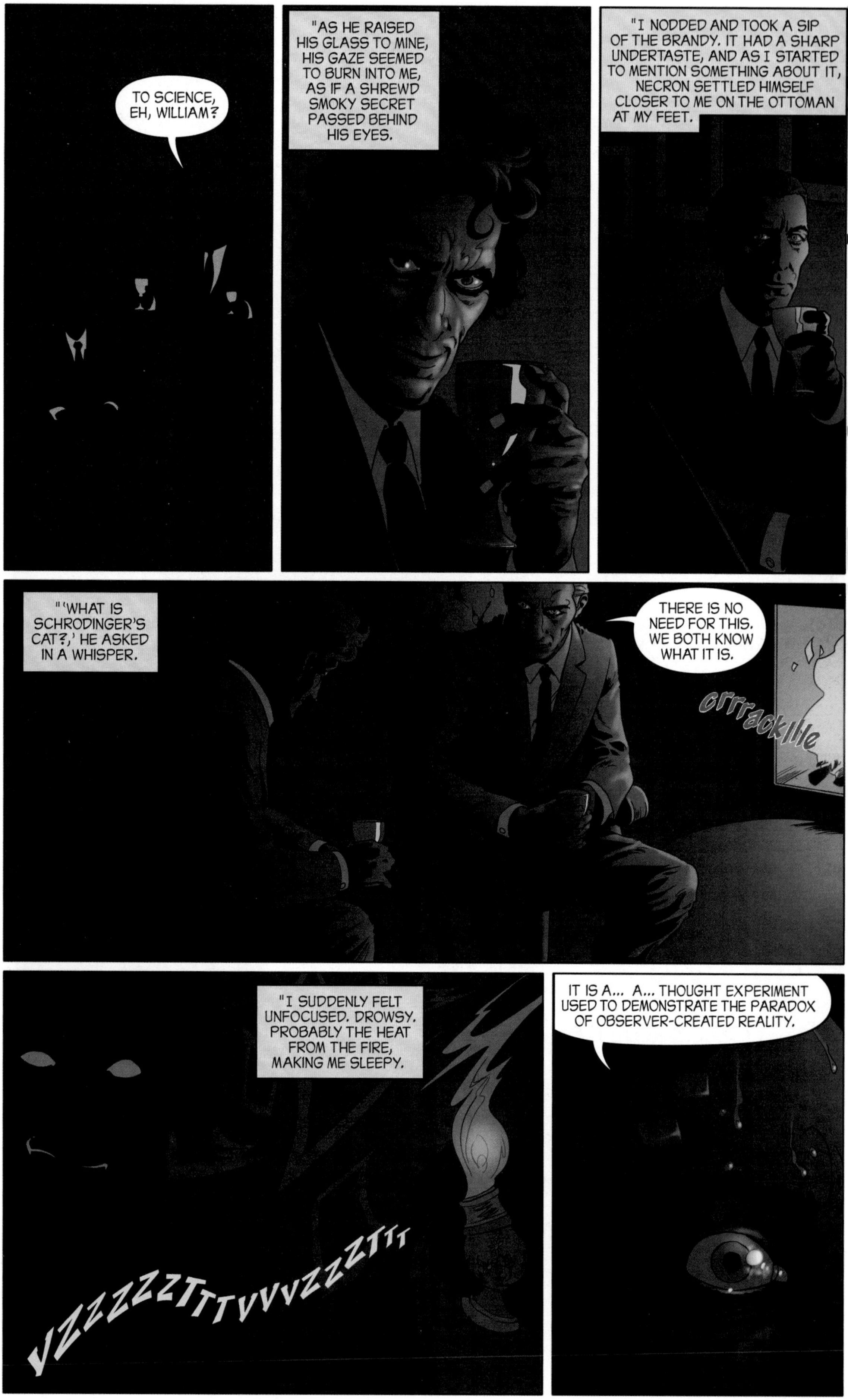
TO SCIENCE, EH, WILLIAM?
"AS HE RAISED HIS GLASS TO MINE, HIS GAZE SEEMED TO BURN INTO ME, AS IF A SHREWD SMOKY SECRET PASSED BEHIND HIS EYES.
"I NODDED AND TOOK A SIP OF THE BRANDY. IT HAD A SHARP UNDERTASTE, AND AS I STARTED TO MENTION SOMETHING ABOUT IT, NECRON SETTLED HIMSELF CLOSER TO ME ON THE OTTOMAN AT MY FEET.
"'WHAT IS SCHRODINGER'S CAT?,' HE ASKED IN A WHISPER.
THERE IS NO NEED FOR THIS. WE BOTH KNOW WHAT IT IS.
CRRRACKLLLE
"I SUDDENLY FELT UNFOCUSED. DROWSY. PROBABLY THE HEAT FROM THE FIRE, MAKING ME SLEEPY.
VZZZZZZTTTTVVVVZZZZTTT
IT IS A... A... THOUGHT EXPERIMENT USED TO DEMONSTRATE THE PARADOX OF OBSERVER-CREATED REALITY.

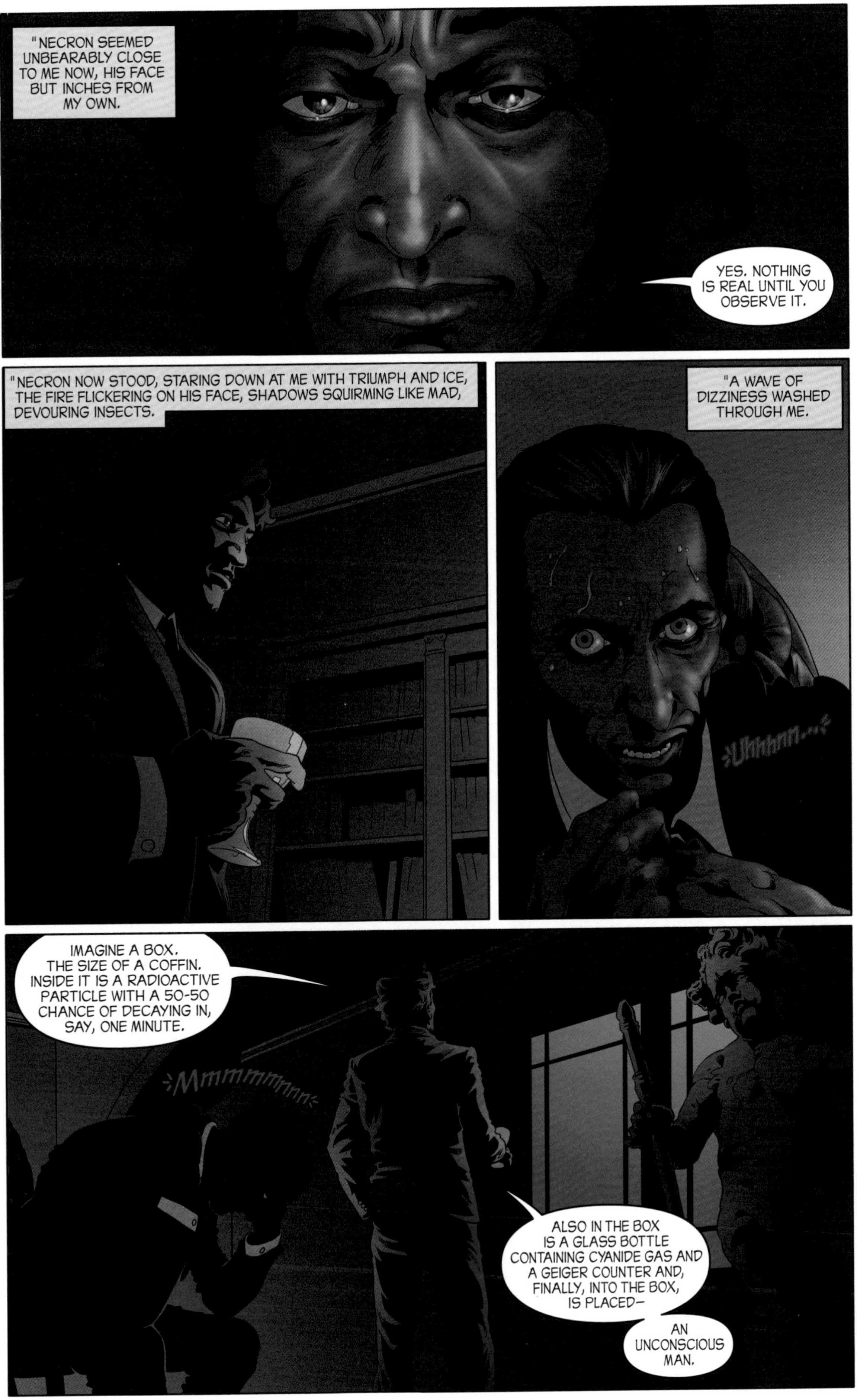

"NECRON SEEMED UNBEARABLY CLOSE TO ME NOW, HIS FACE BUT INCHES FROM MY OWN.
YES. NOTHING IS REAL UNTIL YOU OBSERVE IT.
"NECRON NOW STOOD, STARING DOWN AT ME WITH TRIUMPH AND ICE, THE FIRE FLICKERING ON HIS FACE, SHADOWS SQUIRMING LIKE MAD, DEVOURING INSECTS.
"A WAVE OF DIZZINESS WASHED THROUGH ME.
Uhhhnn...
IMAGINE A BOX. THE SIZE OF A COFFIN. INSIDE IT IS A RADIOACTIVE PARTICLE WITH A 50-50 CHANCE OF DECAYING IN, SAY, ONE MINUTE.
Mmmmmnnn
ALSO IN THE BOX IS A GLASS BOTTLE CONTAINING CYANIDE GAS AND A GEIGER COUNTER AND, FINALLY, INTO THE BOX, IS PLACED—
AN UNCONSCIOUS MAN.

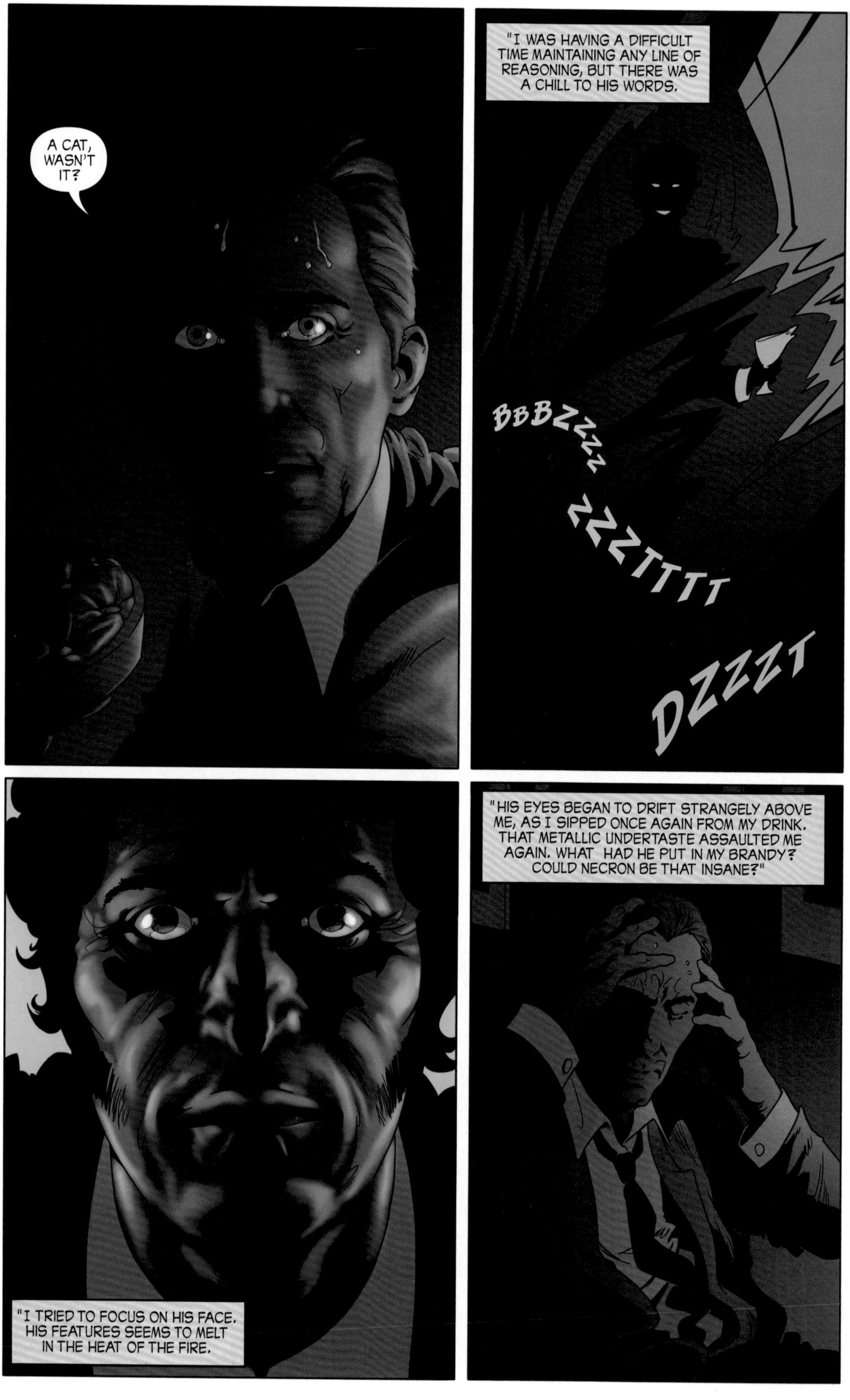

A CAT, WASN'T IT?
"I WAS HAVING A DIFFICULT TIME MAINTAINING ANY LINE OF REASONING, BUT THERE WAS A CHILL TO HIS WORDS.
BBBZzzz
ZZZTTTTT
DZZZT
"I TRIED TO FOCUS ON HIS FACE. HIS FEATURES SEEMS TO MELT IN THE HEAT OF THE FIRE.
"HIS EYES BEGAN TO DRIFT STRANGELY ABOVE ME, AS I SIPPED ONCE AGAIN FROM MY DRINK. THAT METALLIC UNDERTASTE ASSAULTED ME AGAIN. WHAT HAD HE PUT IN MY BRANDY? COULD NECRON BE THAT INSANE?"

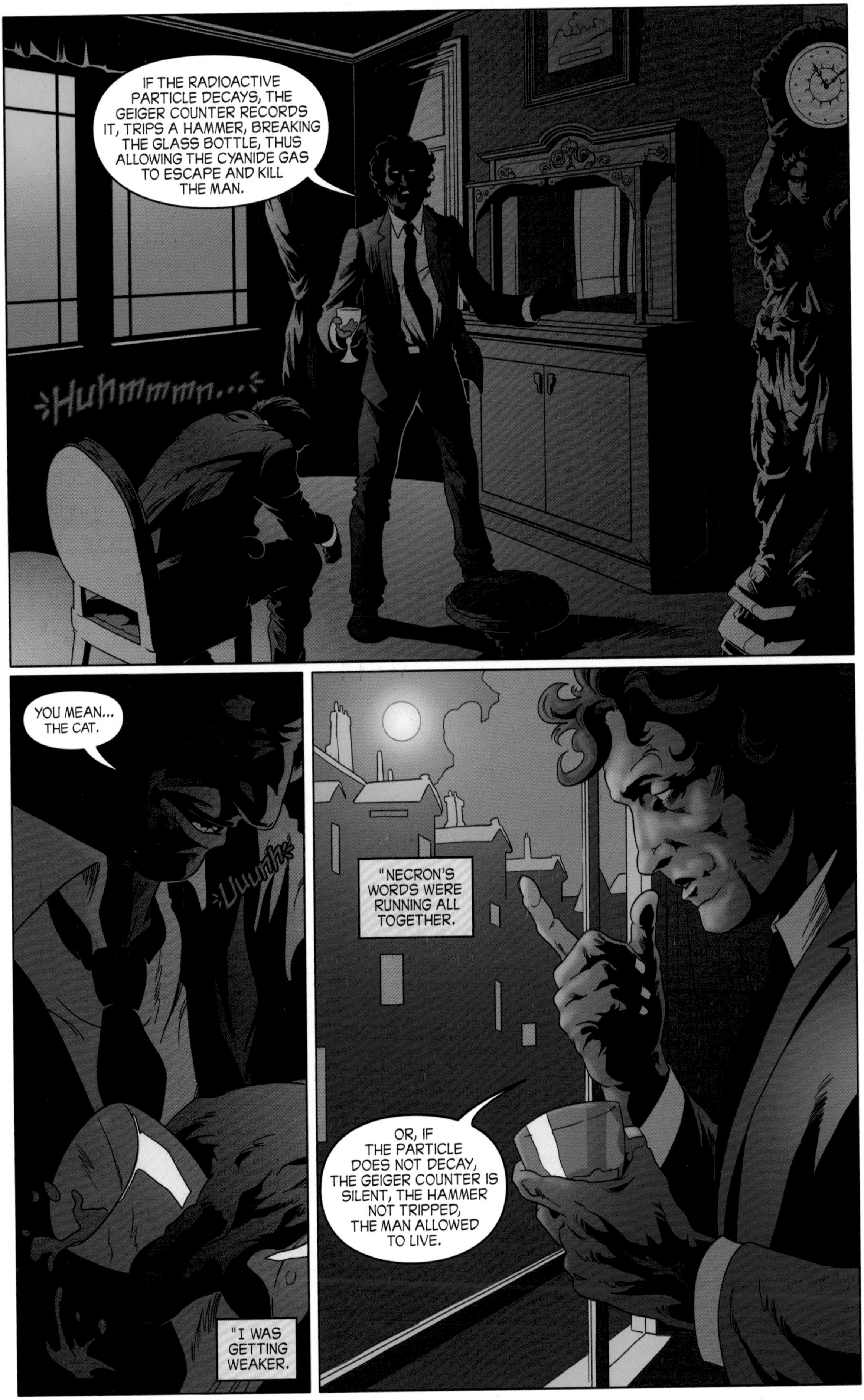
IF THE RADIOACTIVE PARTICLE DECAYS, THE GEIGER COUNTER RECORDS IT, TRIPS A HAMMER, BREAKING THE GLASS BOTTLE, THUS ALLOWING THE CYANIDE GAS TO ESCAPE AND KILL THE MAN.
Huhmmmn...
YOU MEAN... THE CAT.
Uuunh
"I WAS GETTING WEAKER.
"NECRON'S WORDS WERE RUNNING ALL TOGETHER.
OR, IF THE PARTICLE DOES NOT DECAY, THE GEIGER COUNTER IS SILENT, THE HAMMER NOT TRIPPED, THE MAN ALLOWED TO LIVE.

"THE ROOM WAS SPINNING LIKE A CHILD'S MUSIC BOX.

BZZZZZZAAAZZZZTTTTBZZZTTZZZZ

"THE HEAT FROM THE FIREPLACE...

CRACKLE

"NECRON LOOMING ABOVE ME...

"MY EYES BOBBED OPEN, CLOSED.

WHAT DID YOU PUT... IN MY DRINK?

"BUT NECRON IGNORED MY SLURRED QUESTION."

Hsssssh...

CRAKKK

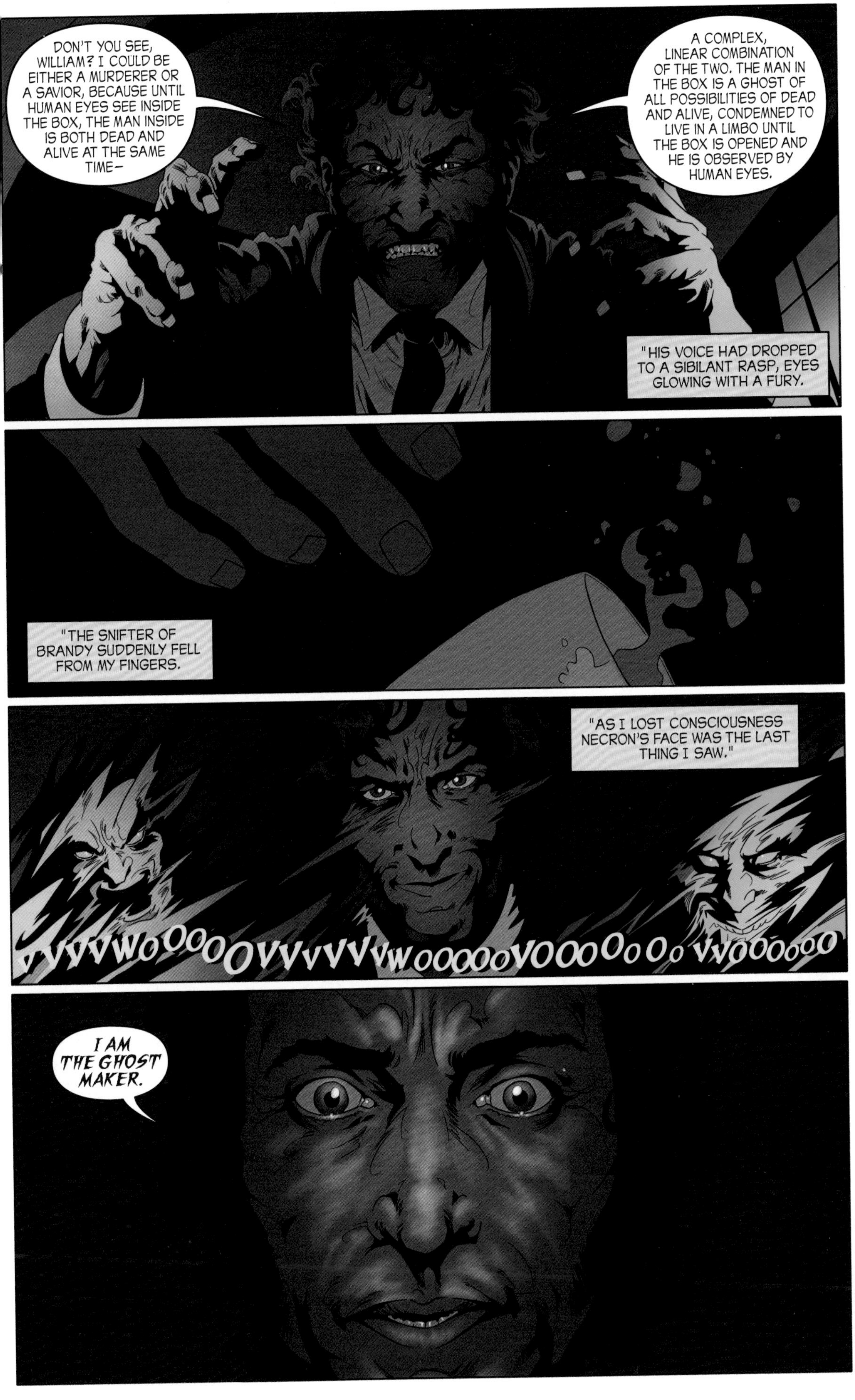

DON'T YOU SEE, WILLIAM? I COULD BE EITHER A MURDERER OR A SAVIOR, BECAUSE UNTIL HUMAN EYES SEE INSIDE THE BOX, THE MAN INSIDE IS BOTH DEAD AND ALIVE AT THE SAME TIME–
A COMPLEX, LINEAR COMBINATION OF THE TWO. THE MAN IN THE BOX IS A GHOST OF ALL POSSIBILITIES OF DEAD AND ALIVE, CONDEMNED TO LIVE IN A LIMBO UNTIL THE BOX IS OPENED AND HE IS OBSERVED BY HUMAN EYES.
"HIS VOICE HAD DROPPED TO A SIBILANT RASP, EYES GLOWING WITH A FURY.
"THE SNIFTER OF BRANDY SUDDENLY FELL FROM MY FINGERS.
"AS I LOST CONSCIOUSNESS NECRON'S FACE WAS THE LAST THING I SAW."
VVVVWOOOOOVVVVVVVWOOOOOVOOOOOOO VVOOOOOOO
I AM THE GHOST MAKER.

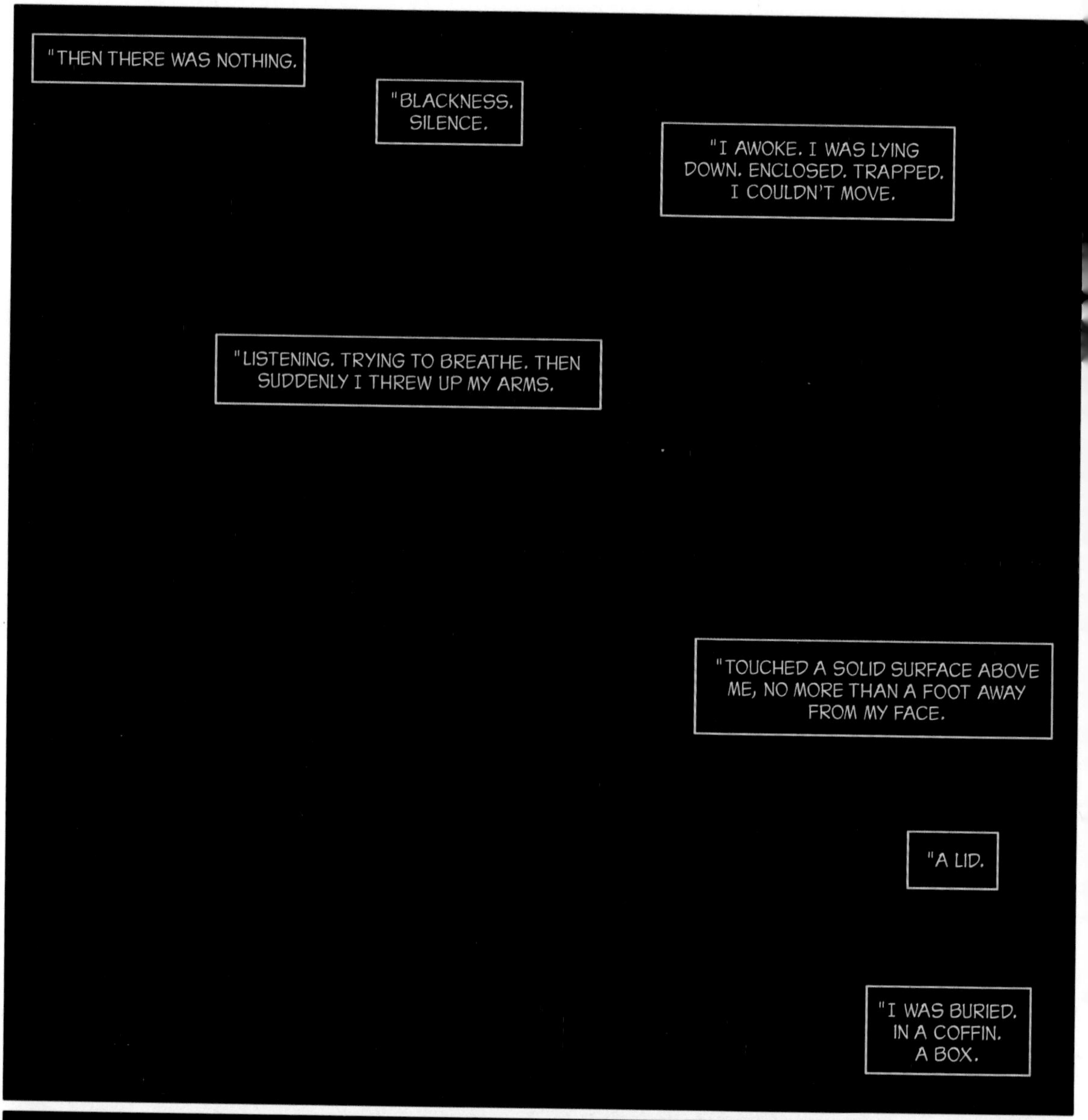
"THEN THERE WAS NOTHING.
"BLACKNESS. SILENCE.
"I AWOKE. I WAS LYING DOWN. ENCLOSED. TRAPPED. I COULDN'T MOVE.
"LISTENING. TRYING TO BREATHE. THEN SUDDENLY I THREW UP MY ARMS.
"TOUCHED A SOLID SURFACE ABOVE ME, NO MORE THAN A FOOT AWAY FROM MY FACE.
"A LID.
"I WAS BURIED. IN A COFFIN. A BOX.

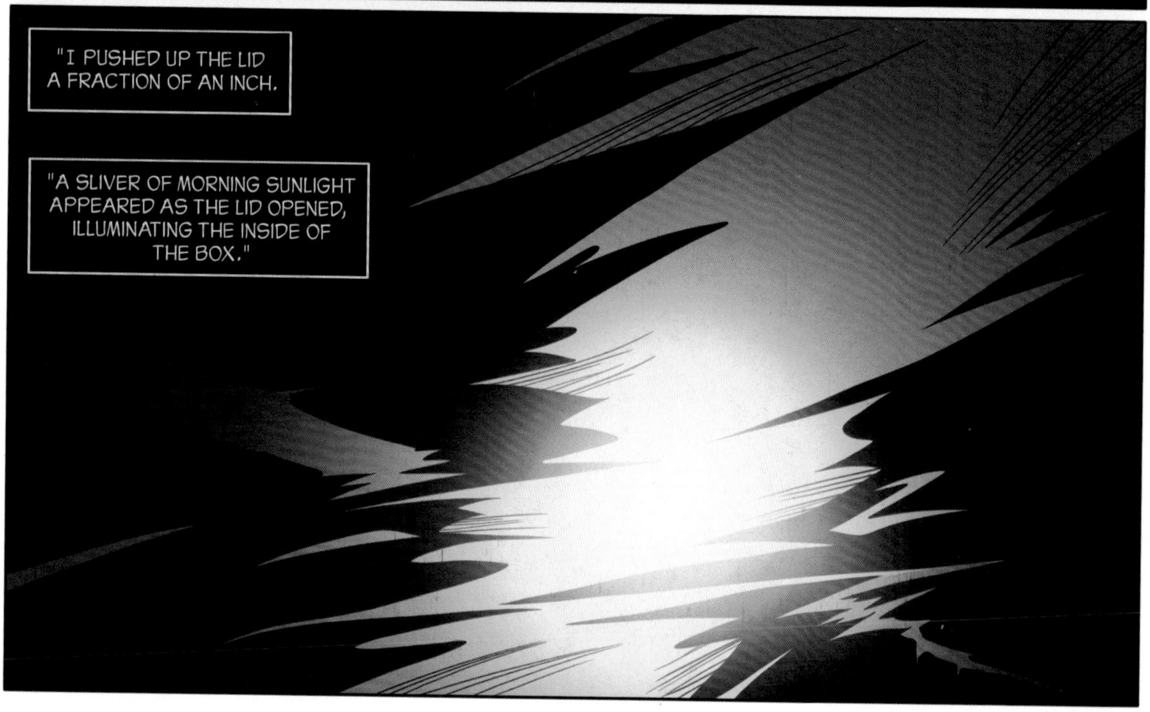
"I PUSHED UP THE LID A FRACTION OF AN INCH.
"A SLIVER OF MORNING SUNLIGHT APPEARED AS THE LID OPENED, ILLUMINATING THE INSIDE OF THE BOX."

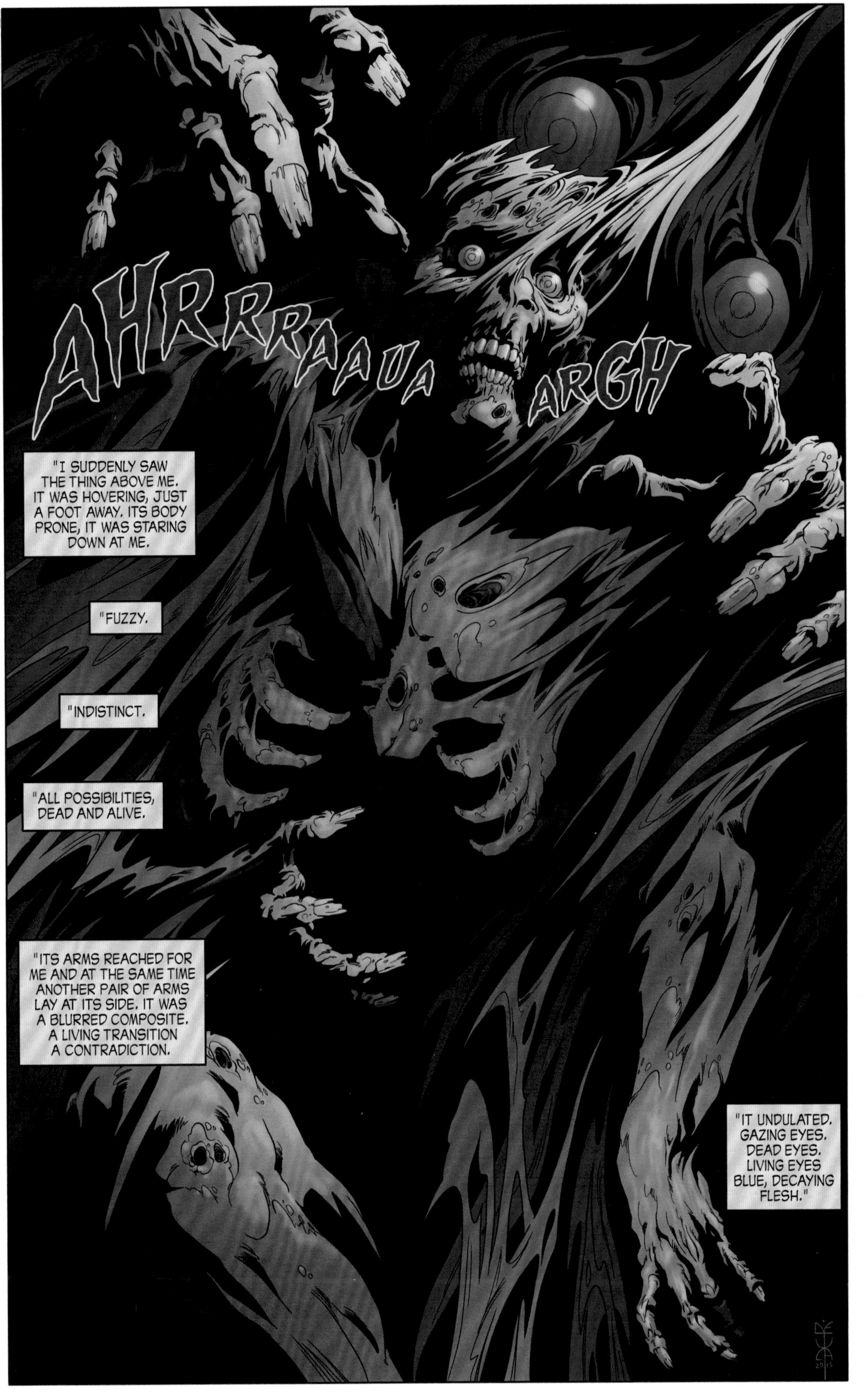
AHRRRAAUA ARGH
"I SUDDENLY SAW THE THING ABOVE ME. IT WAS HOVERING, JUST A FOOT AWAY. ITS BODY PRONE, IT WAS STARING DOWN AT ME.
"FUZZY.
"INDISTINCT.
"ALL POSSIBILITIES, DEAD AND ALIVE.
"ITS ARMS REACHED FOR ME AND AT THE SAME TIME ANOTHER PAIR OF ARMS LAY AT ITS SIDE. IT WAS A BLURRED COMPOSITE. A LIVING TRANSITION A CONTRADICTION.
"IT UNDULATED. GAZING EYES. DEAD EYES. LIVING EYES BLUE, DECAYING FLESH."

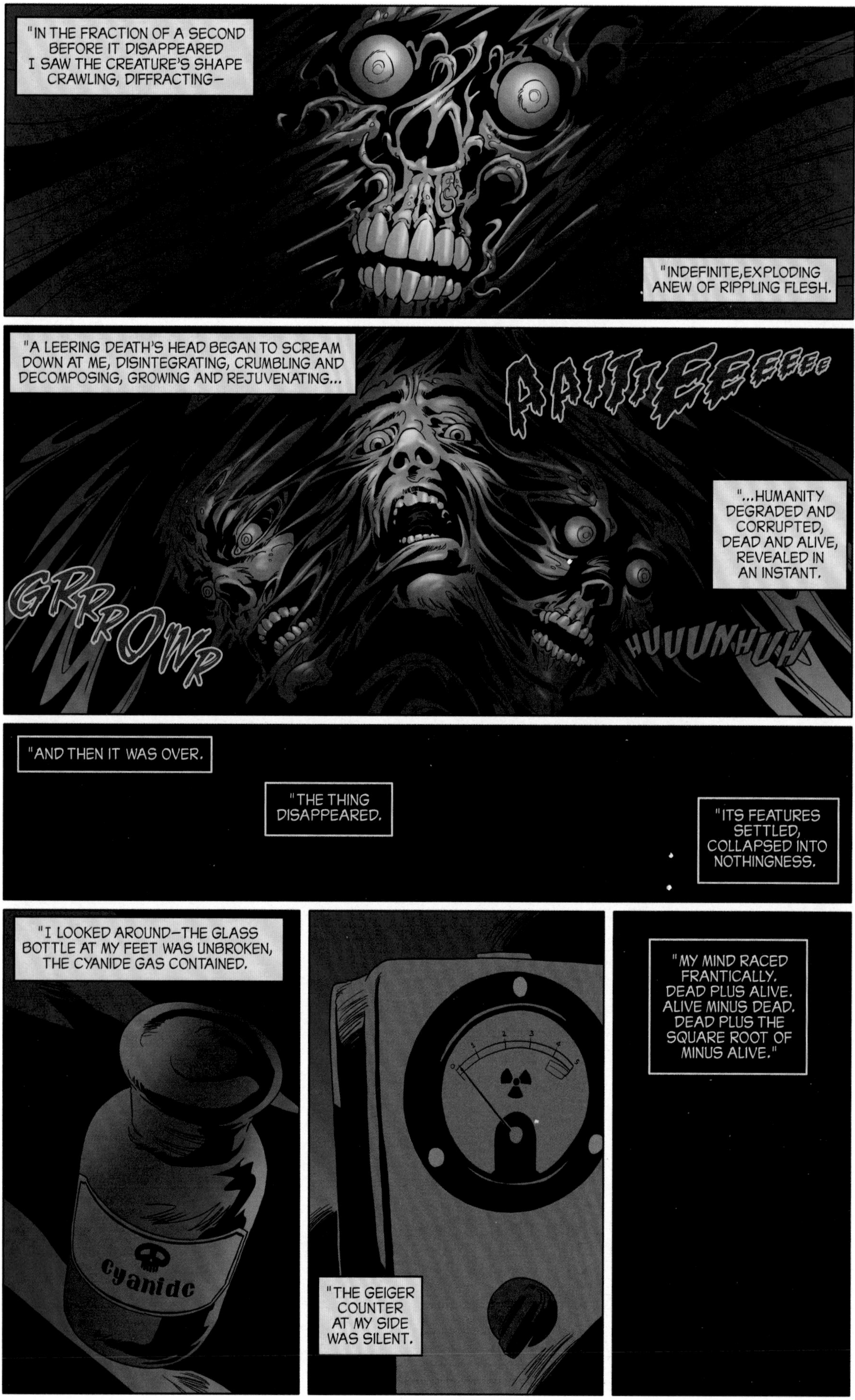

"IN THE FRACTION OF A SECOND BEFORE IT DISAPPEARED I SAW THE CREATURE'S SHAPE CRAWLING, DIFFRACTING–
"INDEFINITE, EXPLODING ANEW OF RIPPLING FLESH.
"A LEERING DEATH'S HEAD BEGAN TO SCREAM DOWN AT ME, DISINTEGRATING, CRUMBLING AND DECOMPOSING, GROWING AND REJUVENATING...
AAIIIIEEEEEEE
"...HUMANITY DEGRADED AND CORRUPTED, DEAD AND ALIVE, REVEALED IN AN INSTANT.
GRRROWR
HUUUNHUH
"AND THEN IT WAS OVER.
"THE THING DISAPPEARED.
"ITS FEATURES SETTLED, COLLAPSED INTO NOTHINGNESS.
"I LOOKED AROUND–THE GLASS BOTTLE AT MY FEET WAS UNBROKEN, THE CYANIDE GAS CONTAINED.
cyanide
"THE GEIGER COUNTER AT MY SIDE WAS SILENT.
"MY MIND RACED FRANTICALLY. DEAD PLUS ALIVE. ALIVE MINUS DEAD. DEAD PLUS THE SQUARE ROOT OF MINUS ALIVE."

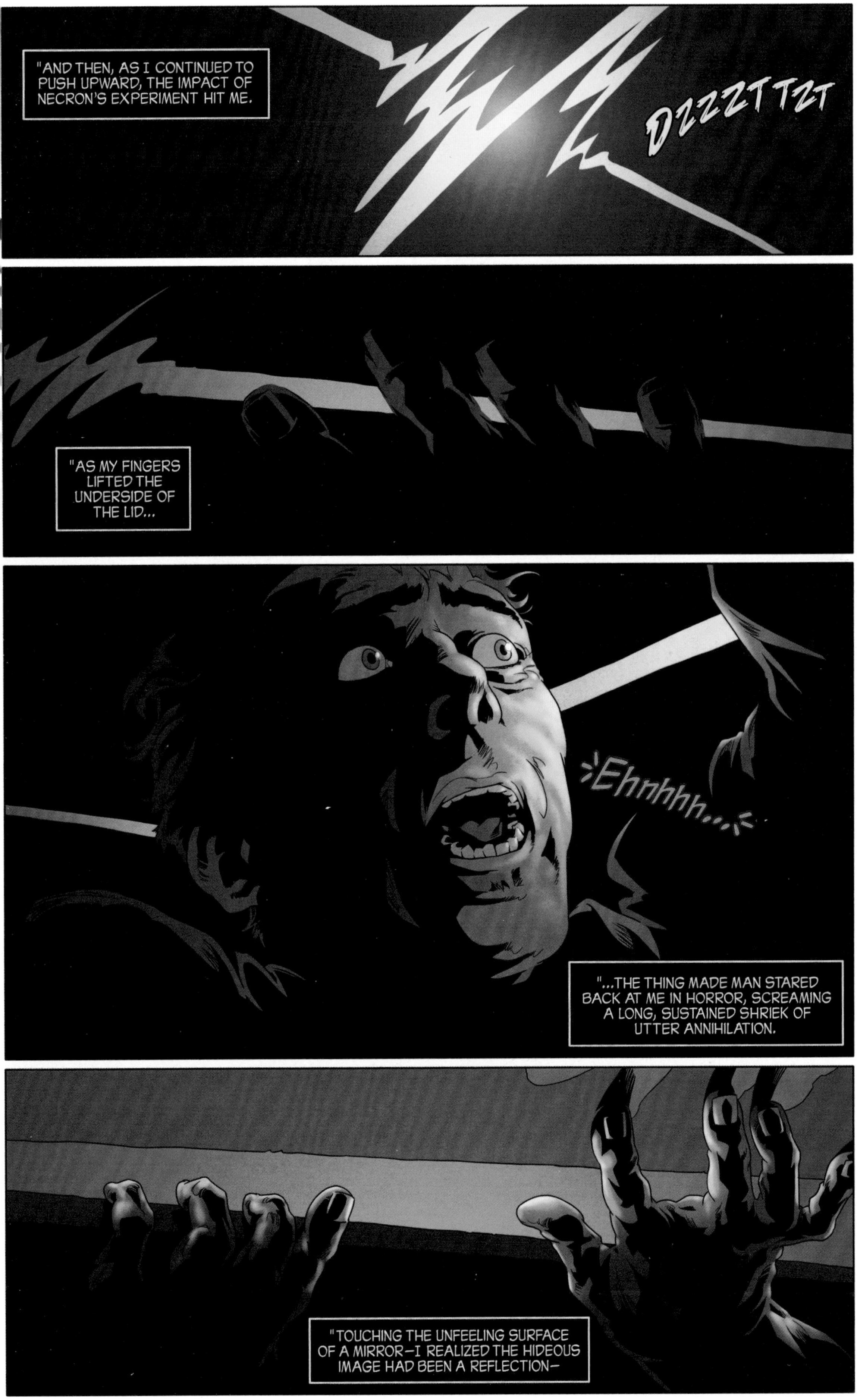
"AND THEN, AS I CONTINUED TO PUSH UPWARD, THE IMPACT OF NECRON'S EXPERIMENT HIT ME.
DZZZTTZT
"AS MY FINGERS LIFTED THE UNDERSIDE OF THE LID...
Ehnhhh...
"...THE THING MADE MAN STARED BACK AT ME IN HORROR, SCREAMING A LONG, SUSTAINED SHRIEK OF UTTER ANNIHILATION.
"TOUCHING THE UNFEELING SURFACE OF A MIRROR—I REALIZED THE HIDEOUS IMAGE HAD BEEN A REFLECTION—

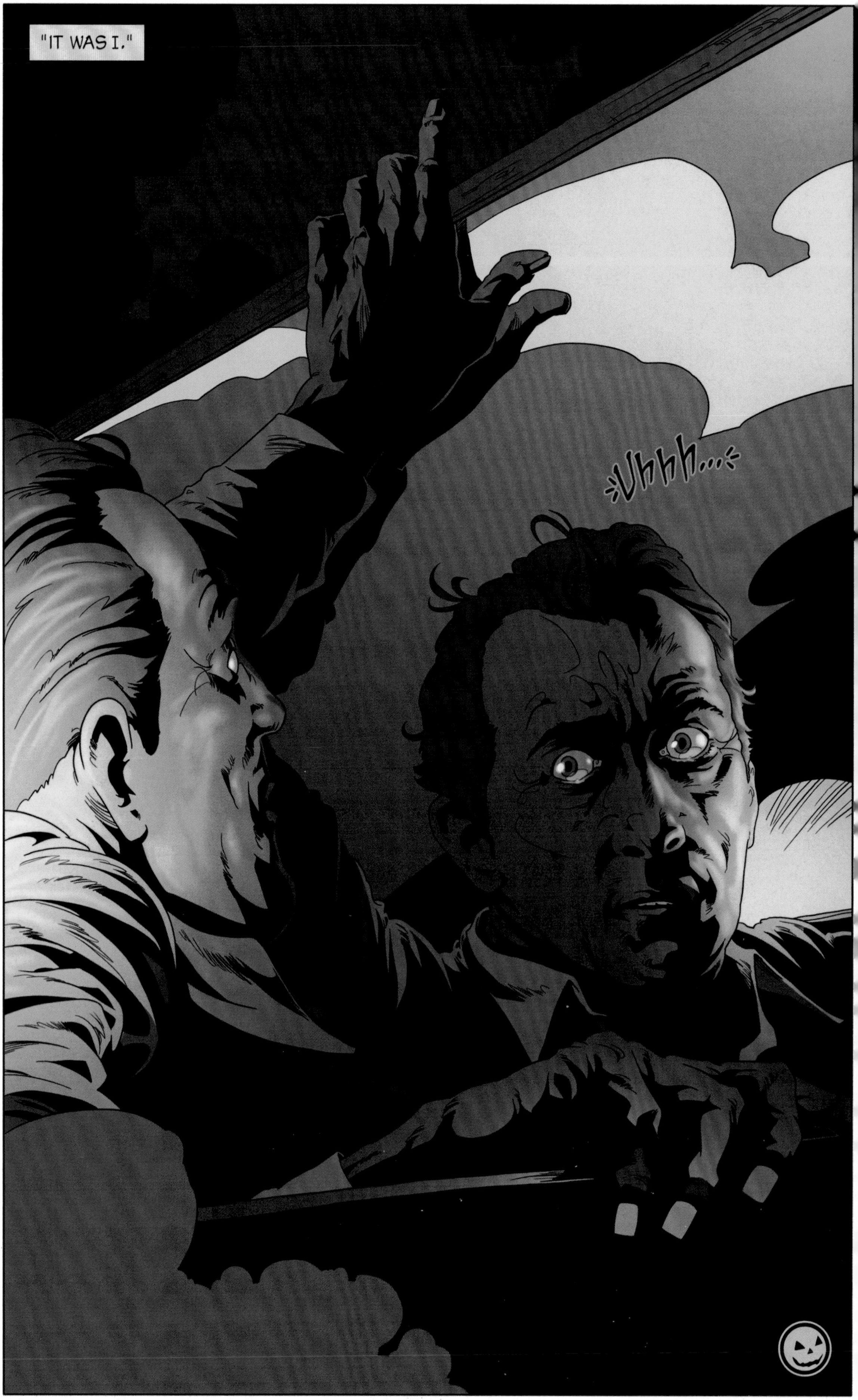
"IT WAS I."
Uhhh...

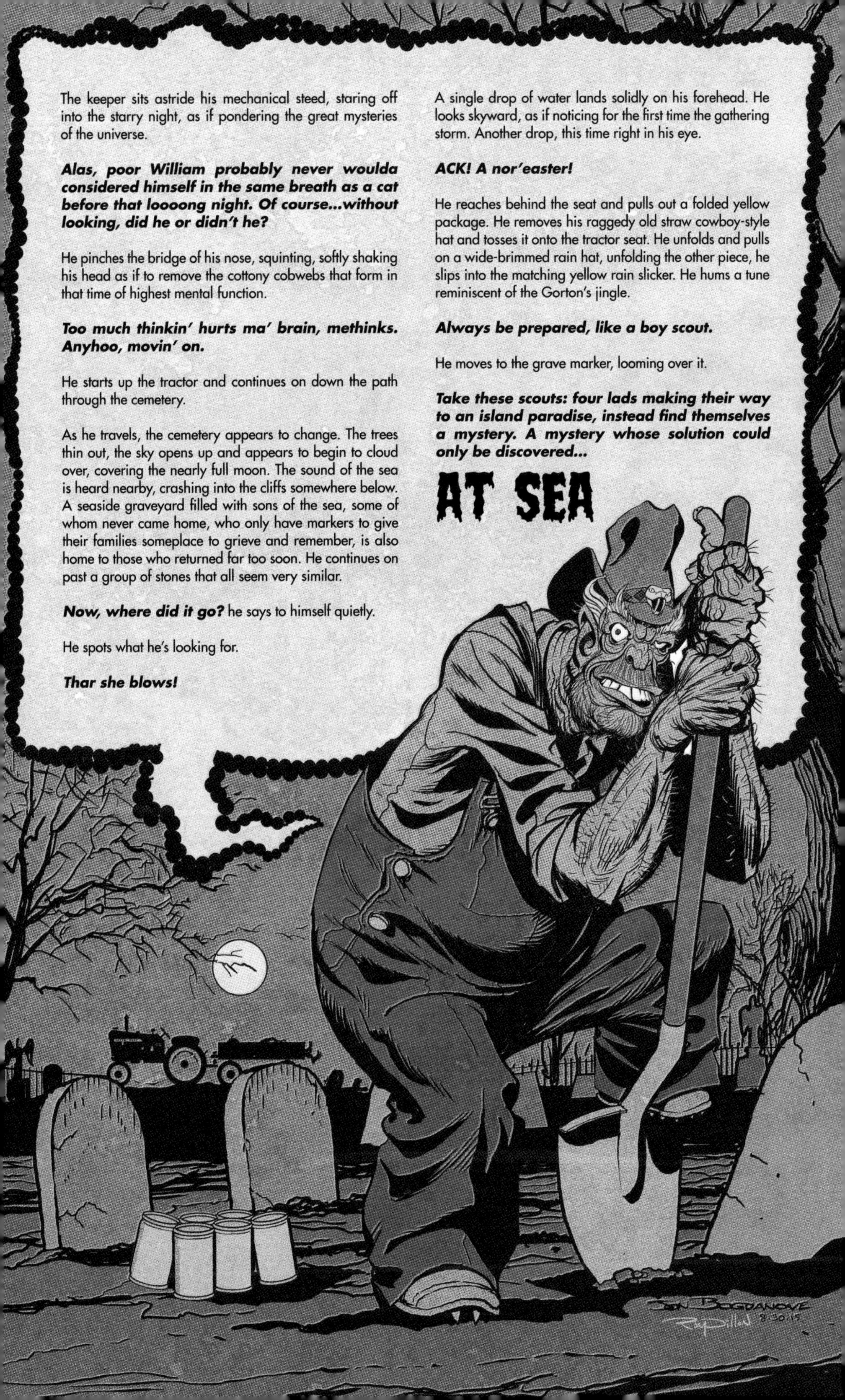
The keeper sits astride his mechanical steed, staring off into the starry night, as if pondering the great mysteries of the universe.
Alas, poor William probably never woulda considered himself in the same breath as a cat before that loooong night. Of course...without looking, did he or didn't he?
He pinches the bridge of his nose, squinting, softly shaking his head as if to remove the cottony cobwebs that form in that time of highest mental function.
Too much thinkin' hurts ma' brain, methinks. Anyhoo, movin' on.
He starts up the tractor and continues on down the path through the cemetery.
As he travels, the cemetery appears to change. The trees thin out, the sky opens up and appears to begin to cloud over, covering the nearly full moon. The sound of the sea is heard nearby, crashing into the cliffs somewhere below. A seaside graveyard filled with sons of the sea, some of whom never came home, who only have markers to give their families someplace to grieve and remember, is also home to those who returned far too soon. He continues on past a group of stones that all seem very similar.
Now, where did it go? he says to himself quietly.
He spots what he's looking for.
Thar she blows!
A single drop of water lands solidly on his forehead. He looks skyward, as if noticing for the first time the gathering storm. Another drop, this time right in his eye.
ACK! A nor'easter!
He reaches behind the seat and pulls out a folded yellow package. He removes his raggedy old straw cowboy-style hat and tosses it onto the tractor seat. He unfolds and pulls on a wide-brimmed rain hat, unfolding the other piece, he slips into the matching yellow rain slicker. He hums a tune reminiscent of the Gorton's jingle.
Always be prepared, like a boy scout.
He moves to the grave marker, looming over it.
Take these scouts: four lads making their way to an island paradise, instead find themselves a mystery. A mystery whose solution could only be discovered...
AT SEA

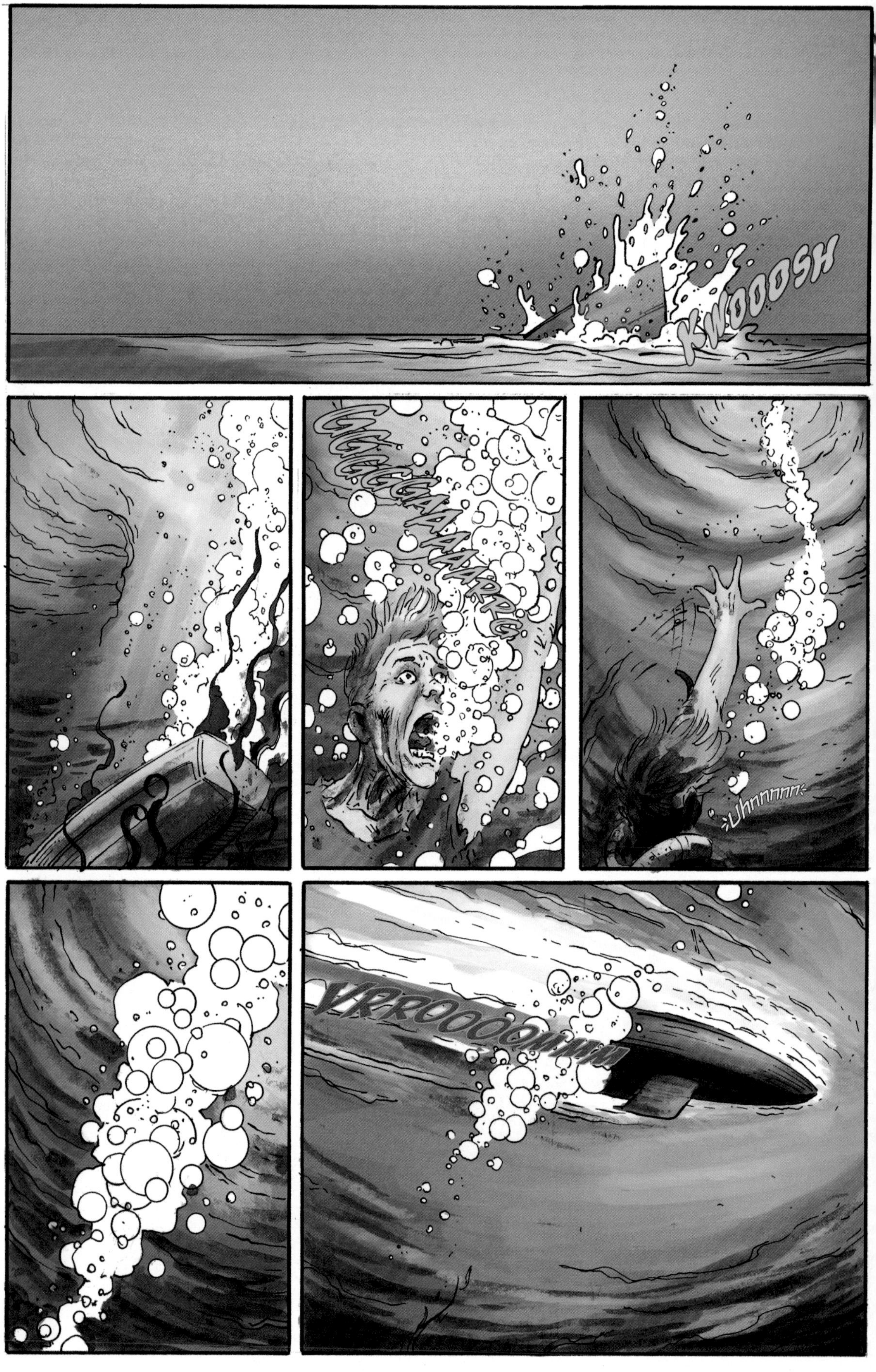
KWOOOSH
GGGGGAAAAARRG
Uhnnnnn
VRROOOOOMMMM

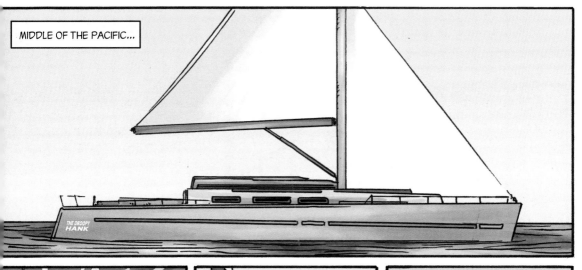
MIDDLE OF THE PACIFIC...

PLSH

FINALLY.

SPLASH SPLASH

SPLASH

GARY? MIKEY?

WHAT ARE YOU YELLING ABOUT?

YES, IT'S OKAY TO PEE IN THE OCEAN.

HUH. COULD'VE SWORN...

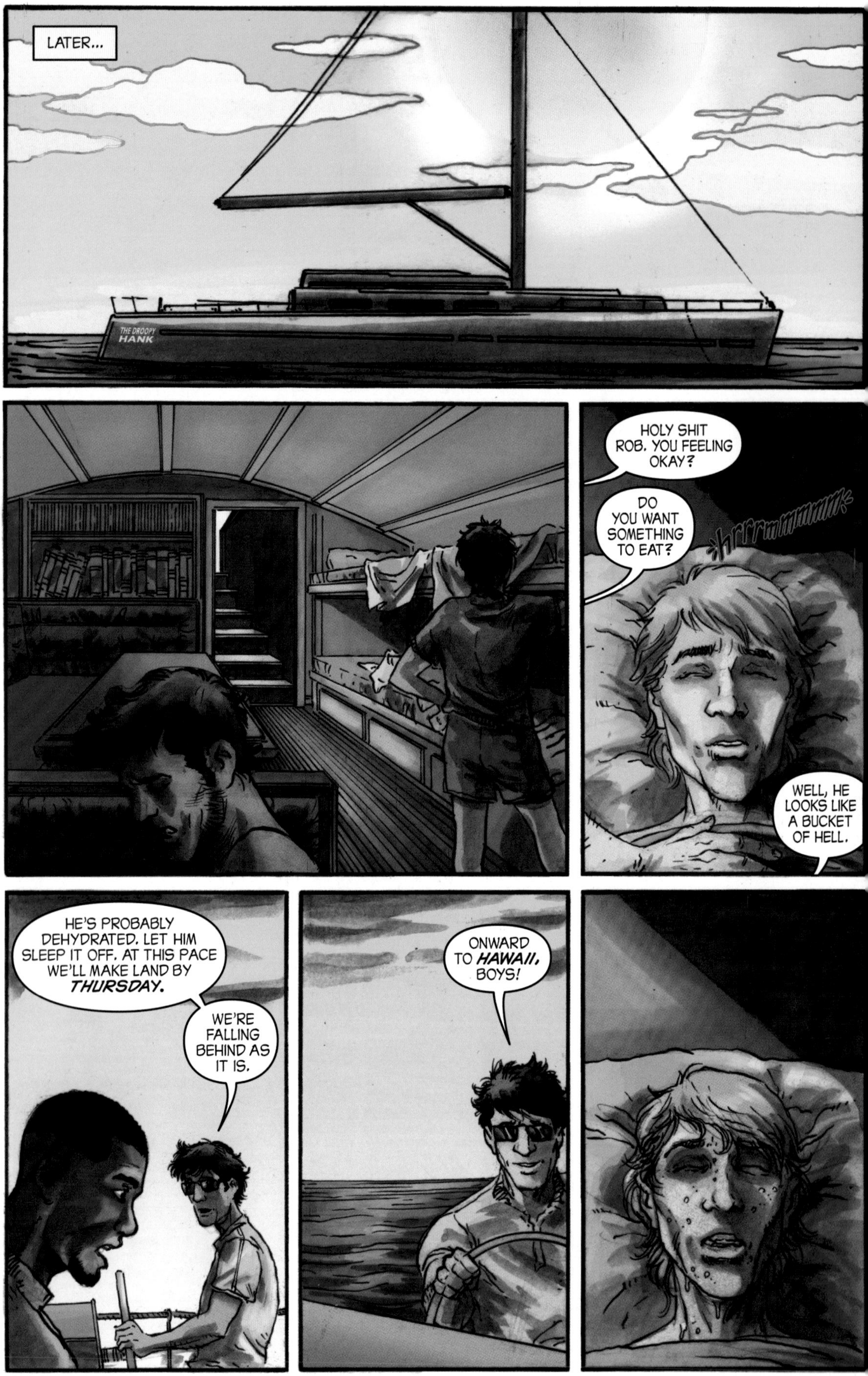
LATER...
THE DROOPY HANK
HOLY SHIT ROB. YOU FEELING OKAY?
DO YOU WANT SOMETHING TO EAT?
hrrrmmmmm
WELL, HE LOOKS LIKE A BUCKET OF HELL.
HE'S PROBABLY DEHYDRATED. LET HIM SLEEP IT OFF. AT THIS PACE WE'LL MAKE LAND BY THURSDAY.
WE'RE FALLING BEHIND AS IT IS.
ONWARD TO HAWAII, BOYS!

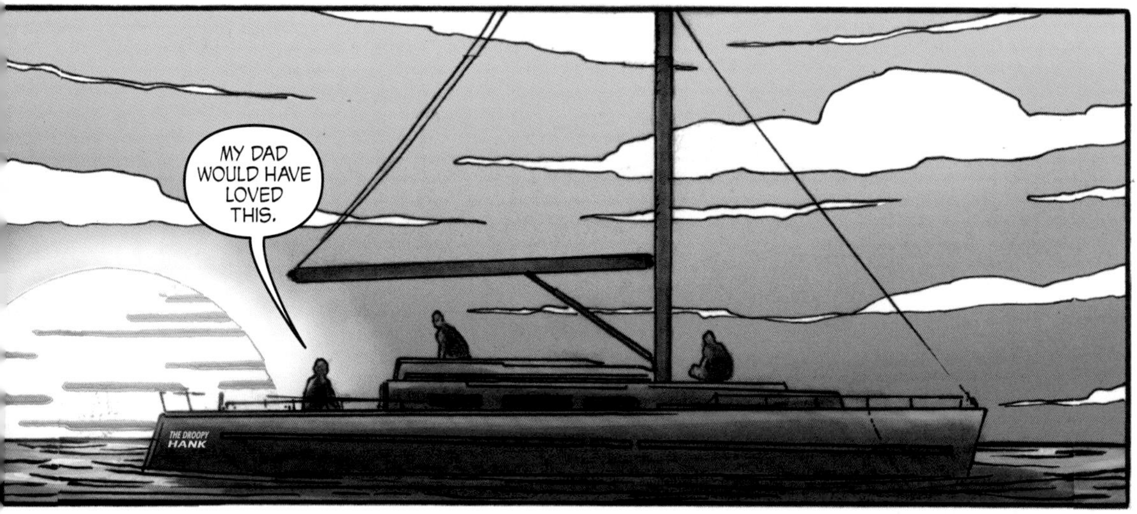
MY DAD WOULD HAVE LOVED THIS.
THE DROOPY HANK

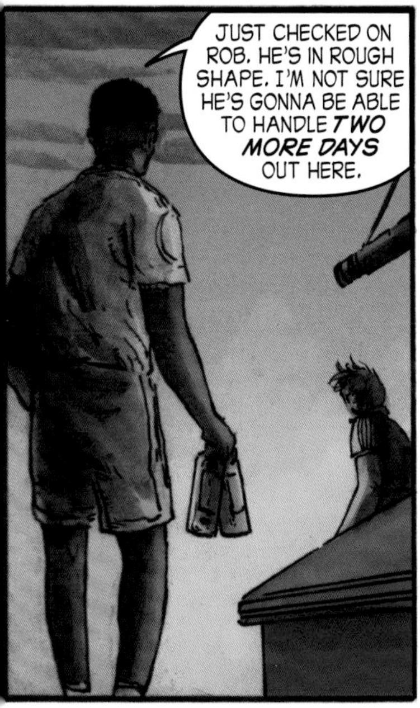
JUST CHECKED ON ROB. HE'S IN ROUGH SHAPE. I'M NOT SURE HE'S GONNA BE ABLE TO HANDLE *TWO MORE DAYS* OUT HERE.

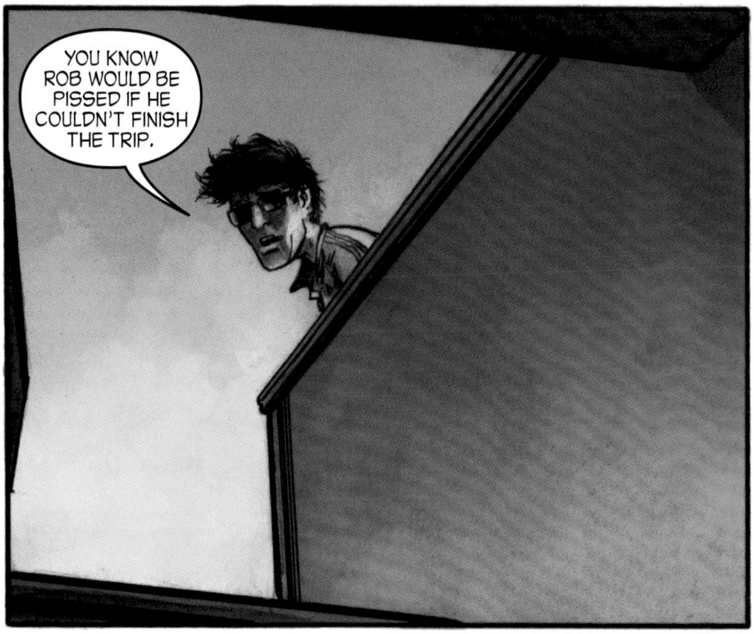
YOU KNOW ROB WOULD BE PISSED IF HE COULDN'T FINISH THE TRIP.

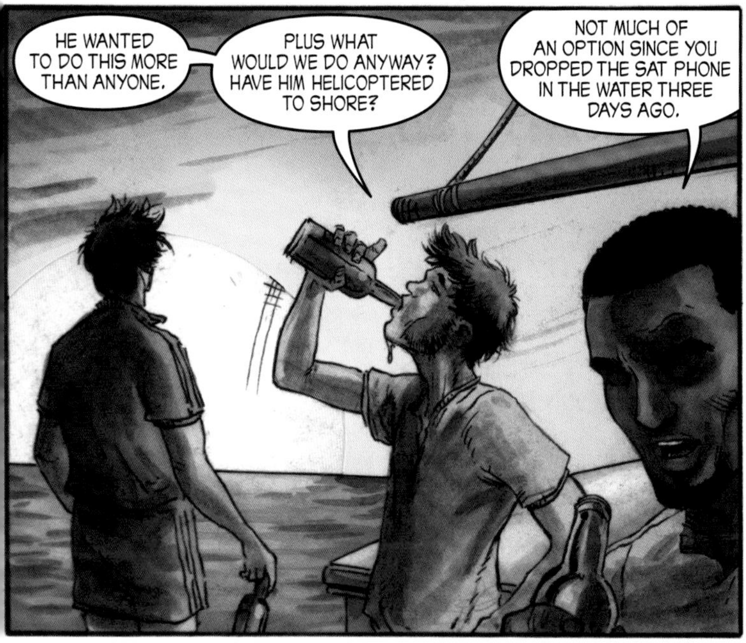
HE WANTED TO DO THIS MORE THAN ANYONE.
PLUS WHAT WOULD WE DO ANYWAY? HAVE HIM HELICOPTERED TO SHORE?
NOT MUCH OF AN OPTION SINCE YOU DROPPED THE SAT PHONE IN THE WATER THREE DAYS AGO.

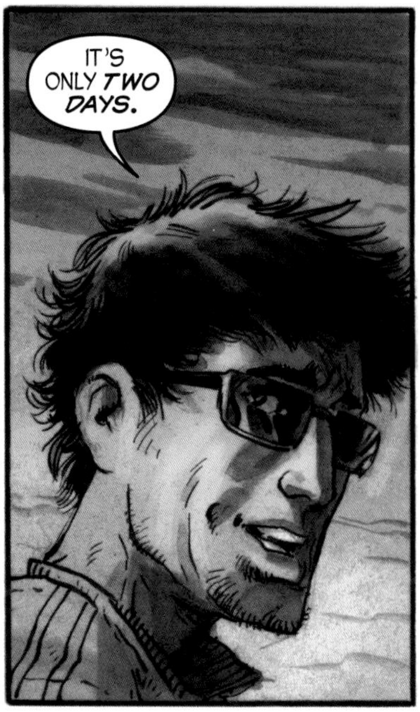
IT'S ONLY *TWO DAYS.*

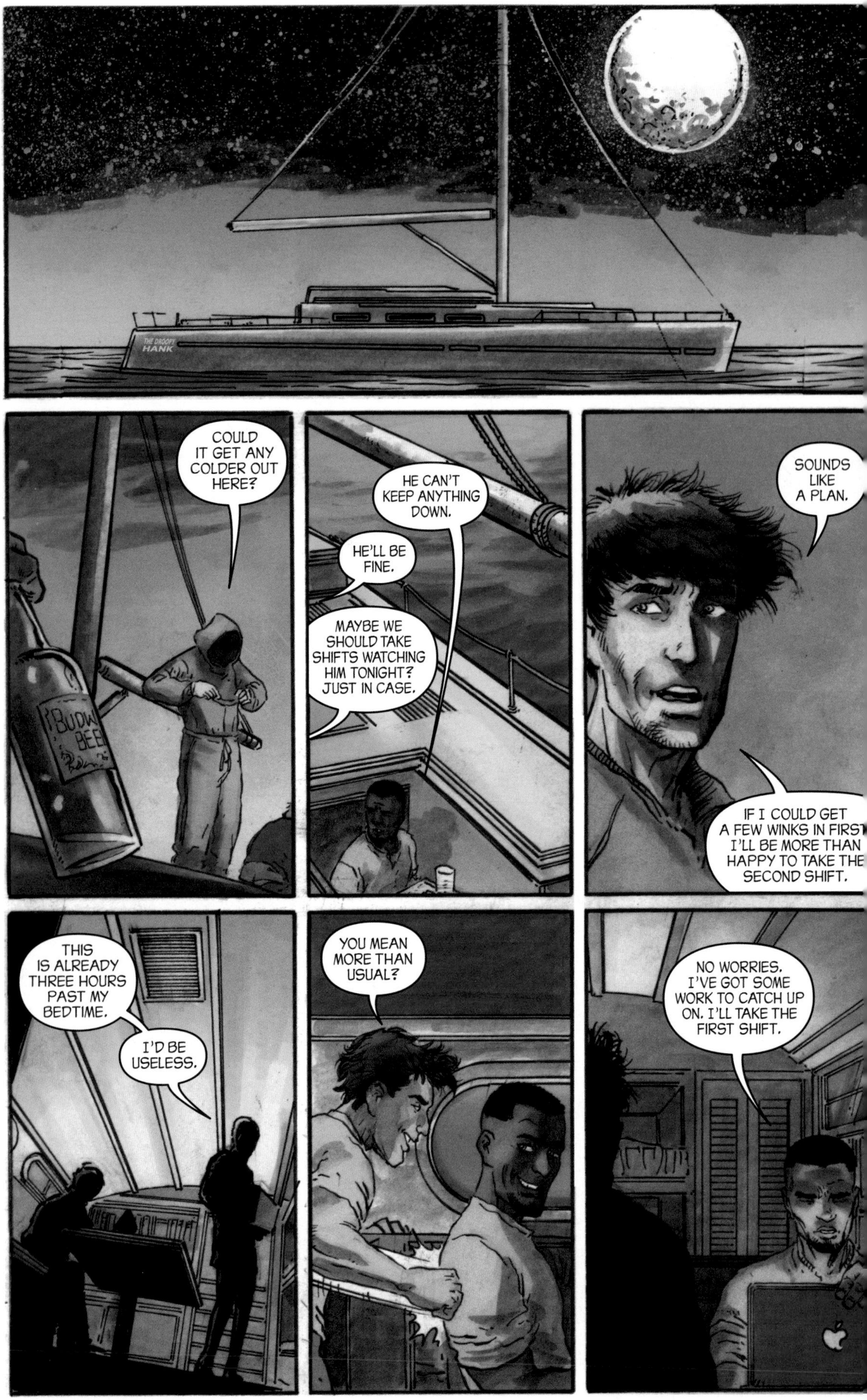
THE DROOPY HANK
COULD IT GET ANY COLDER OUT HERE?
BUDW BEE
HE CAN'T KEEP ANYTHING DOWN.
HE'LL BE FINE.
MAYBE WE SHOULD TAKE SHIFTS WATCHING HIM TONIGHT? JUST IN CASE.
SOUNDS LIKE A PLAN.
IF I COULD GET A FEW WINKS IN FIRST I'LL BE MORE THAN HAPPY TO TAKE THE SECOND SHIFT.
THIS IS ALREADY THREE HOURS PAST MY BEDTIME.
I'D BE USELESS.
YOU MEAN MORE THAN USUAL?
NO WORRIES. I'VE GOT SOME WORK TO CATCH UP ON. I'LL TAKE THE FIRST SHIFT.

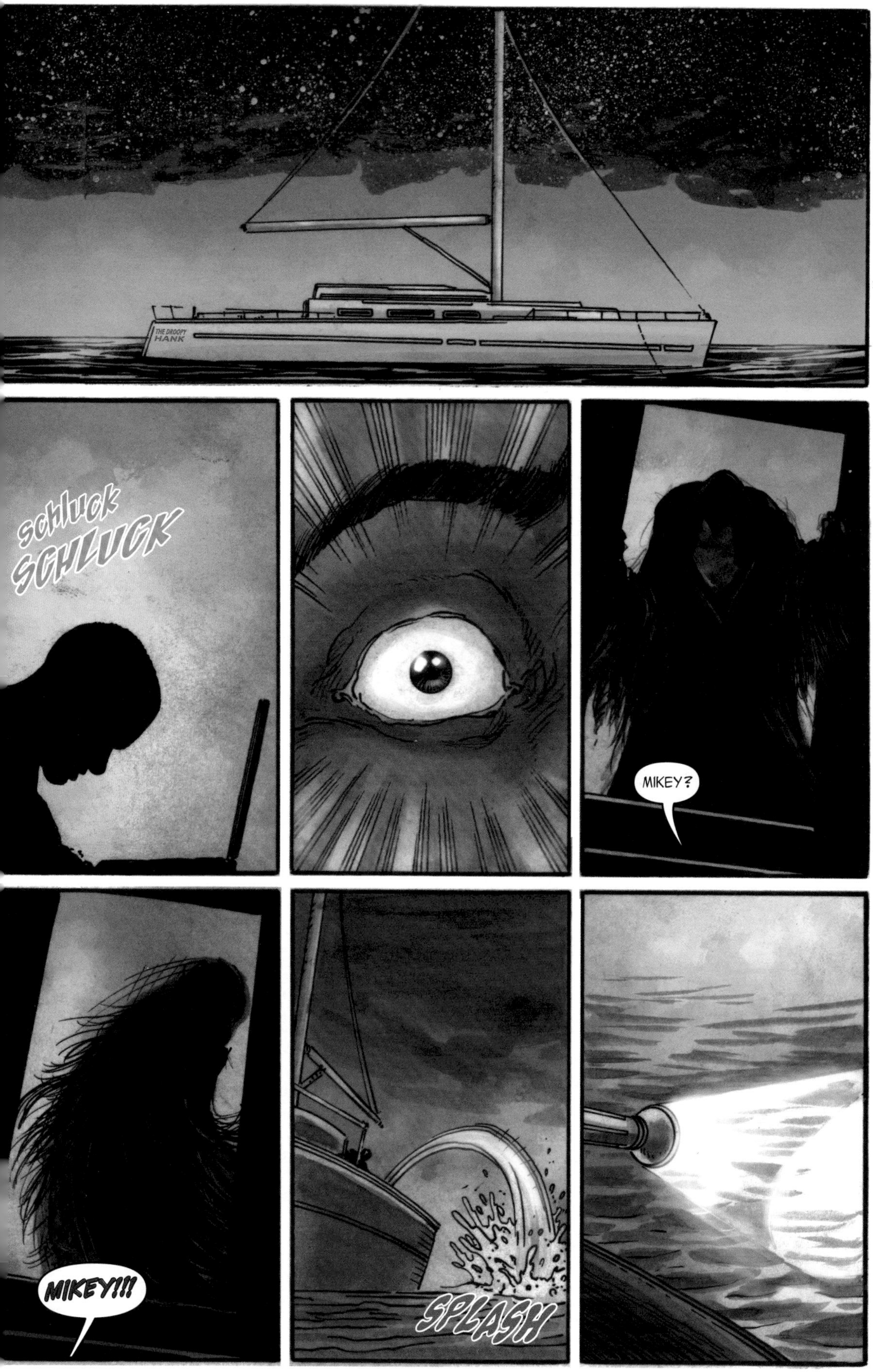
THE DROOPY HANK
SCHLUCK
SCHLUCK
MIKEY?
MIKEY!!!
SPLASH

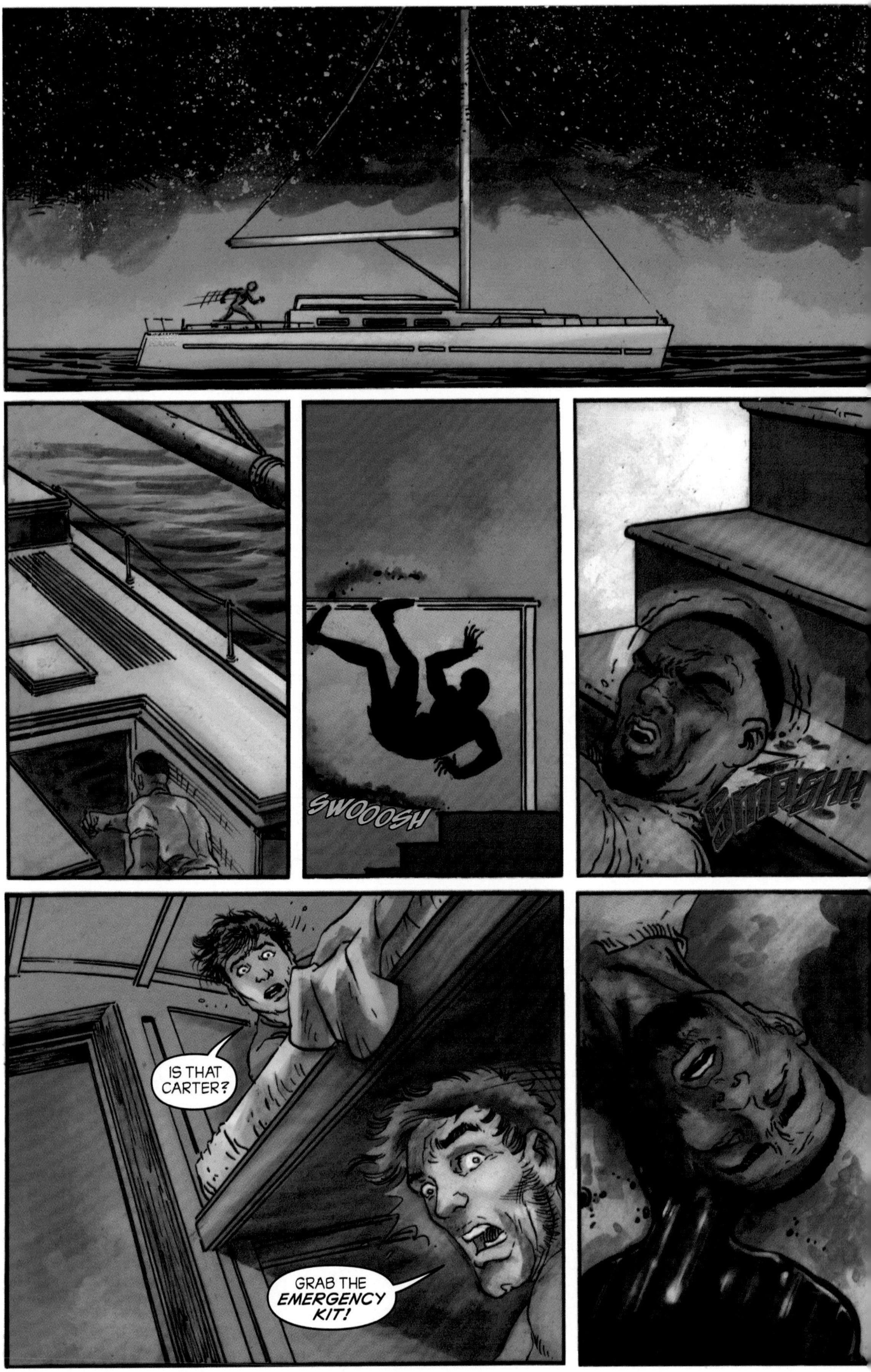
SWOOOSH
SMASHH!
IS THAT CARTER?
GRAB THE *EMERGENCY KIT!*

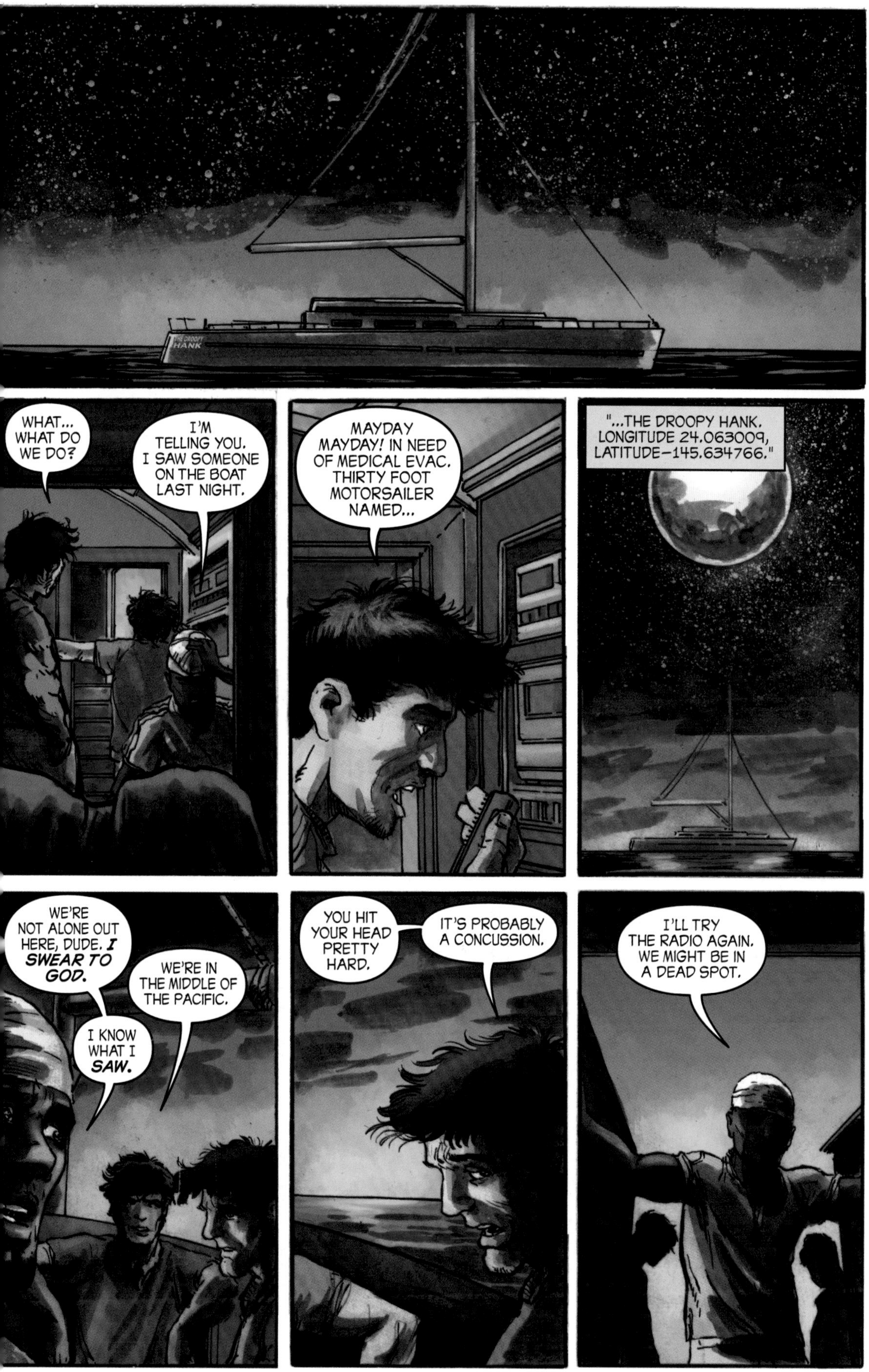
THE DROOPY HANK
WHAT... WHAT DO WE DO?
I'M TELLING YOU. I SAW SOMEONE ON THE BOAT LAST NIGHT.
MAYDAY MAYDAY! IN NEED OF MEDICAL EVAC. THIRTY FOOT MOTORSAILER NAMED...
"...THE DROOPY HANK. LONGITUDE 24.063009, LATITUDE–145.634766."
WE'RE NOT ALONE OUT HERE, DUDE. I SWEAR TO GOD.
WE'RE IN THE MIDDLE OF THE PACIFIC.
I KNOW WHAT I SAW.
YOU HIT YOUR HEAD PRETTY HARD.
IT'S PROBABLY A CONCUSSION.
I'LL TRY THE RADIO AGAIN. WE MIGHT BE IN A DEAD SPOT.

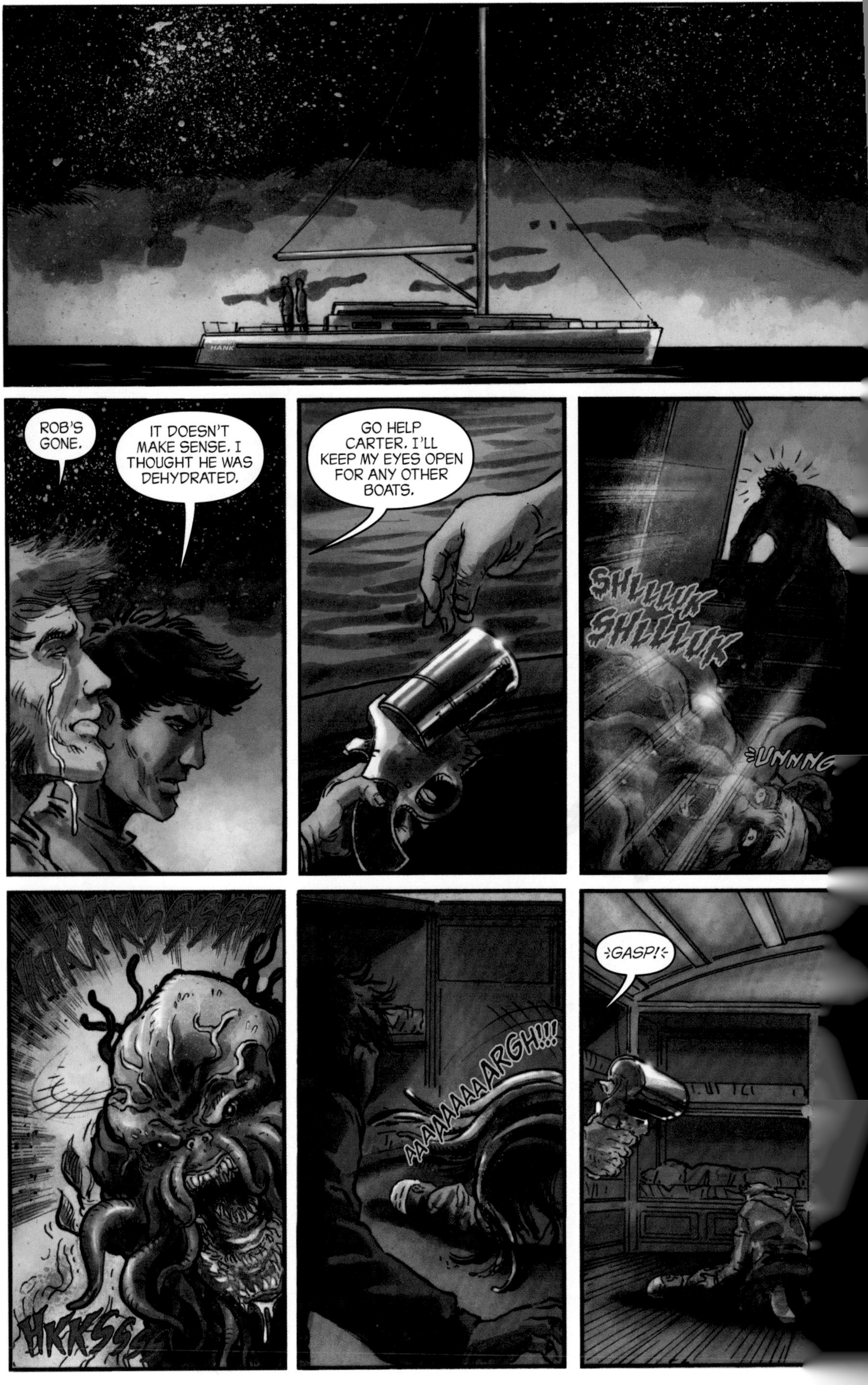
ROB'S GONE.
IT DOESN'T MAKE SENSE. I THOUGHT HE WAS DEHYDRATED.
GO HELP CARTER. I'LL KEEP MY EYES OPEN FOR ANY OTHER BOATS.
SHLLLUK
SHLLLUK
UNNNG
HKKSSS
AAAAAAAAARGH!!!
GASP!

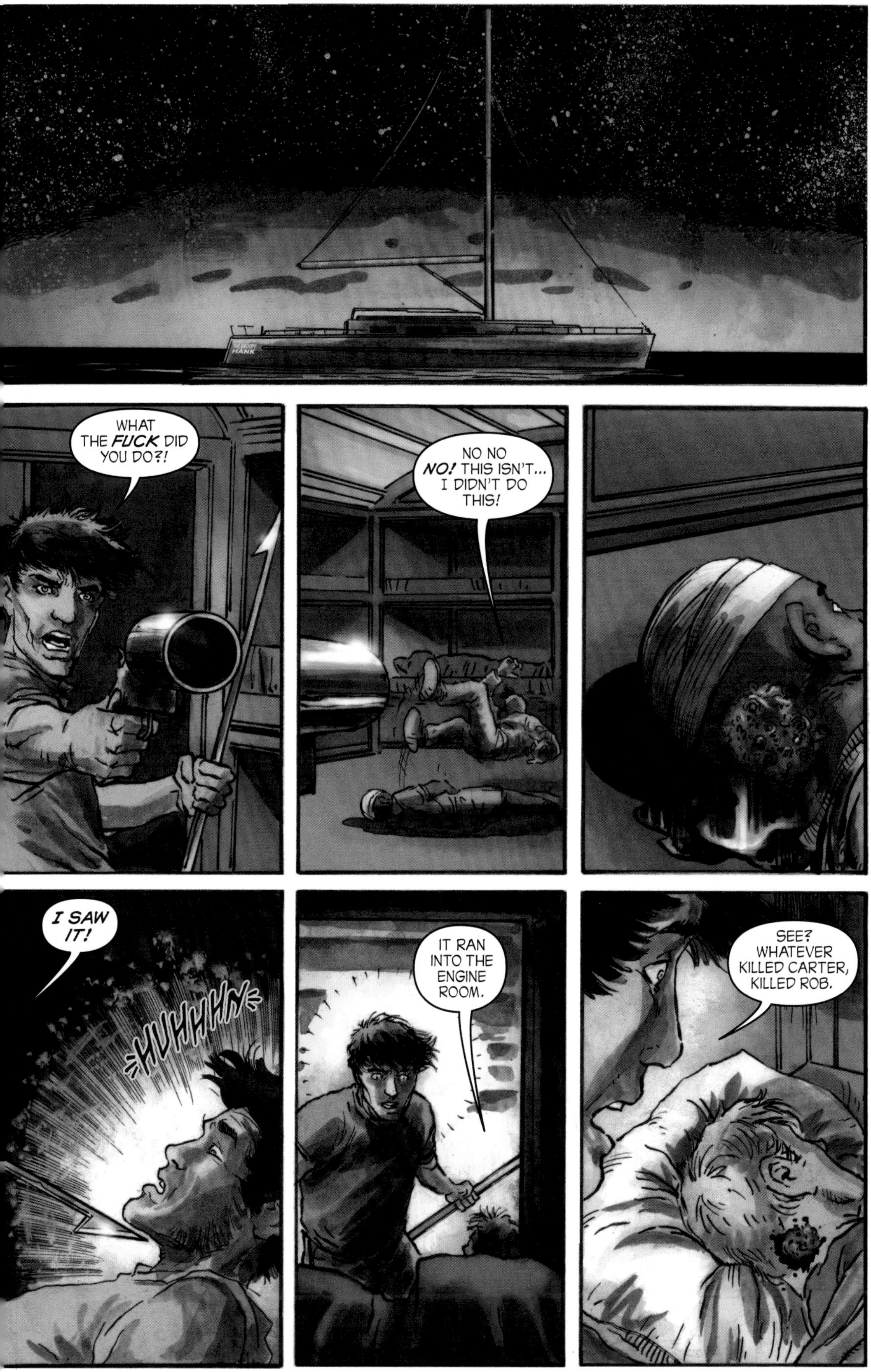
WHAT THE FUCK DID YOU DO?!
NO NO NO! THIS ISN'T... I DIDN'T DO THIS!
I SAW IT!
HUHHHH
IT RAN INTO THE ENGINE ROOM.
SEE? WHATEVER KILLED CARTER, KILLED ROB.

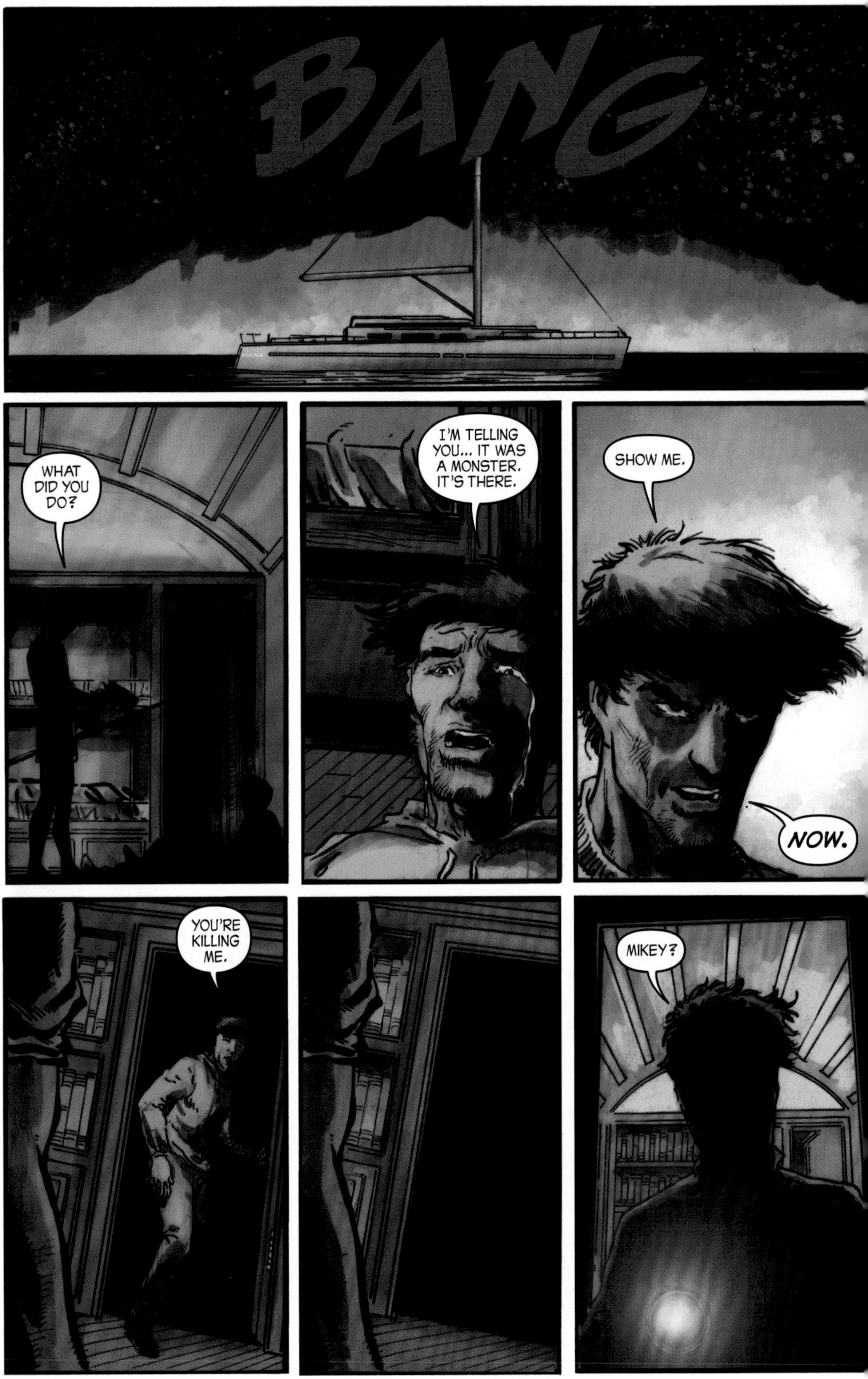
BANG
WHAT DID YOU DO?
I'M TELLING YOU... IT WAS A MONSTER. IT'S THERE.
SHOW ME.
NOW.
YOU'RE KILLING ME.
MIKEY?

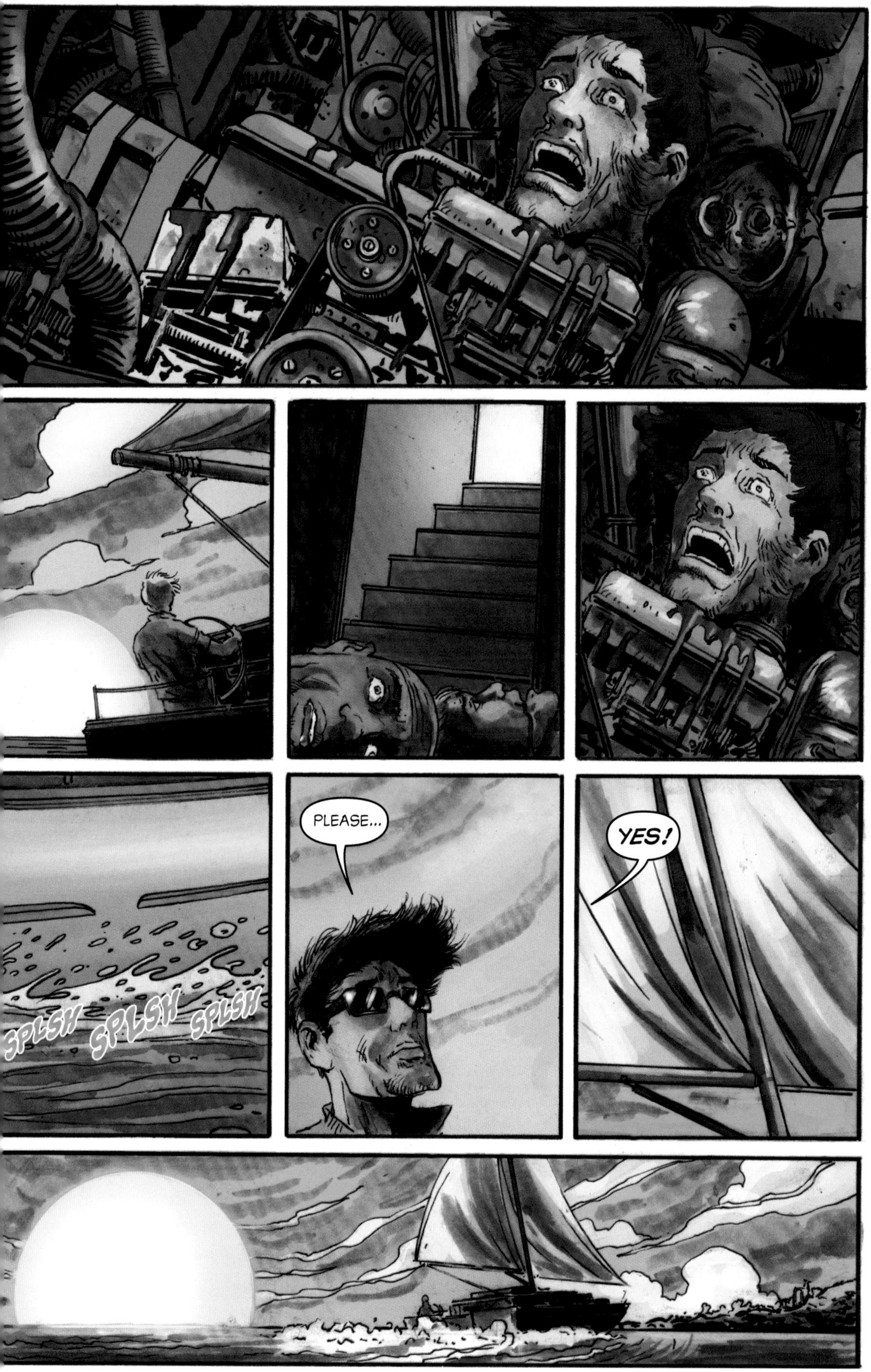
SPLSH SPLSH SPLSH
PLEASE...
YES!

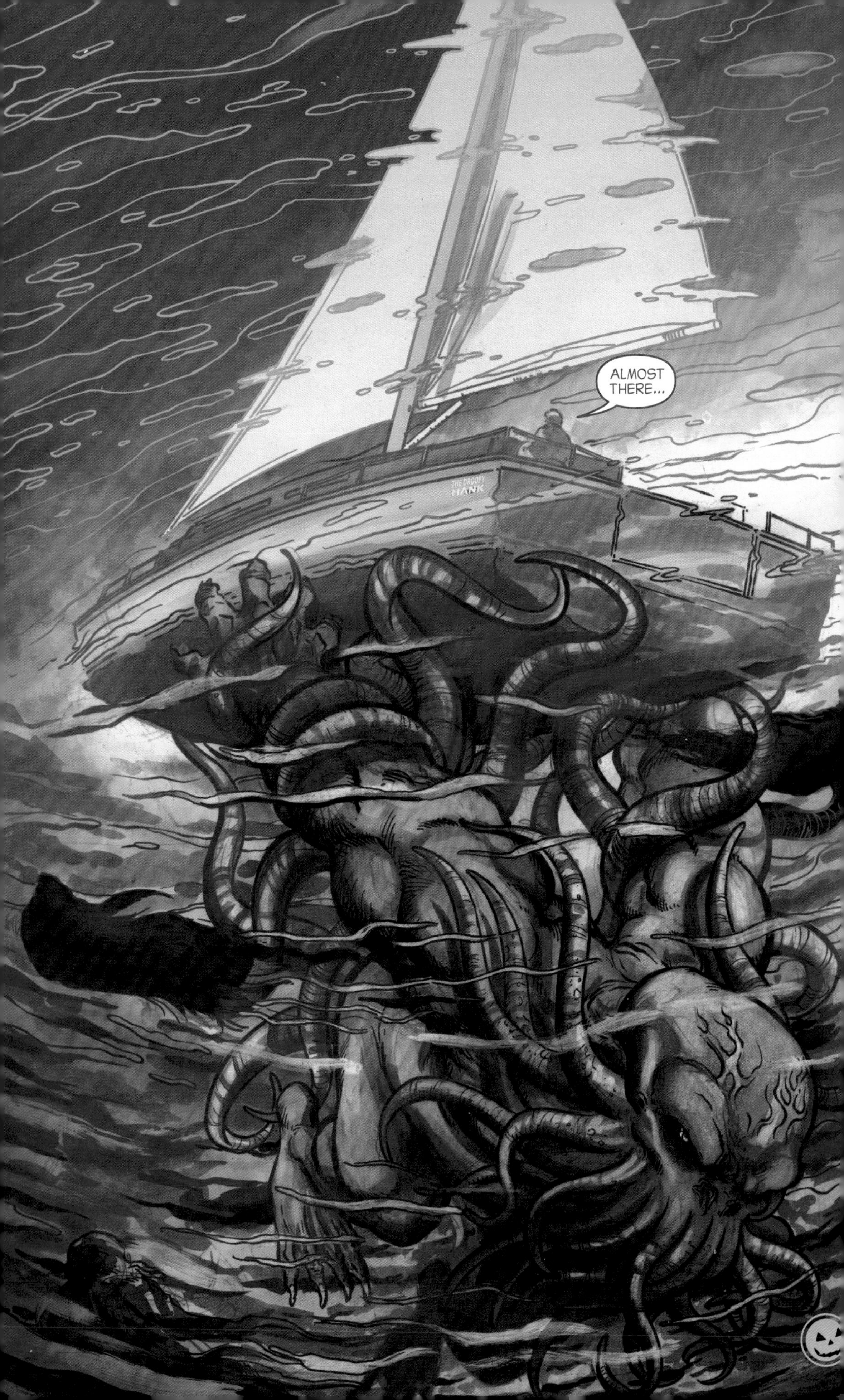
ALMOST THERE...
THE DROOPY
HANK

The rain continues to fall at the seaside graveyard. The keeper is working on one of his least favorite tasks, washing off the graffiti that the local teens "tag" on every clean, open surface in town. The cemetery, with its remote location and lack of ready monitoring, is always a prime candidate for a little street art. He scrubs with vigor at the "Willie loves Betty" heart with arrows.

Darn kids.

Oh, you're back. How'd you like that one? Not your usual old fishing trip, eh? One might even say...it sucked...if one was likely to make jokes of that nature.

Just as sharply as it began, the rain begins to slow as he walks back over to the tractor. He glances up at the clearing sky.

Well, that's more like it.

Taking off the rain jacket and hat, he tosses them into the trailer with the tools.

He hops back onto the tractor and pulls it around in a 180 degree turn, heading back the way he came. Soon, the surroundings are changing again. The trees return, and the stones become less constant and a bit more chaotic in their placement. He comes to a large open clearing amongst the regular markers.

Ah, here we are. Our next tale is a very special one, indeed. Why's that, you ask?

He gestures to the open, grassy area in which he now stands.

Well, simple...because it happened right here, on this very spot!

A story like so many stories before it, that proves once again that knowledge truly IS power. And when it's all over, you'll know the most important piece of information in this tale. You'll know what...

BUNNY DIDN'T TELL US

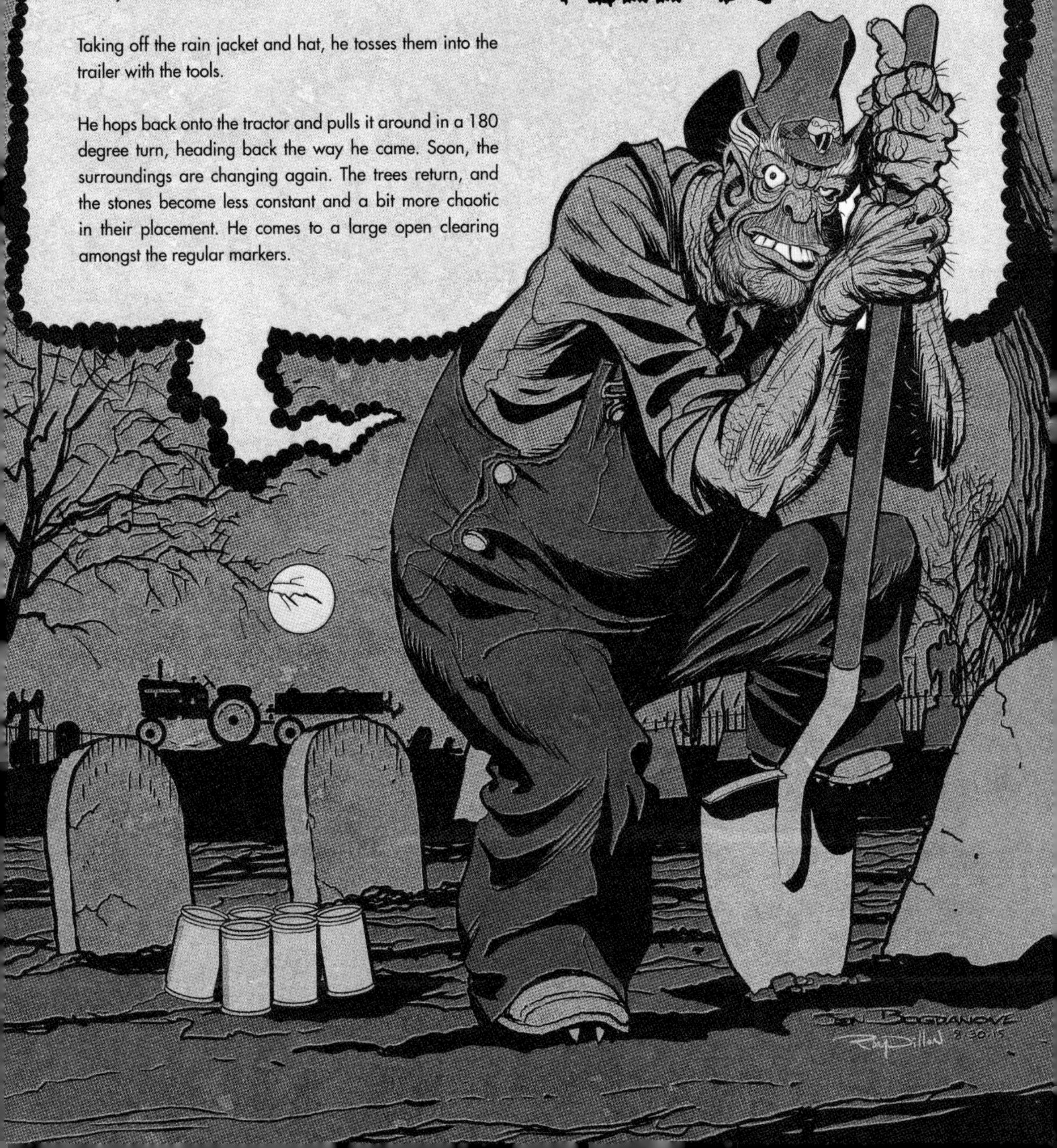

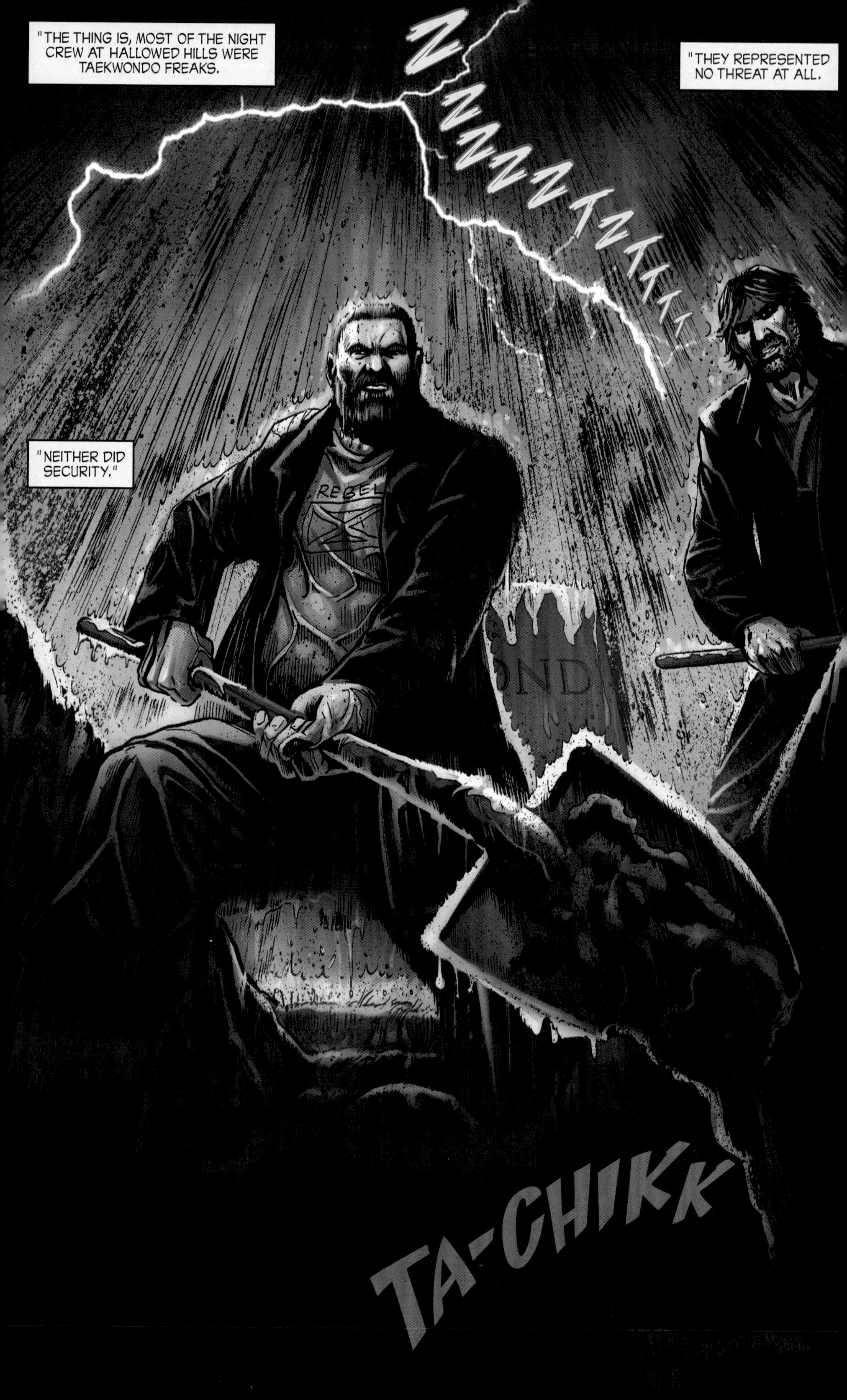
"THE THING IS, MOST OF THE NIGHT CREW AT HALLOWED HILLS WERE TAEKWONDO FREAKS.
ZZZZZZZZAKKKKK
"THEY REPRESENTED NO THREAT AT ALL.
"NEITHER DID SECURITY."
REBEL
TA-CHIKK

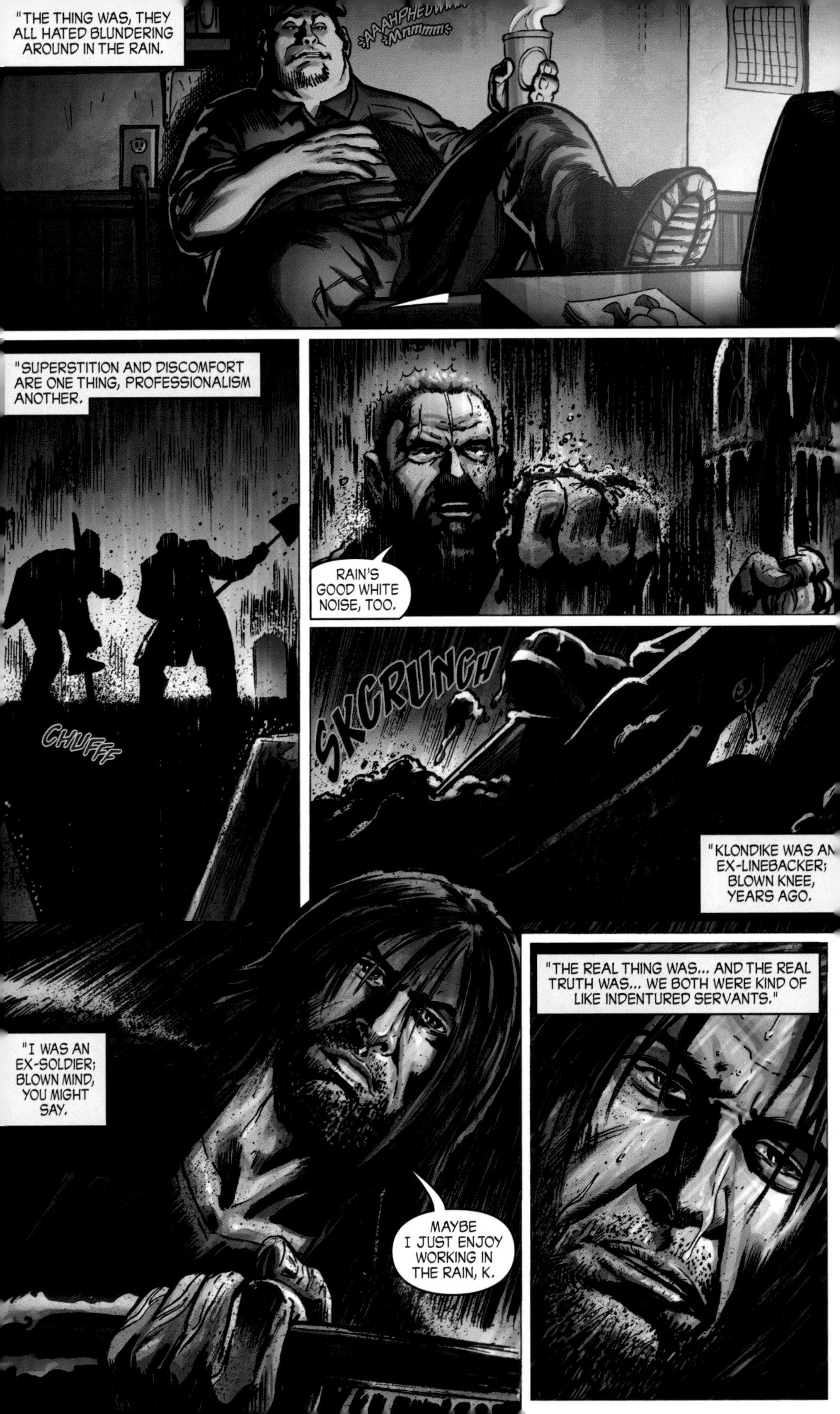
"THE THING WAS, THEY ALL HATED BLUNDERING AROUND IN THE RAIN.
Mnmmm
"SUPERSTITION AND DISCOMFORT ARE ONE THING, PROFESSIONALISM ANOTHER.
CHUFFF
RAIN'S GOOD WHITE NOISE, TOO.
SKGRUNCH
"KLONDIKE WAS A
EX-LINEBACKER; BLOWN KNEE, YEARS AGO.
"I WAS AN EX-SOLDIER; BLOWN MIND, YOU MIGHT SAY.
MAYBE I JUST ENJOY WORKING IN THE RAIN, K.
"THE REAL THING WAS... AND THE REAL TRUTH WAS... WE BOTH WERE KIND OF LIKE INDENTURED SERVANTS."

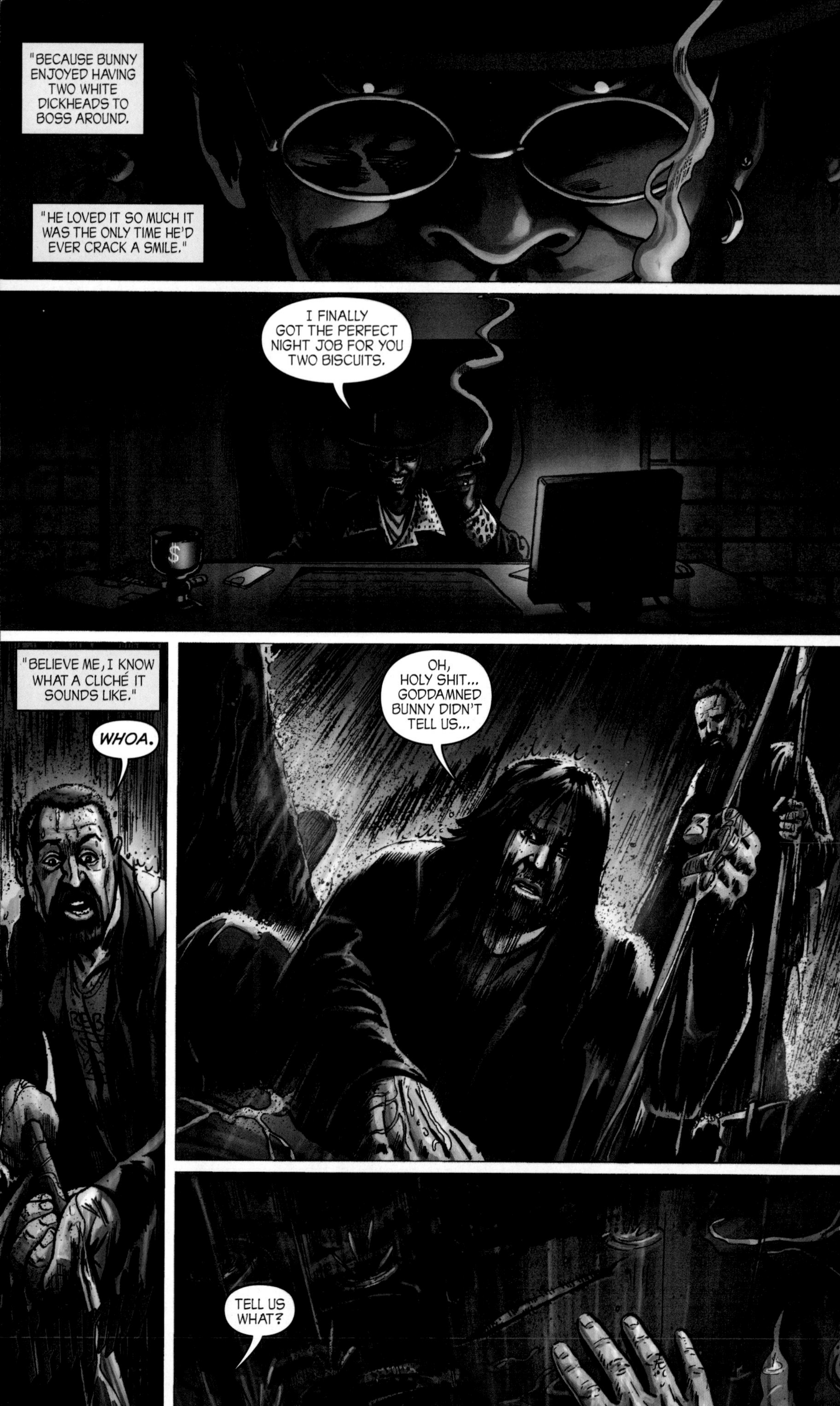
"BECAUSE BUNNY ENJOYED HAVING TWO WHITE DICKHEADS TO BOSS AROUND.
"HE LOVED IT SO MUCH IT WAS THE ONLY TIME HE'D EVER CRACK A SMILE."
I FINALLY GOT THE PERFECT NIGHT JOB FOR YOU TWO BISCUITS.
"BELIEVE ME, I KNOW WHAT A CLICHÉ IT SOUNDS LIKE."
WHOA.
OH, HOLY SHIT... GODDAMNED BUNNY DIDN'T TELL US...
TELL US WHAT?

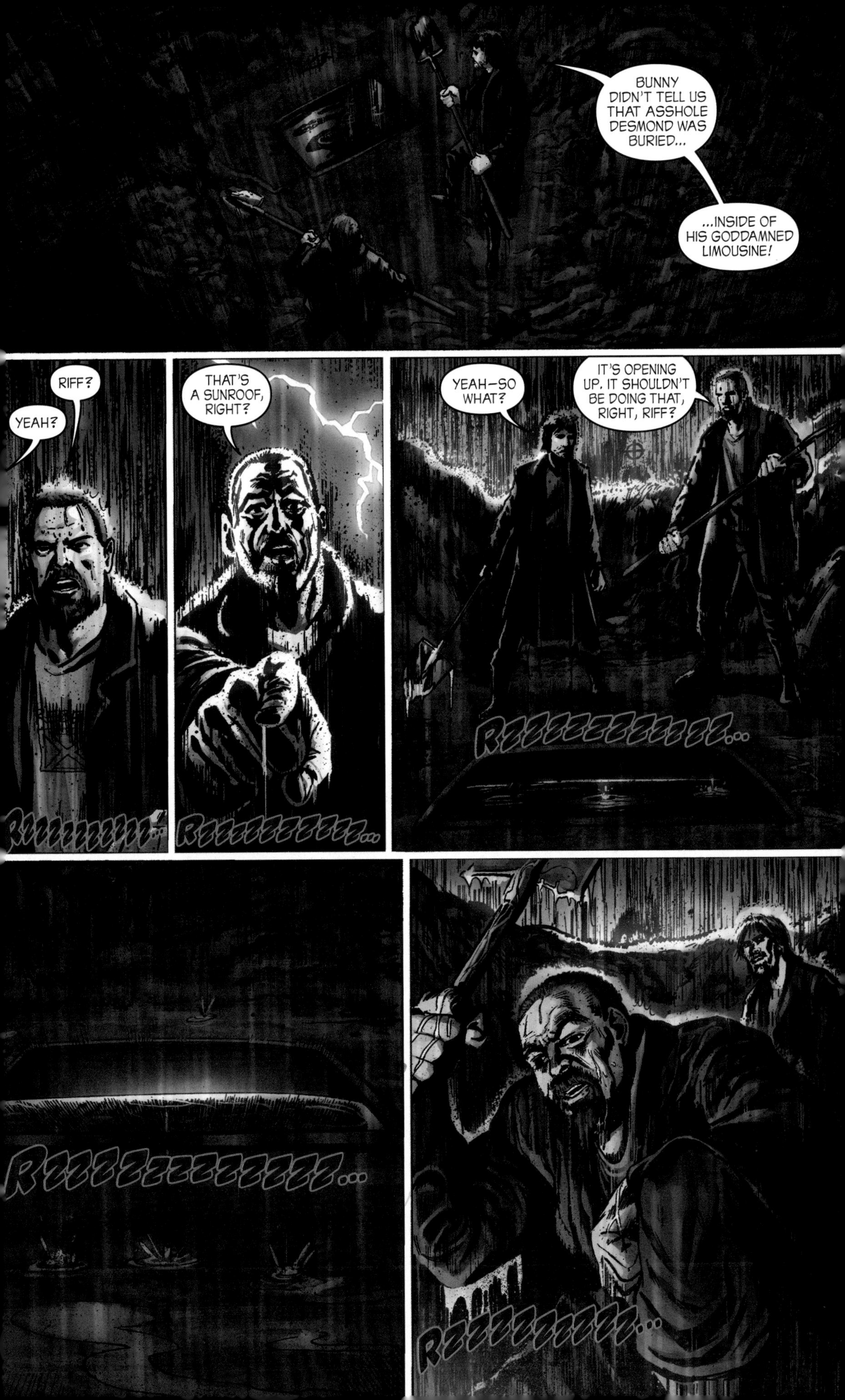
BUNNY DIDN'T TELL US THAT ASSHOLE DESMOND WAS BURIED...
...INSIDE OF HIS GODDAMNED LIMOUSINE!
RIFF?
YEAH?
RZZZZZZZZZ
THAT'S A SUNROOF, RIGHT?
RZZZZZZZZZZ...
YEAH—SO WHAT?
IT'S OPENING UP. IT SHOULDN'T BE DOING THAT, RIGHT, RIFF?
RZZZZZZZZZZZZ...
RZZZZZZZZZZZZZZ...
RZZZZZZZZZZ...

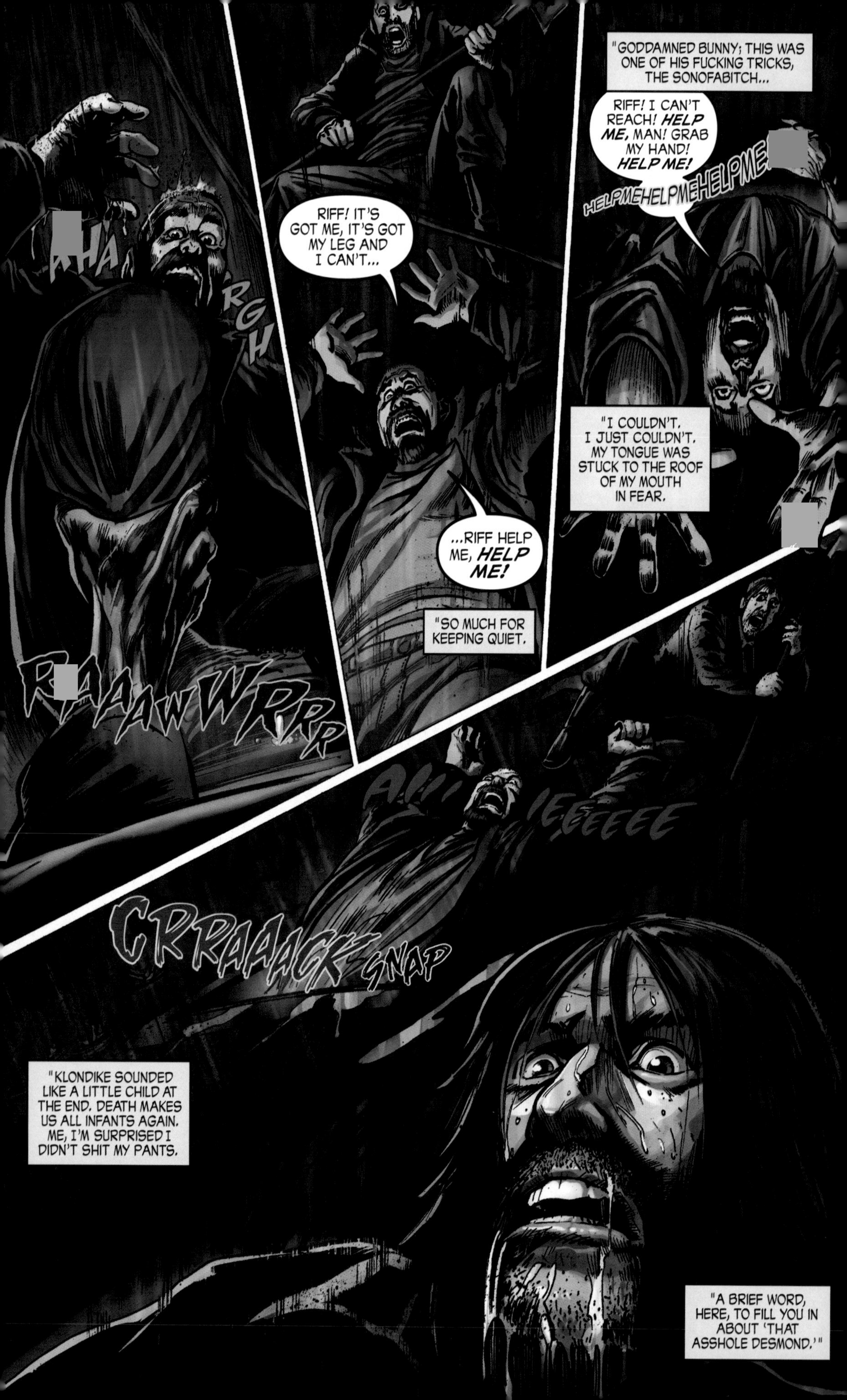

HA
RGH
AAAWRRRR
RIFF! IT'S GOT ME, IT'S GOT MY LEG AND I CAN'T...
...RIFF HELP ME, **HELP ME!**
"SO MUCH FOR KEEPING QUIET.
"GODDAMNED BUNNY; THIS WAS ONE OF HIS FUCKING TRICKS, THE SONOFABITCH...
RIFF! I CAN'T REACH! **HELP ME,** MAN! GRAB MY HAND! **HELP ME!**
HELPMEHELPMEHELPME
"I COULDN'T. I JUST COULDN'T. MY TONGUE WAS STUCK TO THE ROOF OF MY MOUTH IN FEAR.
EEEEEE
CRRAAACK
SNAP
"KLONDIKE SOUNDED LIKE A LITTLE CHILD AT THE END. DEATH MAKES US ALL INFANTS AGAIN. ME, I'M SURPRISED I DIDN'T SHIT MY PANTS.
"A BRIEF WORD, HERE, TO FILL YOU IN ABOUT 'THAT ASSHOLE DESMOND.'"

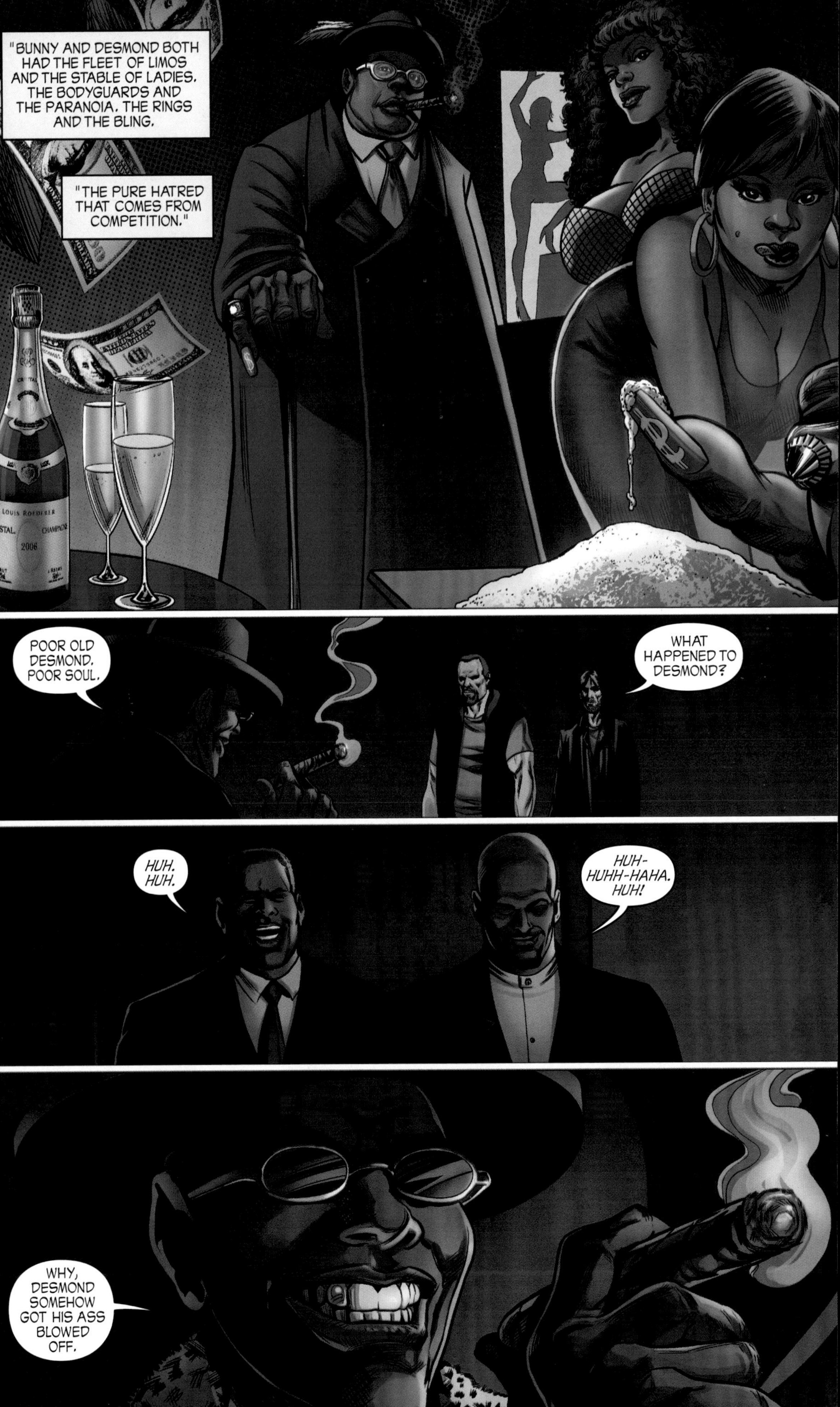
"BUNNY AND DESMOND BOTH HAD THE FLEET OF LIMOS AND THE STABLE OF LADIES. THE BODYGUARDS AND THE PARANOIA. THE RINGS AND THE BLING.
"THE PURE HATRED THAT COMES FROM COMPETITION."
POOR OLD DESMOND. POOR SOUL.
WHAT HAPPENED TO DESMOND?
HUH. HUH.
HUH-HUHH-HAHA. HUH!
WHY, DESMOND SOMEHOW GOT HIS ASS BLOWED OFF.

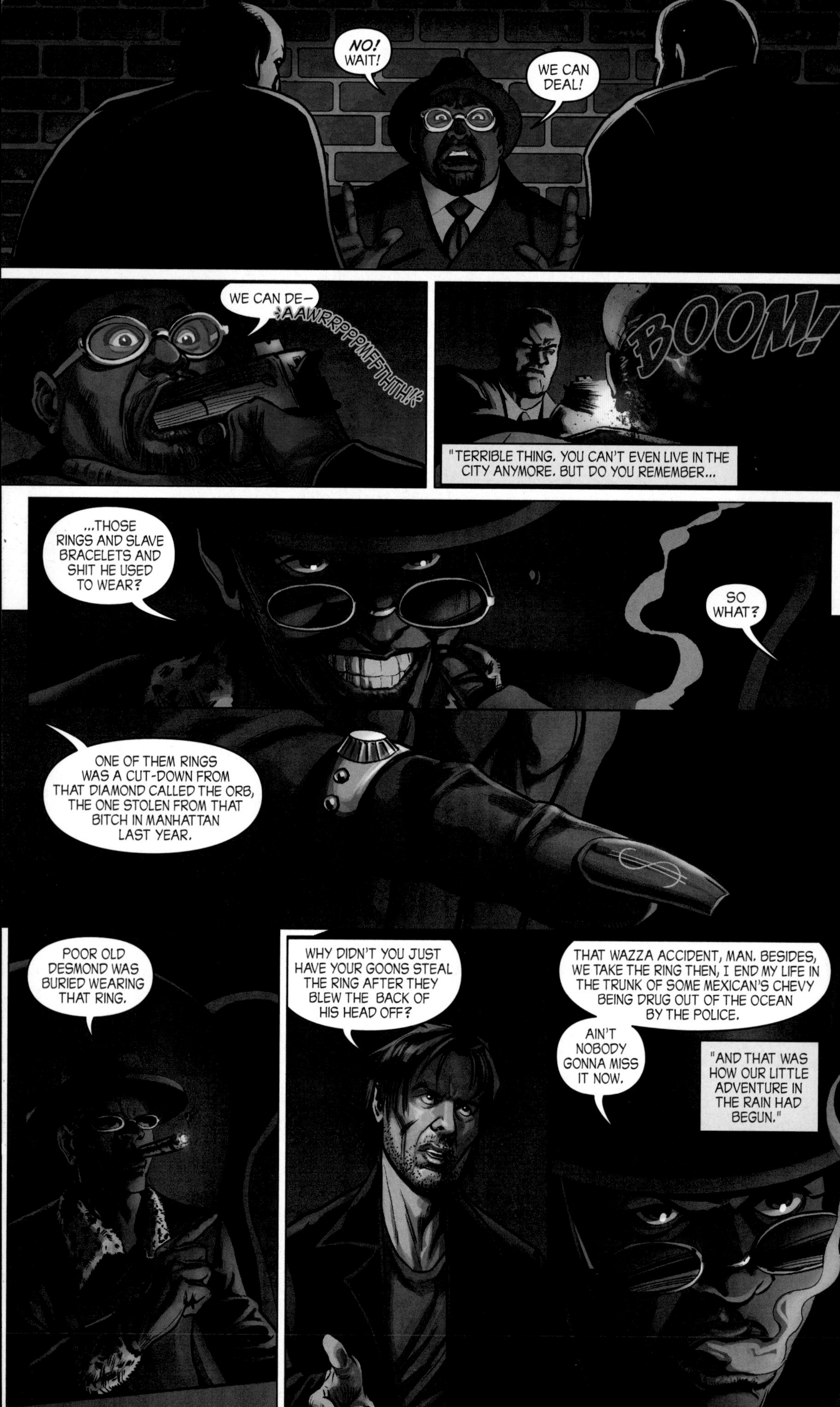
NO! WAIT!
WE CAN DEAL!
WE CAN DE—
—AAWRRPPPMFFTHTH!!
BOOM!
"TERRIBLE THING. YOU CAN'T EVEN LIVE IN THE CITY ANYMORE. BUT DO YOU REMEMBER...
...THOSE RINGS AND SLAVE BRACELETS AND SHIT HE USED TO WEAR?
SO WHAT?
ONE OF THEM RINGS WAS A CUT-DOWN FROM THAT DIAMOND CALLED THE ORB, THE ONE STOLEN FROM THAT BITCH IN MANHATTAN LAST YEAR.
POOR OLD DESMOND WAS BURIED WEARING THAT RING.
WHY DIDN'T YOU JUST HAVE YOUR GOONS STEAL THE RING AFTER THEY BLEW THE BACK OF HIS HEAD OFF?
THAT WAZZA ACCIDENT, MAN. BESIDES, WE TAKE THE RING THEN, I END MY LIFE IN THE TRUNK OF SOME MEXICAN'S CHEVY BEING DRUG OUT OF THE OCEAN BY THE POLICE.
AIN'T NOBODY GONNA MISS IT NOW.
"AND THAT WAS HOW OUR LITTLE ADVENTURE IN THE RAIN HAD BEGUN."

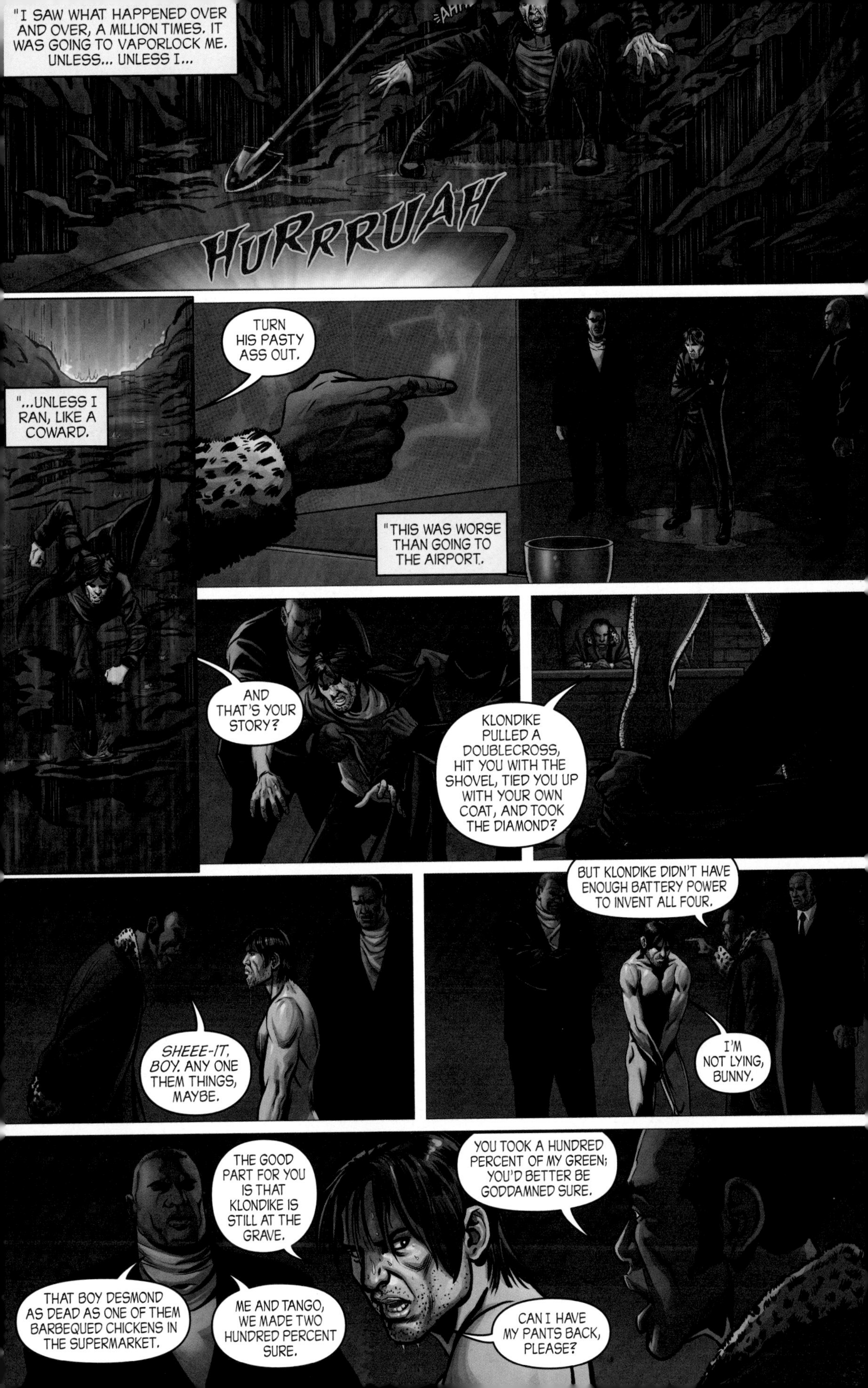
"I SAW WHAT HAPPENED OVER AND OVER, A MILLION TIMES. IT WAS GOING TO VAPORLOCK ME. UNLESS... UNLESS I...
HURRRUAH
"...UNLESS I RAN, LIKE A COWARD.
TURN HIS PASTY ASS OUT.
"THIS WAS WORSE THAN GOING TO THE AIRPORT.
AND THAT'S YOUR STORY?
KLONDIKE PULLED A DOUBLECROSS, HIT YOU WITH THE SHOVEL, TIED YOU UP WITH YOUR OWN COAT, AND TOOK THE DIAMOND?
SHEEE-IT, BOY. ANY ONE THEM THINGS, MAYBE.
BUT KLONDIKE DIDN'T HAVE ENOUGH BATTERY POWER TO INVENT ALL FOUR.
I'M NOT LYING, BUNNY.
THE GOOD PART FOR YOU IS THAT KLONDIKE IS STILL AT THE GRAVE.
YOU TOOK A HUNDRED PERCENT OF MY GREEN; YOU'D BETTER BE GODDAMNED SURE.
THAT BOY DESMOND AS DEAD AS ONE OF THEM BARBEQUED CHICKENS IN THE SUPERMARKET.
ME AND TANGO, WE MADE TWO HUNDRED PERCENT SURE.
CAN I HAVE MY PANTS BACK, PLEASE?

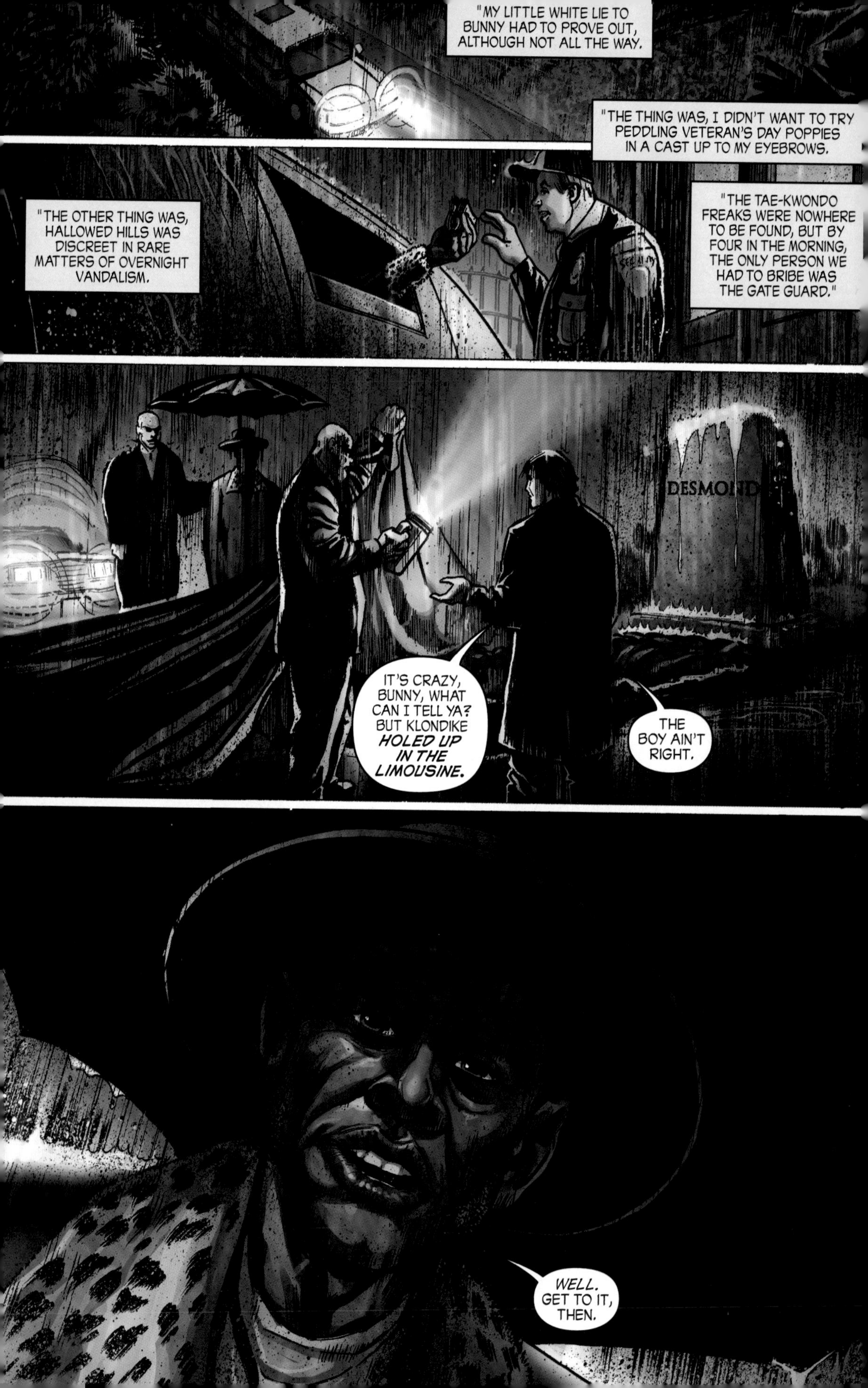
"MY LITTLE WHITE LIE TO BUNNY HAD TO PROVE OUT, ALTHOUGH NOT ALL THE WAY.
"THE THING WAS, I DIDN'T WANT TO TRY PEDDLING VETERAN'S DAY POPPIES IN A CAST UP TO MY EYEBROWS.
"THE OTHER THING WAS, HALLOWED HILLS WAS DISCREET IN RARE MATTERS OF OVERNIGHT VANDALISM.
"THE TAE-KWONDO FREAKS WERE NOWHERE TO BE FOUND, BUT BY FOUR IN THE MORNING, THE ONLY PERSON WE HAD TO BRIBE WAS THE GATE GUARD."
DESMOND
IT'S CRAZY, BUNNY, WHAT CAN I TELL YA? BUT KLONDIKE HOLED UP IN THE LIMOUSINE.
THE BOY AIN'T RIGHT.
WELL. GET TO IT, THEN.

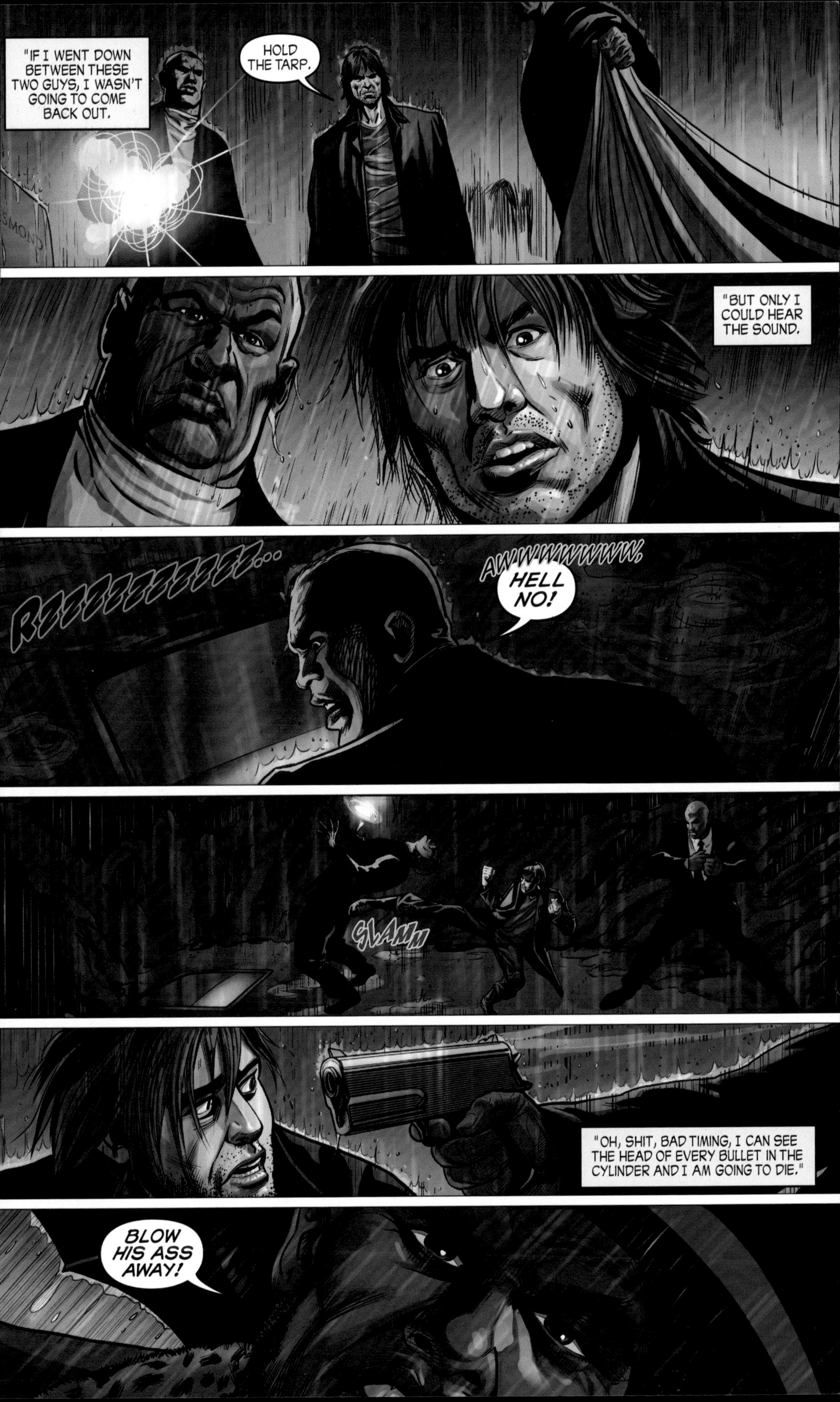
"IF I WENT DOWN BETWEEN THESE TWO GUYS, I WASN'T GOING TO COME BACK OUT.
HOLD THE TARP.
"BUT ONLY I COULD HEAR THE SOUND.
RZZZZZZZZZZZ...
AWWWWWWWW,
HELL NO!
SWAMM
"OH, SHIT, BAD TIMING, I CAN SEE THE HEAD OF EVERY BULLET IN THE CYLINDER AND I AM GOING TO DIE."
BLOW HIS ASS AWAY!

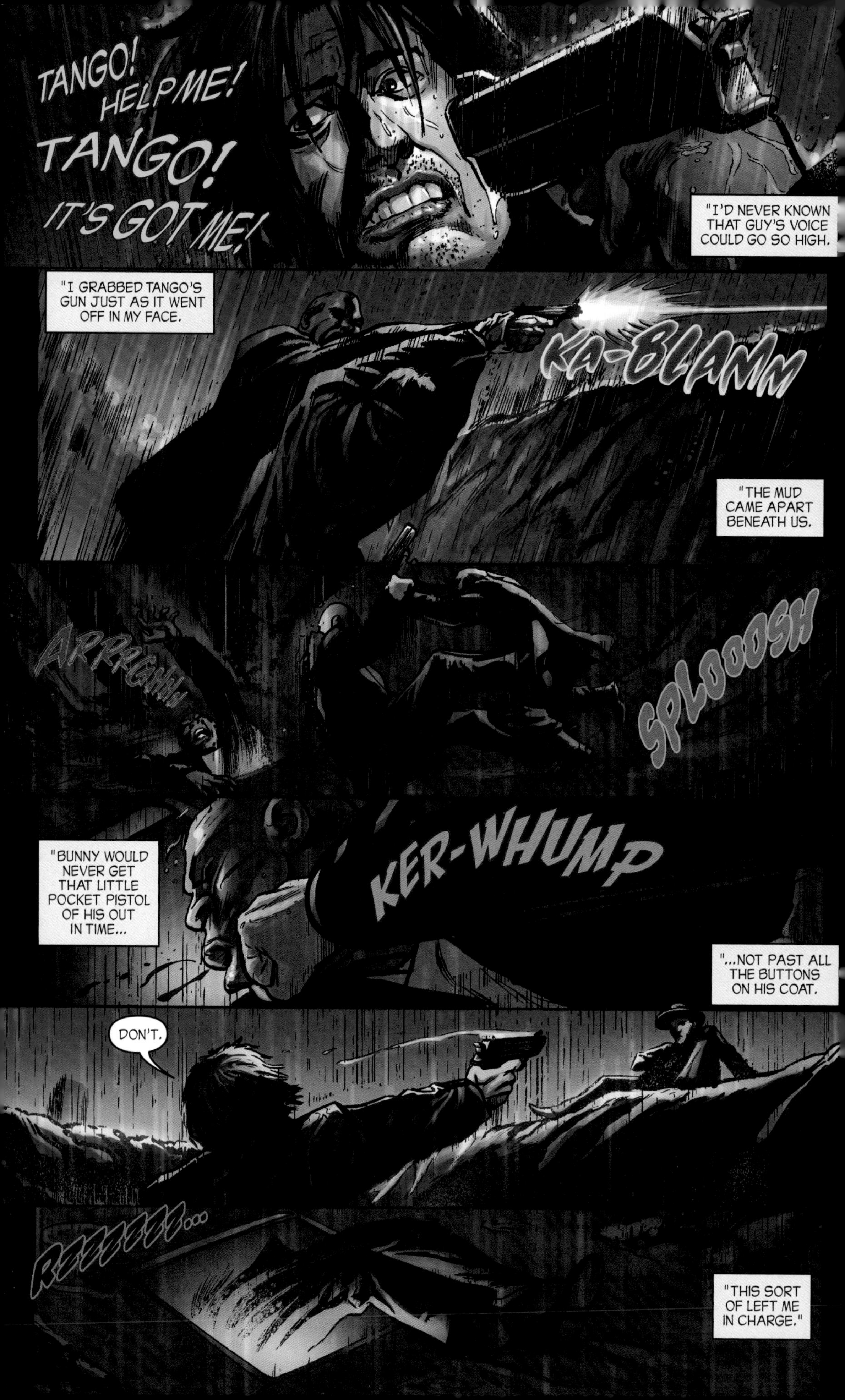
TANGO! HELP ME! TANGO! IT'S GOT ME!
"I'D NEVER KNOWN THAT GUY'S VOICE COULD GO SO HIGH.
"I GRABBED TANGO'S GUN JUST AS IT WENT OFF IN MY FACE.
KA-BLAMM
"THE MUD CAME APART BENEATH US.
ARRRGHH
SPLOOOSH
"BUNNY WOULD NEVER GET THAT LITTLE POCKET PISTOL OF HIS OUT IN TIME...
KER-WHUMP
"...NOT PAST ALL THE BUTTONS ON HIS COAT.
DON'T.
"THIS SORT OF LEFT ME IN CHARGE."

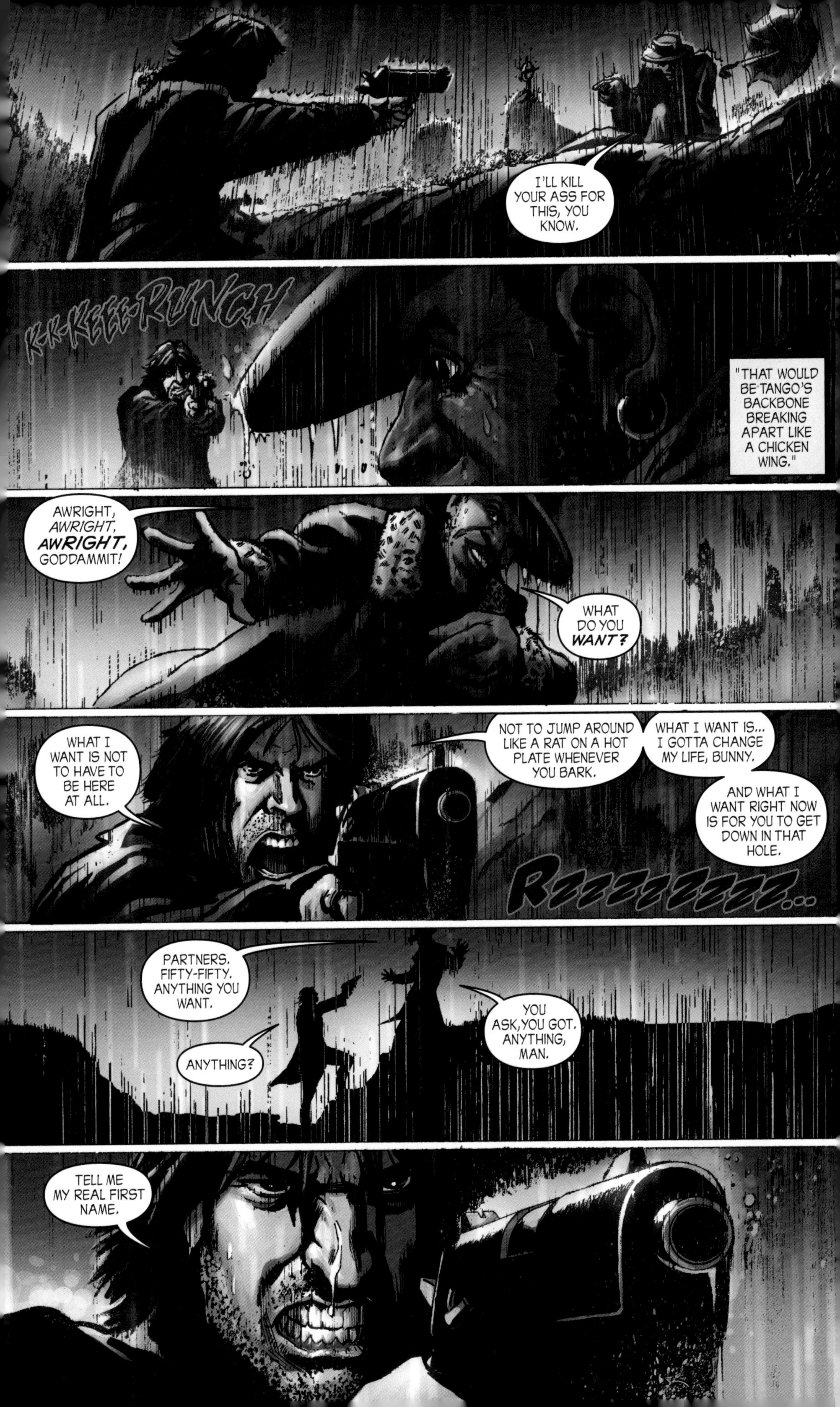

I'LL KILL YOUR ASS FOR THIS, YOU KNOW.
K-K-KEEE-RUNCH
"THAT WOULD BE TANGO'S BACKBONE BREAKING APART LIKE A CHICKEN WING."
AWRIGHT, AWRIGHT, AWRIGHT, GODDAMMIT!
WHAT DO YOU WANT?
WHAT I WANT IS NOT TO HAVE TO BE HERE AT ALL.
NOT TO JUMP AROUND LIKE A RAT ON A HOT PLATE WHENEVER YOU BARK.
WHAT I WANT IS... I GOTTA CHANGE MY LIFE, BUNNY.
AND WHAT I WANT RIGHT NOW IS FOR YOU TO GET DOWN IN THAT HOLE.
RZZZZZZZZ...
PARTNERS. FIFTY-FIFTY. ANYTHING YOU WANT.
YOU ASK, YOU GOT. ANYTHING, MAN.
ANYTHING?
TELL ME MY REAL FIRST NAME.

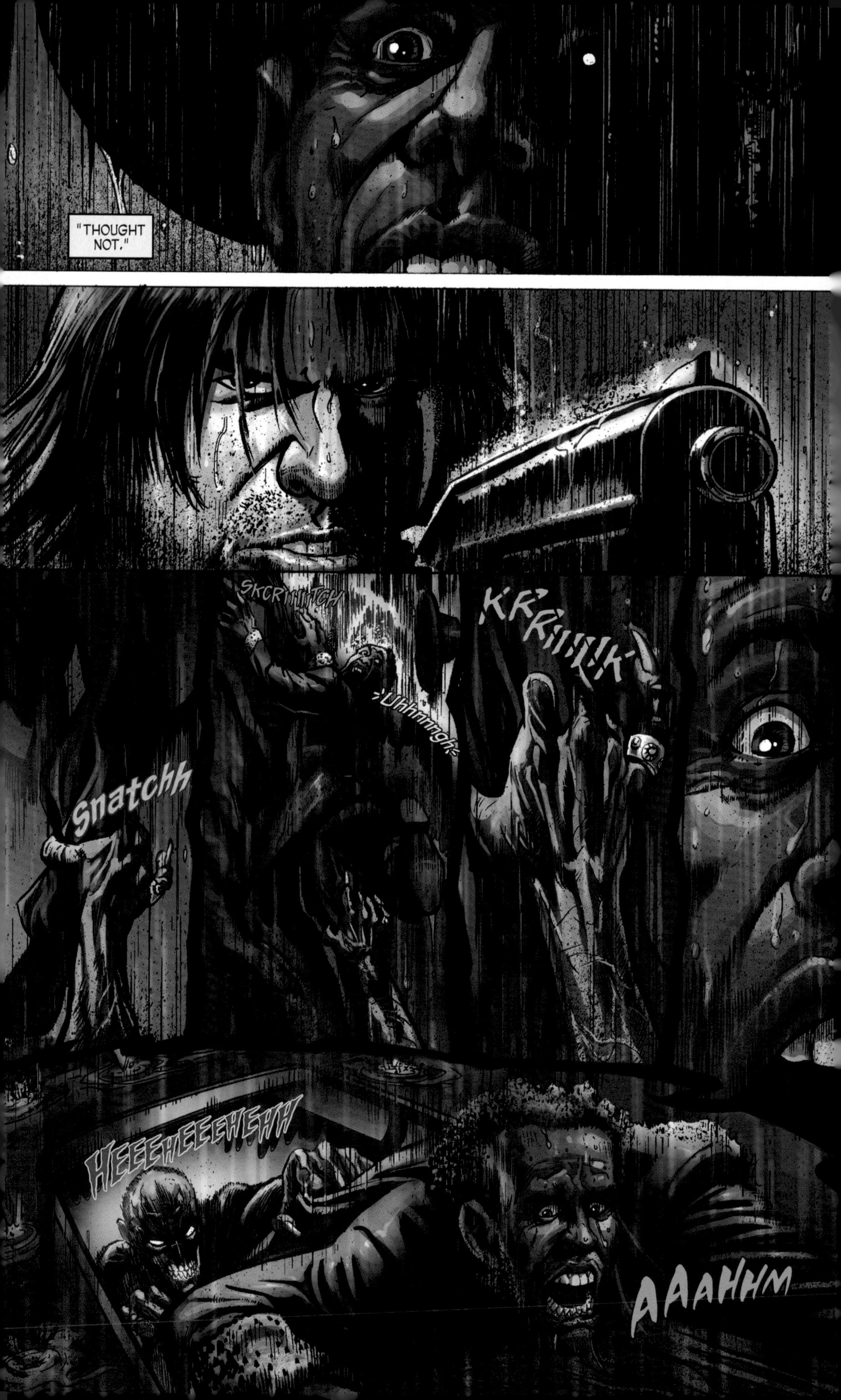

"THOUGHT NOT."
SKCRIIIIITCH
Snatchh
KRRIIIIK
Uhhhnngh
HEEEHEEEHEHH
AAAHHM

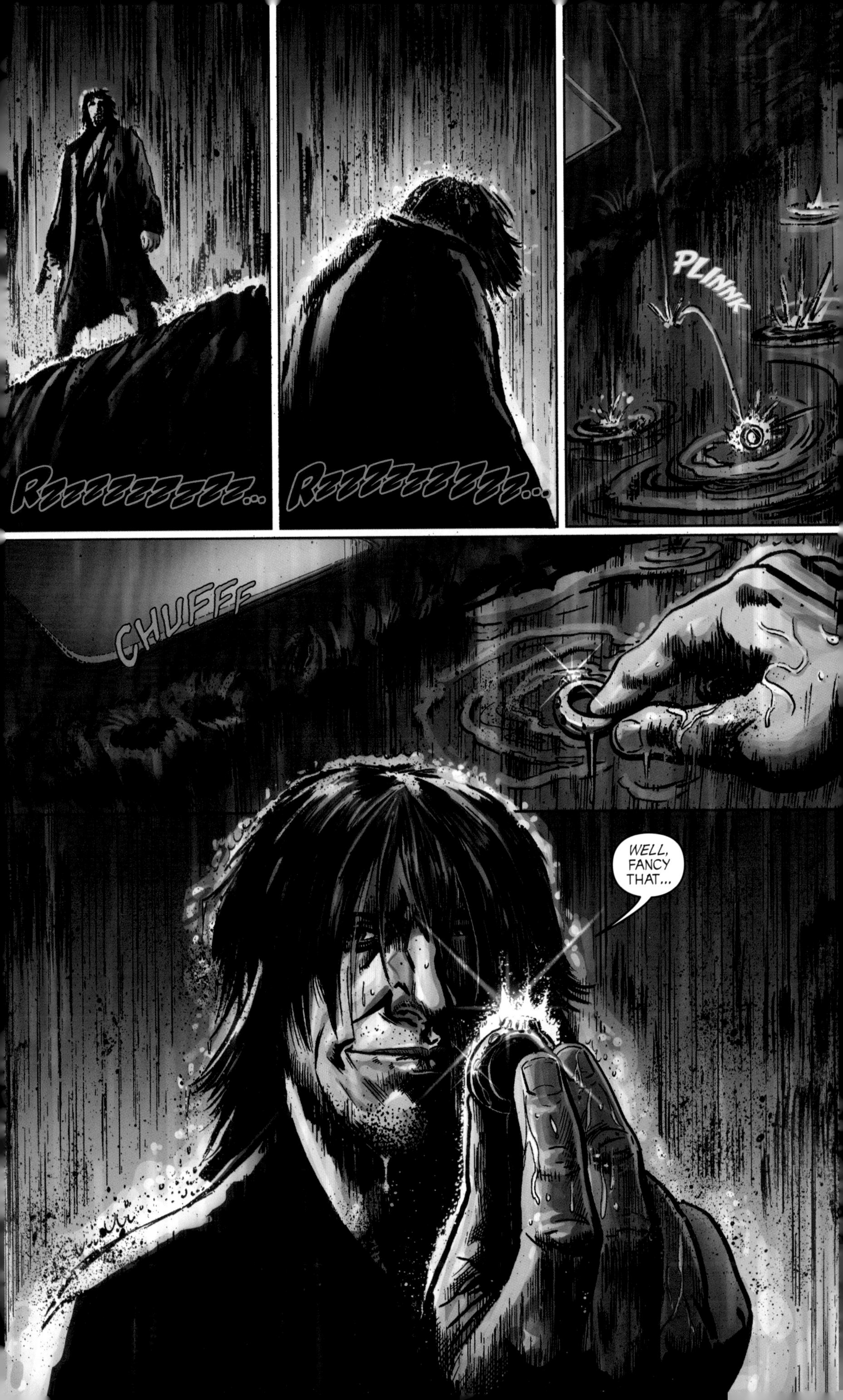
Rzzzzzzzzz...
Rzzzzzzzzzz...
PLINNK
CHUFFF
WELL, FANCY THAT...

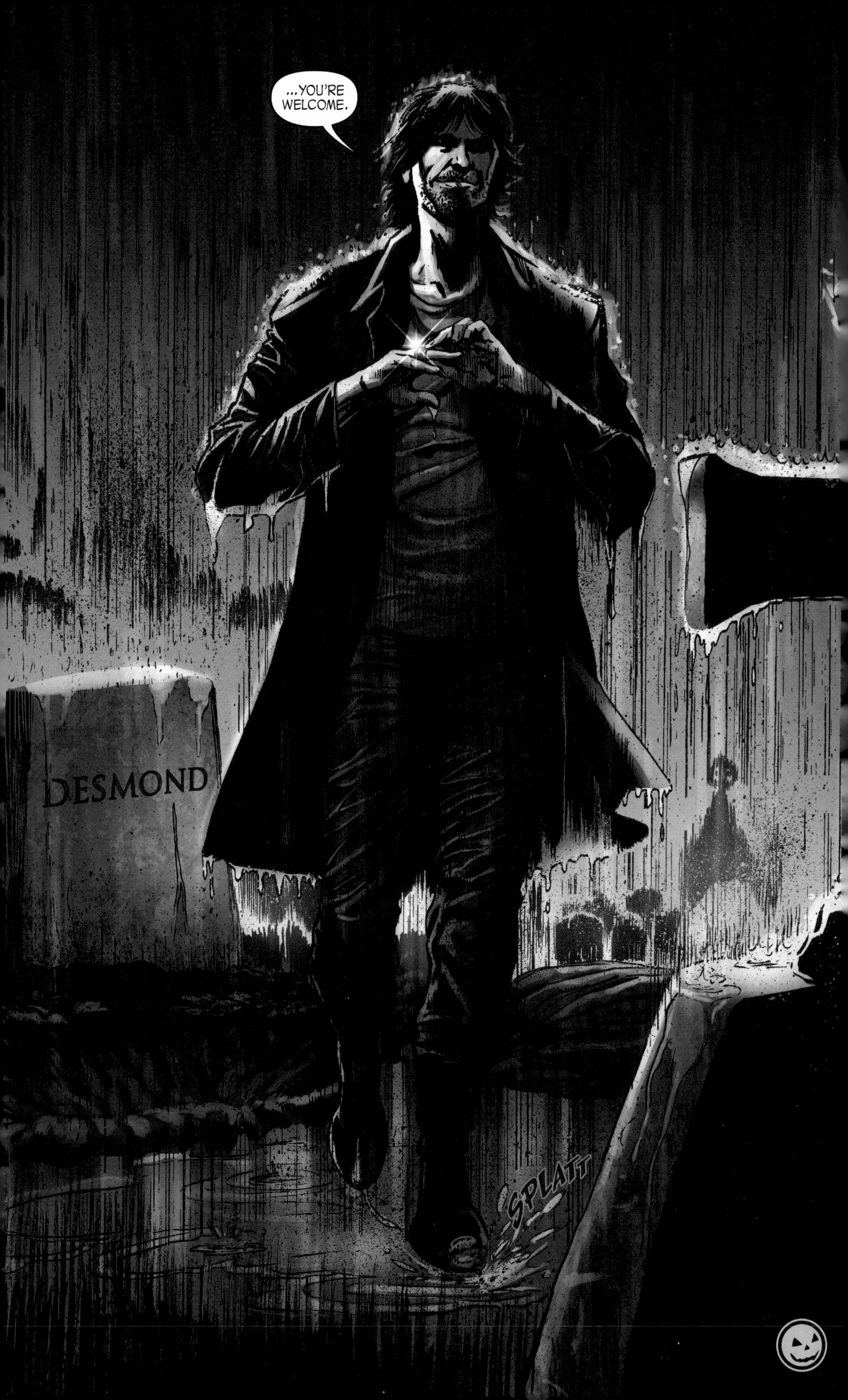
...YOU'RE WELCOME.
DESMOND
SPLATT

Down on all fours, his ear to the ground, like an old Saturday matinee Indian listening for galloping horses, the keeper seems intent on hearing…something.

He quietly "hmphs" to himself.

Returning to his feet, he brushes the loose dirt from his overalls and hands.

I wonder if I kin charge fer overnight parking.

I'll hafta look into that, he mutters to himself.

Back on his tractor, he continues on his nightly journey. As he passes through the next bunch of trees, they seem to part and thin out again as he crests a small rise in the terrain. He continues down the other side, and we find ourselves in an old 'Boot Hill'-style graveyard. A wooden picket fence contains the rows of mixed wooden monuments and small hand-carved stone tablets.

He crests another small rise and stops at an old scrub oak, just tall enough for him to park his tractor beneath. He pokes the brim of his battered old hat upward slightly.

Time fer a little break, I reckon.

He reaches back into the trailer behind him and pulls out an old miner's lunch pail. Black, paint-chipped and dented, it looks as if it has as many miles on it as the keeper does. He pops the latches and reaches in.

You know, there's good folks and there's bad folks. Then, there's just reg'lar people. At the end of the day, it don't matter. They all end up here, one way or another.

He pulls out what appears to be a thick sandwich, wrapped neatly in tin foil.

Take Dean Patricks. He was just one of them reg'lar guys, and look what happened to him.

What's that? Oh, my apologies. I haven't told you that one yet, huh?

He leans back in his seat, kicks his feet up, sandwich in hand.

I'll just grab a bite here while I tell ya' 'bout Dean. A reg'lar guy, maybe even a little like you, who found himself hungry for just a little more in life. So he went looking, and ended up finding…

SOME GRUB

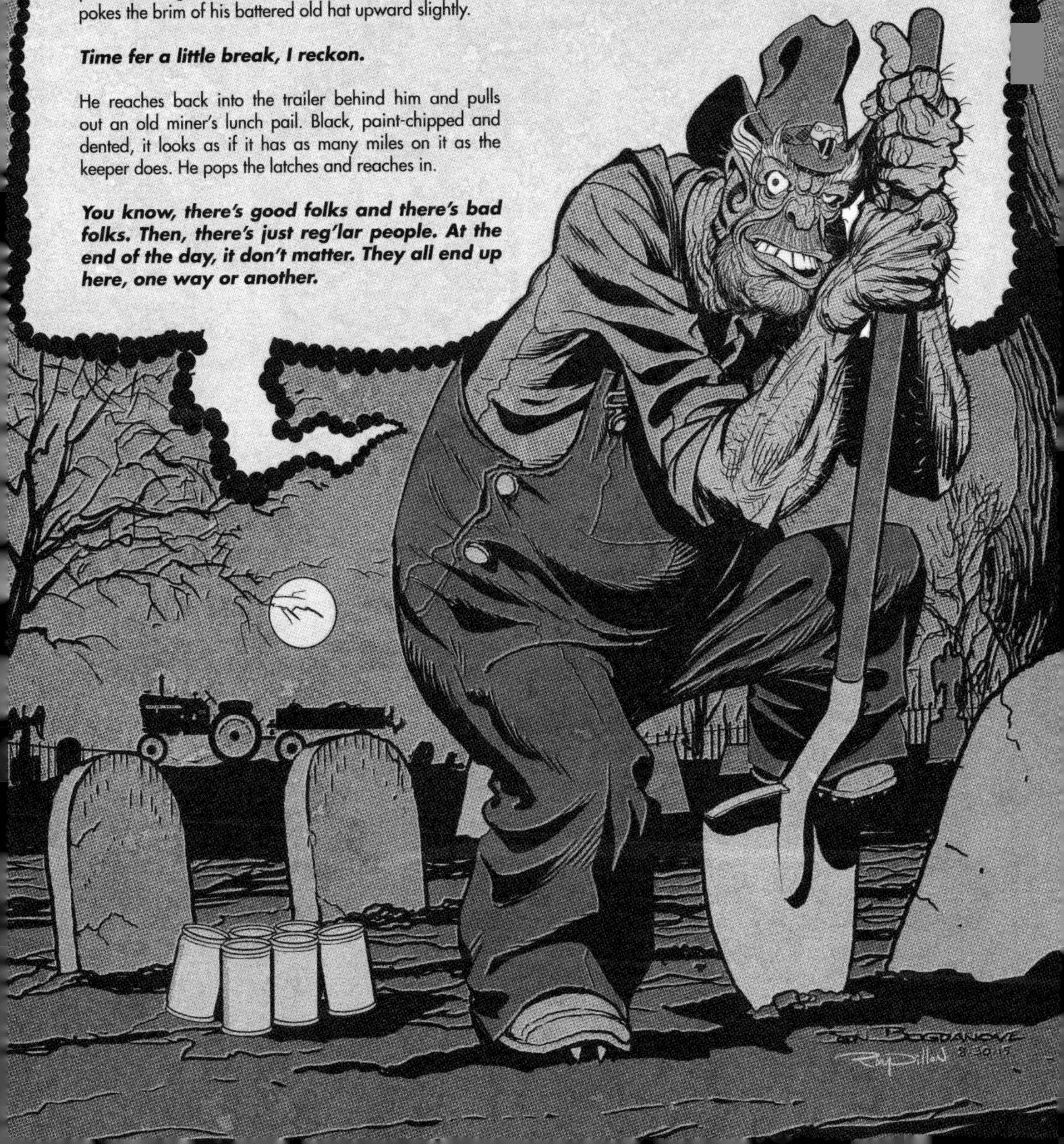

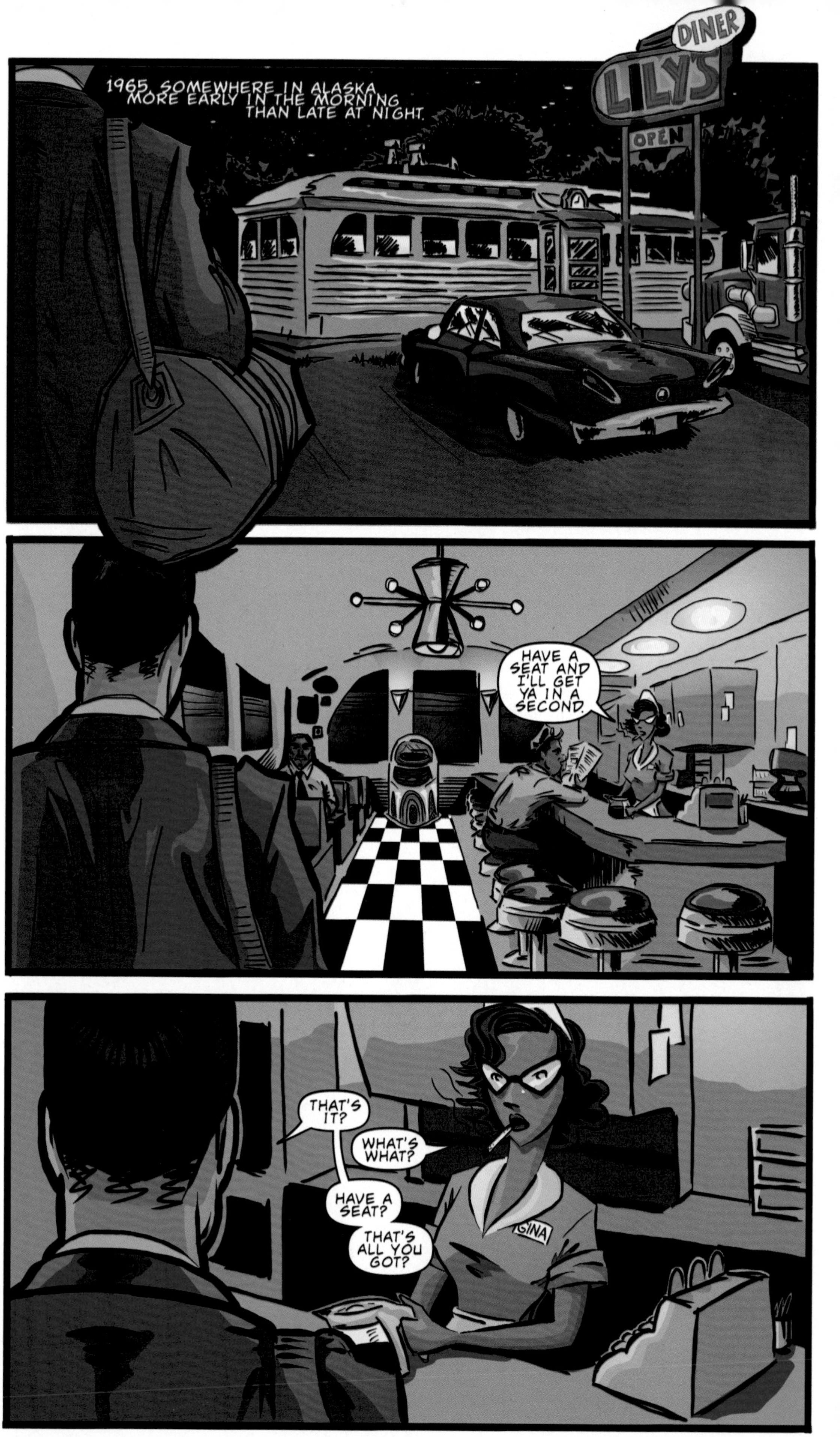

1965, SOMEWHERE IN ALASKA
MORE EARLY IN THE MORNING
THAN LATE AT NIGHT.
DINER
LILY'S
OPEN
HAVE A SEAT AND I'LL GET YA IN A SECOND.
THAT'S IT?
WHAT'S WHAT?
HAVE A SEAT?
THAT'S ALL YOU GOT?
GINA

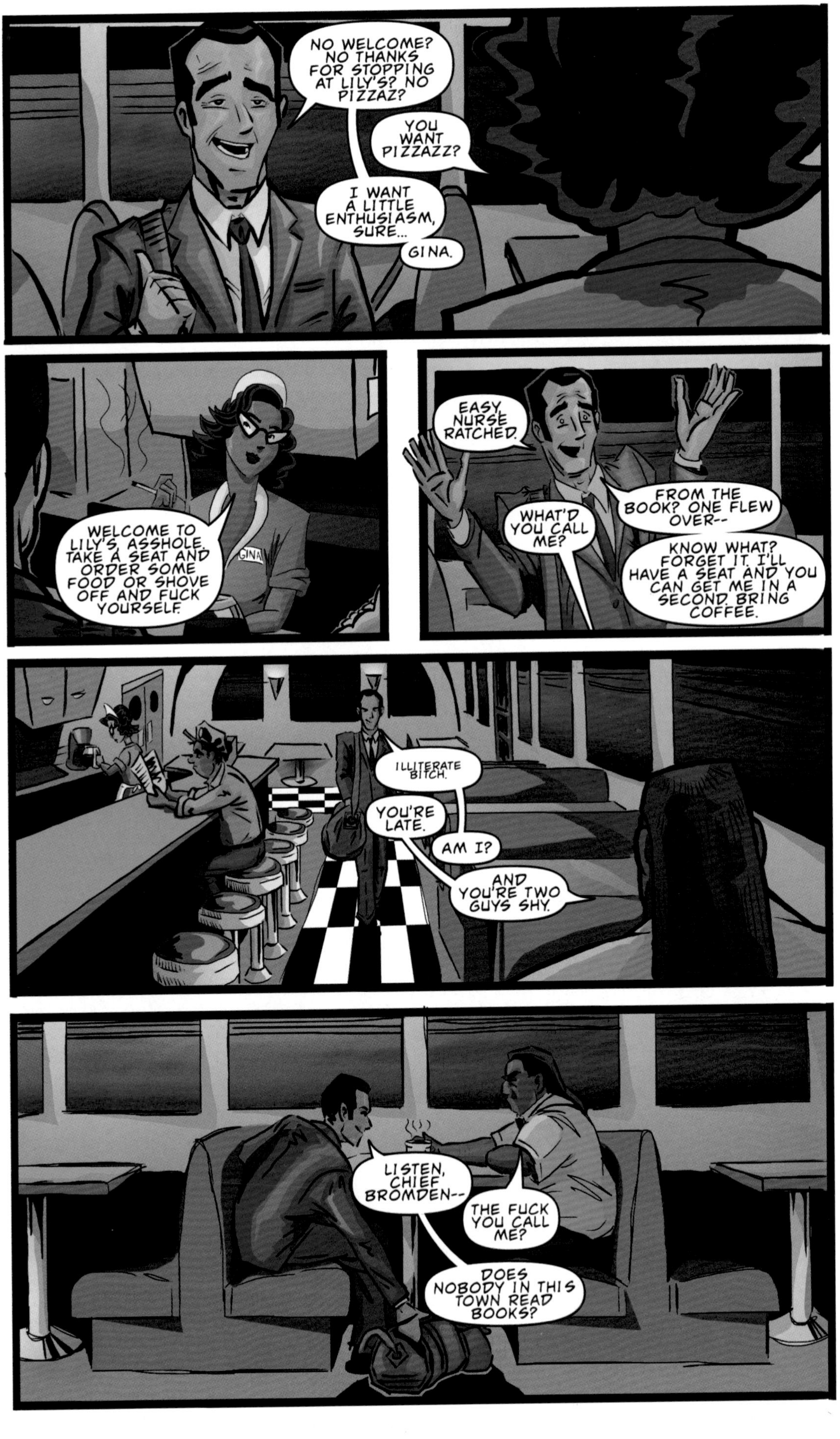
NO WELCOME? NO THANKS FOR STOPPING AT LILY'S? NO PIZZAZ?
YOU WANT PIZZAZZ?
I WANT A LITTLE ENTHUSIASM, SURE...
GINA.
WELCOME TO LILY'S, ASSHOLE. TAKE A SEAT AND ORDER SOME FOOD OR SHOVE OFF AND FUCK YOURSELF.
GINA
EASY, NURSE RATCHED.
WHAT'D YOU CALL ME?
FROM THE BOOK? ONE FLEW OVER--
KNOW WHAT? FORGET IT. I'LL HAVE A SEAT AND YOU CAN GET ME IN A SECOND. BRING COFFEE.
ILLITERATE BITCH.
YOU'RE LATE.
AM I?
AND YOU'RE TWO GUYS SHY.
LISTEN, CHIEF BROMDEN--
THE FUCK YOU CALL ME?
DOES NOBODY IN THIS TOWN READ BOOKS?

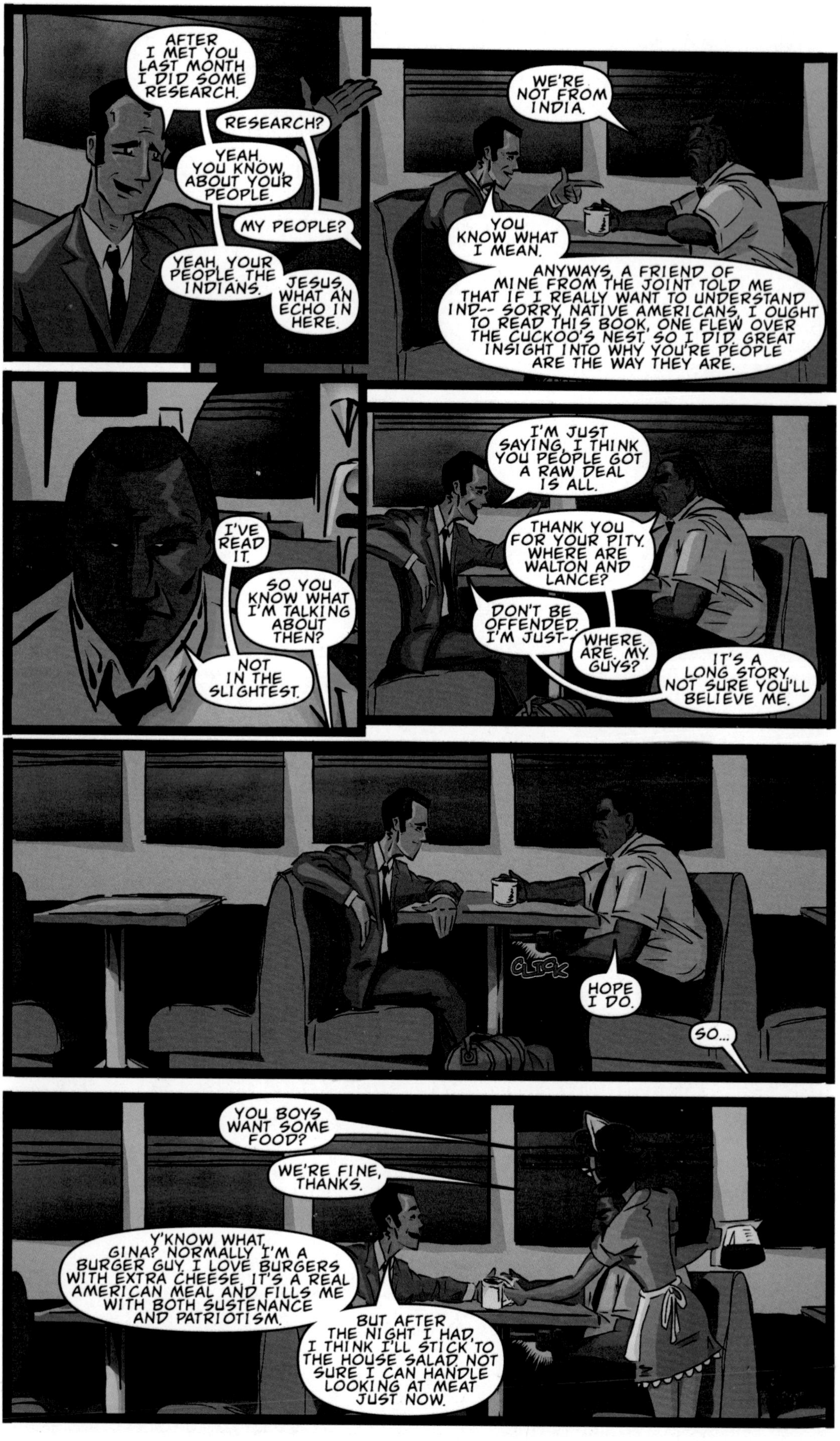
AFTER I MET YOU LAST MONTH I DID SOME RESEARCH.
RESEARCH?
YEAH. YOU KNOW, ABOUT YOUR PEOPLE.
MY PEOPLE?
YEAH, YOUR PEOPLE, THE INDIANS.
JESUS, WHAT AN ECHO IN HERE.
WE'RE NOT FROM INDIA.
YOU KNOW WHAT I MEAN.
ANYWAYS, A FRIEND OF MINE FROM THE JOINT TOLD ME THAT IF I REALLY WANT TO UNDERSTAND IND-- SORRY, NATIVE AMERICANS, I OUGHT TO READ THIS BOOK, ONE FLEW OVER THE CUCKOO'S NEST. SO I DID. GREAT INSIGHT INTO WHY YOU'RE PEOPLE ARE THE WAY THEY ARE.
I'VE READ IT.
SO YOU KNOW WHAT I'M TALKING ABOUT THEN?
NOT IN THE SLIGHTEST.
I'M JUST SAYING, I THINK YOU PEOPLE GOT A RAW DEAL IS ALL.
THANK YOU FOR YOUR PITY. WHERE ARE WALTON AND LANCE?
DON'T BE OFFENDED. I'M JUST--
WHERE ARE MY GUYS?
IT'S A LONG STORY. NOT SURE YOU'LL BELIEVE ME.
CLICK
HOPE I DO.
SO...
YOU BOYS WANT SOME FOOD?
WE'RE FINE, THANKS.
Y'KNOW WHAT, GINA? NORMALLY I'M A BURGER GUY. I LOVE BURGERS WITH EXTRA CHEESE. IT'S A REAL AMERICAN MEAL AND FILLS ME WITH BOTH SUSTENANCE AND PATRIOTISM.
BUT AFTER THE NIGHT I HAD, I THINK I'LL STICK TO THE HOUSE SALAD. NOT SURE I CAN HANDLE LOOKING AT MEAT JUST NOW.

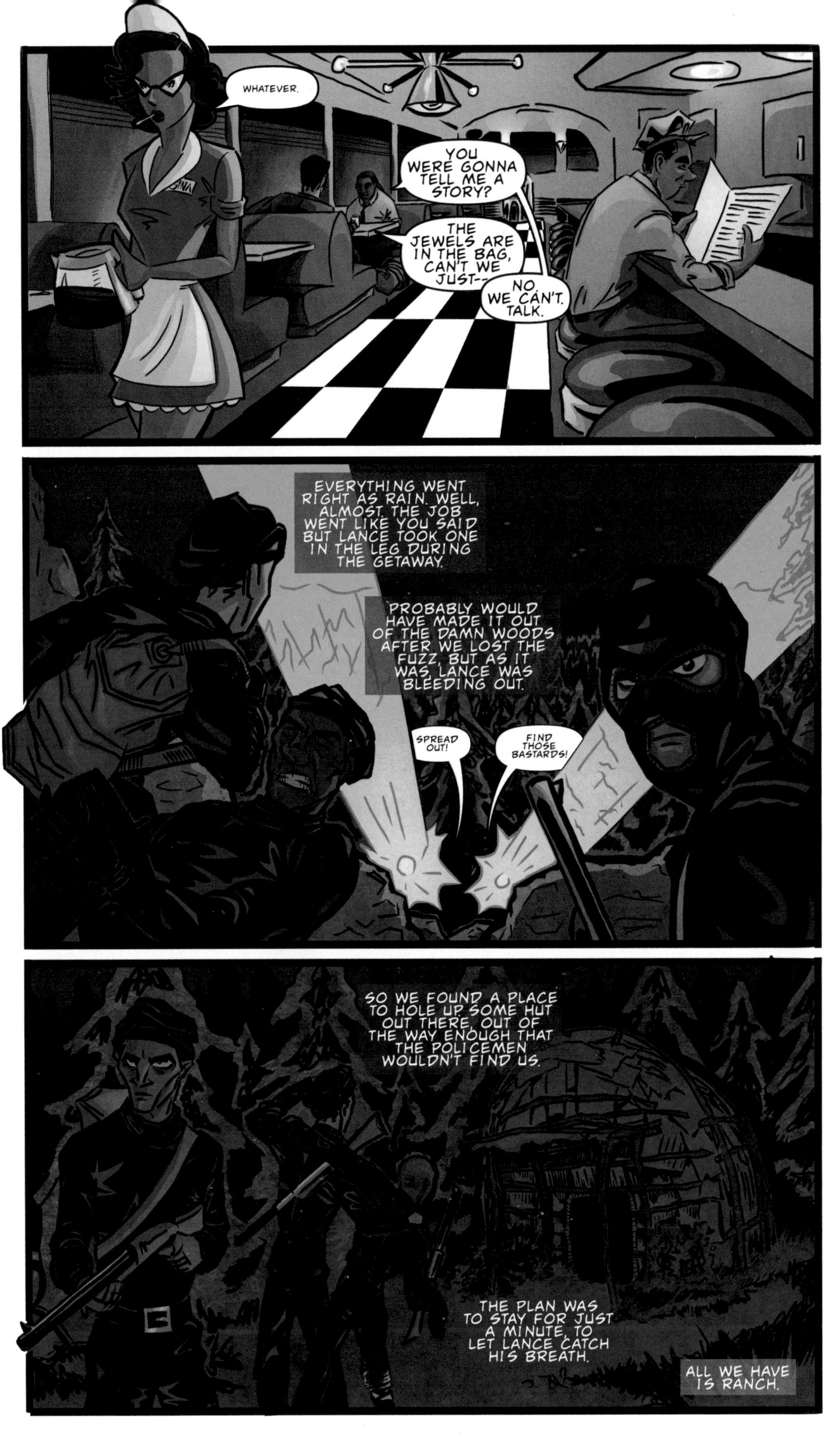
WHATEVER.
YOU WERE GONNA TELL ME A STORY?
THE JEWELS ARE IN THE BAG, CAN'T WE JUST--
NO. WE CAN'T. TALK.
EVERYTHING WENT RIGHT AS RAIN. WELL, ALMOST. THE JOB WENT LIKE YOU SAID BUT LANCE TOOK ONE IN THE LEG DURING THE GETAWAY.
PROBABLY WOULD HAVE MADE IT OUT OF THE DAMN WOODS AFTER WE LOST THE FUZZ, BUT AS IT WAS, LANCE WAS BLEEDING OUT.
SPREAD OUT!
FIND THOSE BASTARDS!
SO WE FOUND A PLACE TO HOLE UP. SOME HUT OUT THERE, OUT OF THE WAY ENOUGH THAT THE POLICEMEN WOULDN'T FIND US.
THE PLAN WAS TO STAY FOR JUST A MINUTE, TO LET LANCE CATCH HIS BREATH.
ALL WE HAVE IS RANCH.

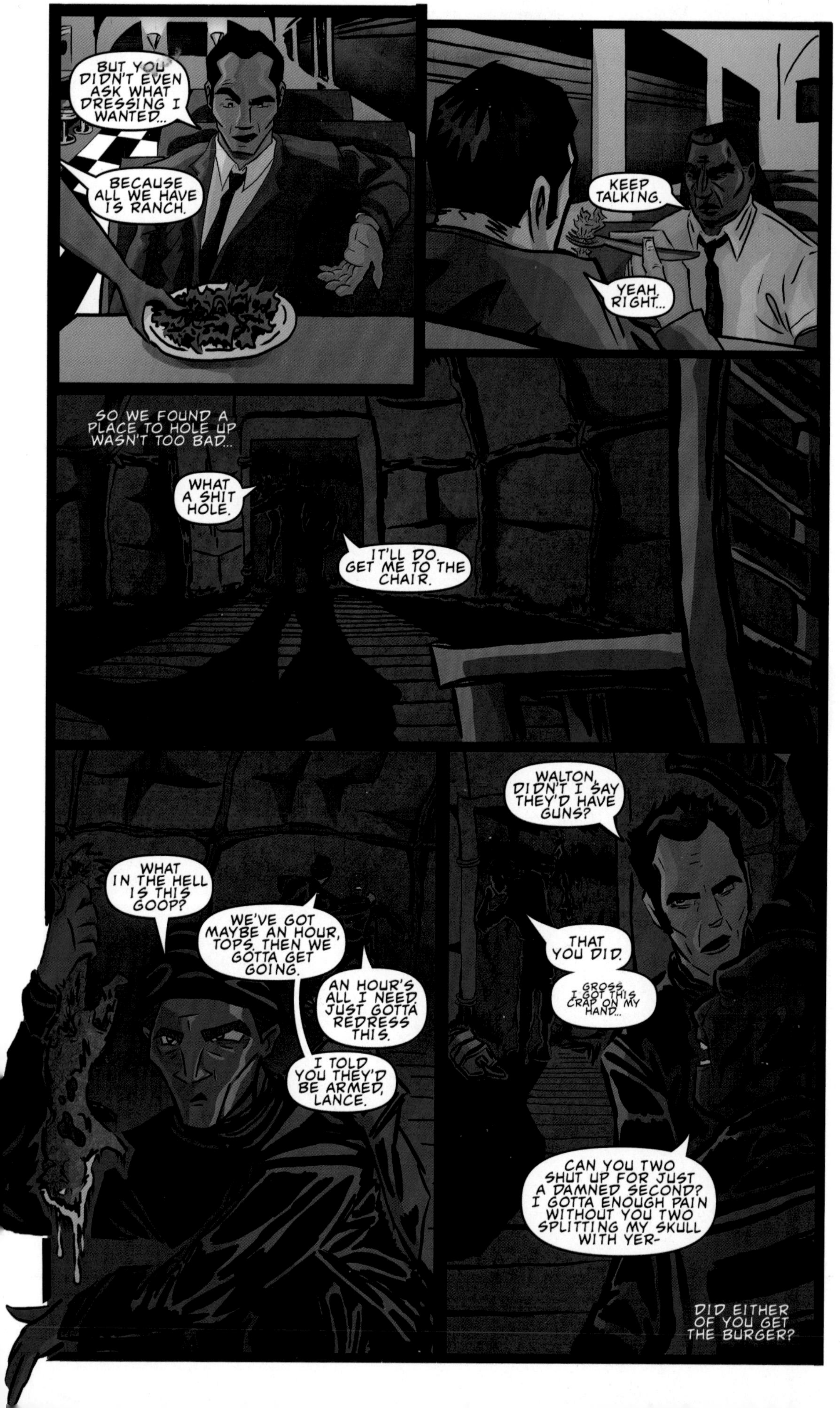
BUT YOU DIDN'T EVEN ASK WHAT DRESSING I WANTED...
BECAUSE ALL WE HAVE IS RANCH.
KEEP TALKING.
YEAH. RIGHT...
SO WE FOUND A PLACE TO HOLE UP WASN'T TOO BAD...
WHAT A SHIT HOLE.
IT'LL DO. GET ME TO THE CHAIR.
WHAT IN THE HELL IS THIS GOOP?
WE'VE GOT MAYBE AN HOUR, TOPS. THEN WE GOTTA GET GOING.
AN HOUR'S ALL I NEED. JUST GOTTA REDRESS THIS.
I TOLD YOU THEY'D BE ARMED, LANCE.
WALTON, DIDN'T I SAY THEY'D HAVE GUNS?
THAT YOU DID.
GROSS. I GOT THIS CRAP ON MY HAND...
CAN YOU TWO SHUT UP FOR JUST A DAMNED SECOND? I GOTTA ENOUGH PAIN WITHOUT YOU TWO SPLITTING MY SKULL WITH YER-
DID EITHER OF YOU GET THE BURGER?

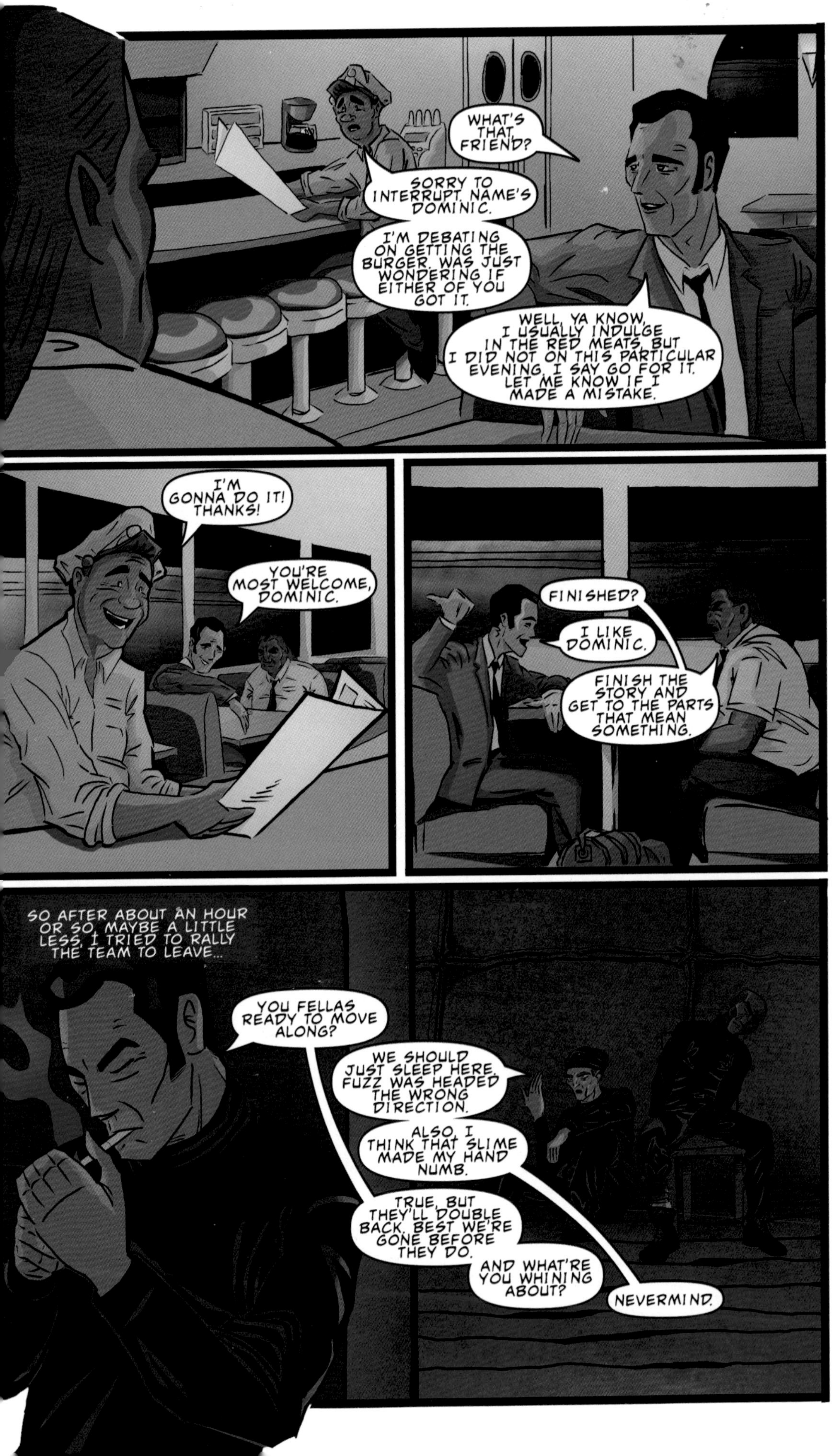
WHAT'S THAT, FRIEND?
SORRY TO INTERRUPT. NAME'S DOMINIC.
I'M DEBATING ON GETTING THE BURGER. WAS JUST WONDERING IF EITHER OF YOU GOT IT.
WELL, YA KNOW, I USUALLY INDULGE IN THE RED MEATS, BUT I DID NOT ON THIS PARTICULAR EVENING. I SAY GO FOR IT. LET ME KNOW IF I MADE A MISTAKE.
I'M GONNA DO IT! THANKS!
YOU'RE MOST WELCOME, DOMINIC.
FINISHED?
I LIKE DOMINIC.
FINISH THE STORY AND GET TO THE PARTS THAT MEAN SOMETHING.
SO AFTER ABOUT AN HOUR OR SO, MAYBE A LITTLE LESS, I TRIED TO RALLY THE TEAM TO LEAVE...
YOU FELLAS READY TO MOVE ALONG?
WE SHOULD JUST SLEEP HERE. FUZZ WAS HEADED THE WRONG DIRECTION.
ALSO, I THINK THAT SLIME MADE MY HAND NUMB.
TRUE, BUT THEY'LL DOUBLE BACK. BEST WE'RE GONE BEFORE THEY DO.
AND WHAT'RE YOU WHINING ABOUT?
NEVERMIND.

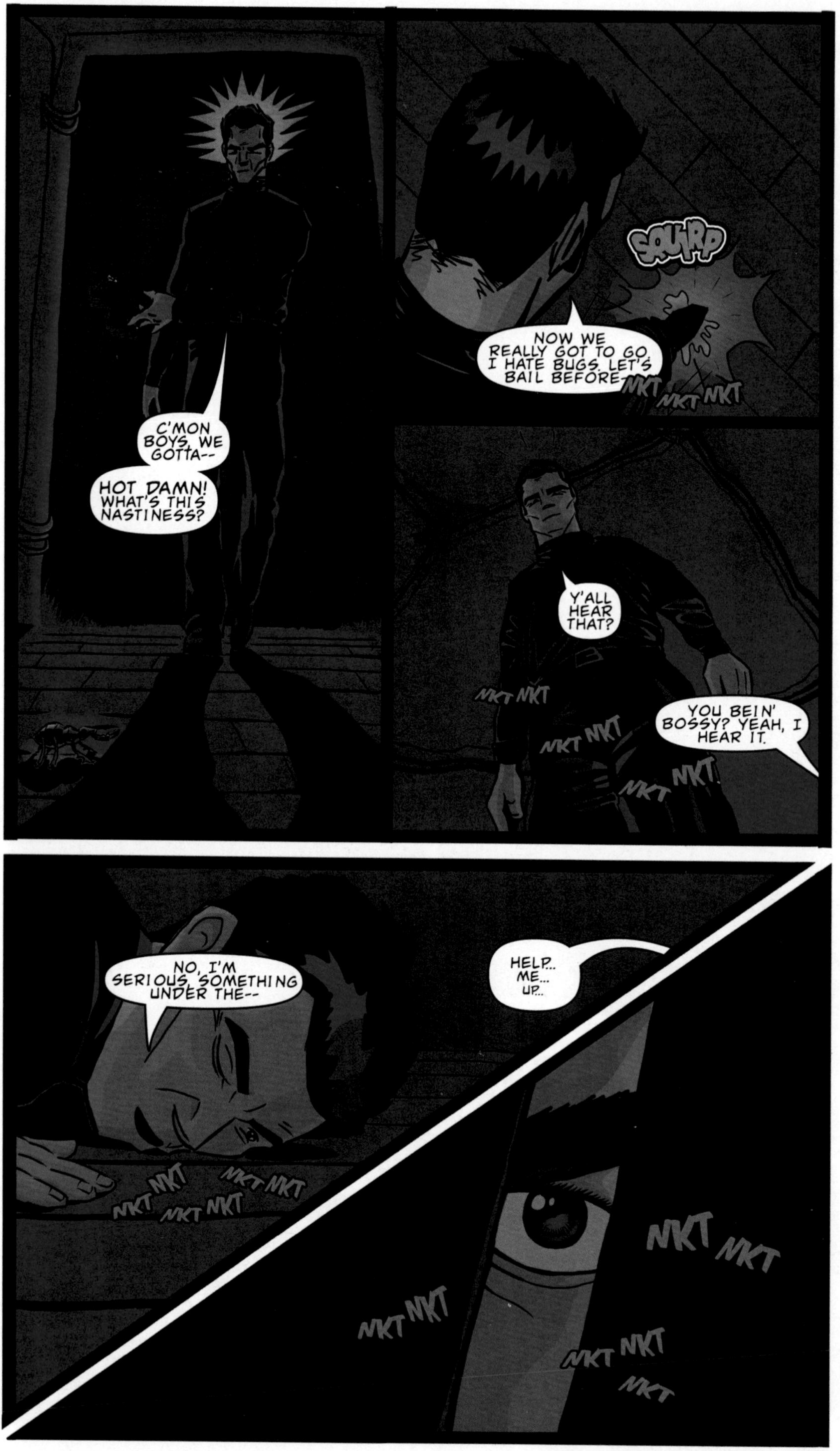
C'MON BOYS, WE GOTTA--
HOT DAMN! WHAT'S THIS NASTINESS?
SQUIRP
NOW WE REALLY GOT TO GO. I HATE BUGS. LET'S BAIL BEFORE--
NKT NKT NKT
Y'ALL HEAR THAT?
NKT NKT
NKT NKT
NKT NKT
YOU BEIN' BOSSY? YEAH, I HEAR IT.
NO, I'M SERIOUS, SOMETHING UNDER THE--
NKT NKT NKT NKT NKT NKT
HELP... ME... UP...
NKT NKT
NKT NKT
NKT NKT
NKT

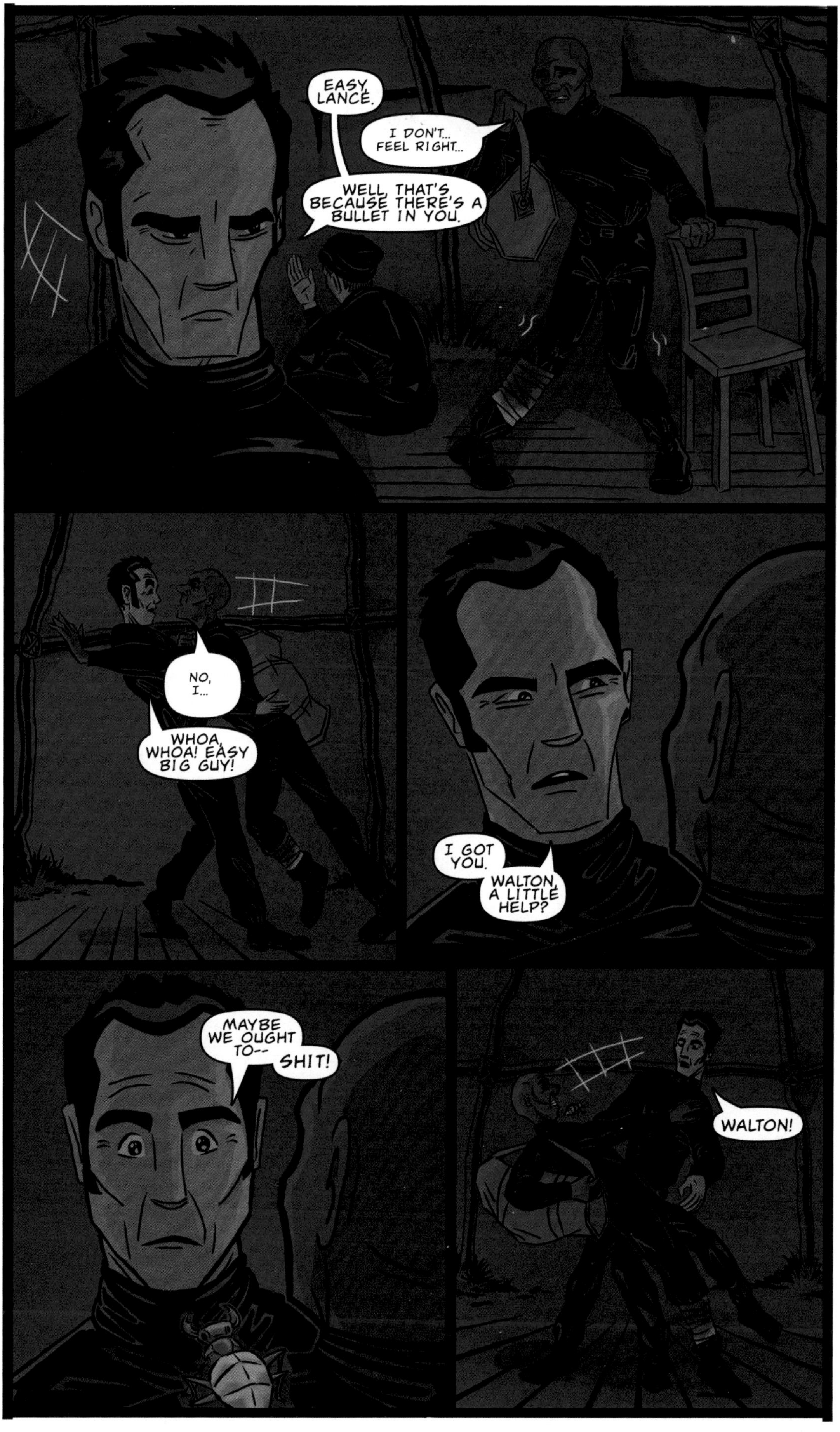
EASY, LANCE.
I DON'T... FEEL RIGHT...
WELL, THAT'S BECAUSE THERE'S A BULLET IN YOU.
NO, I...
WHOA, WHOA! EASY BIG GUY!
I GOT YOU.
WALTON, A LITTLE HELP?
MAYBE WE OUGHT TO--
SHIT!
WALTON!

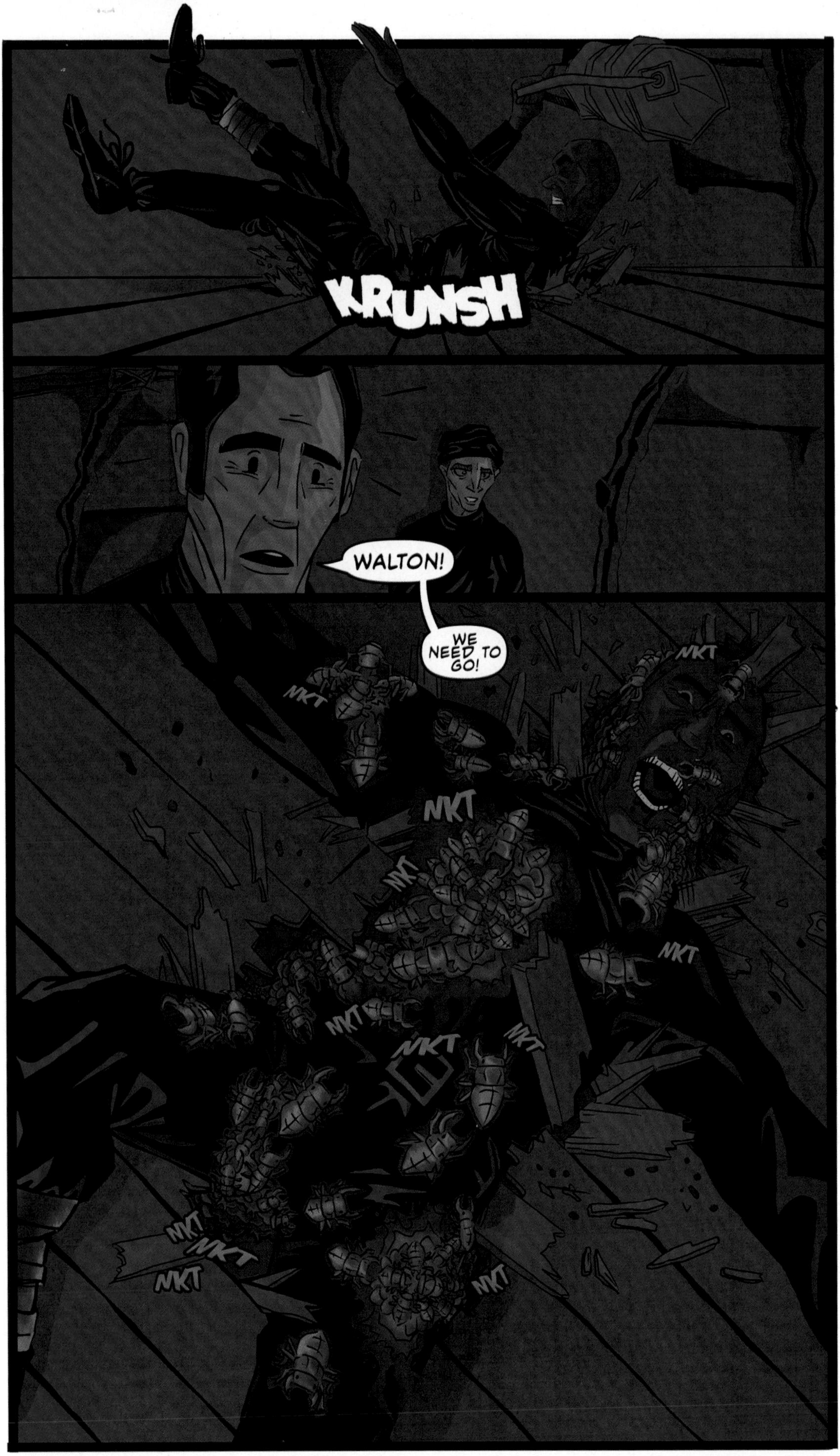
KRUNSH
WALTON!
WE NEED TO GO!
NKT
NKT
NKT
NKT
NKT
NKT
NKT
NKT
NKT
NKT
NKT
NKT

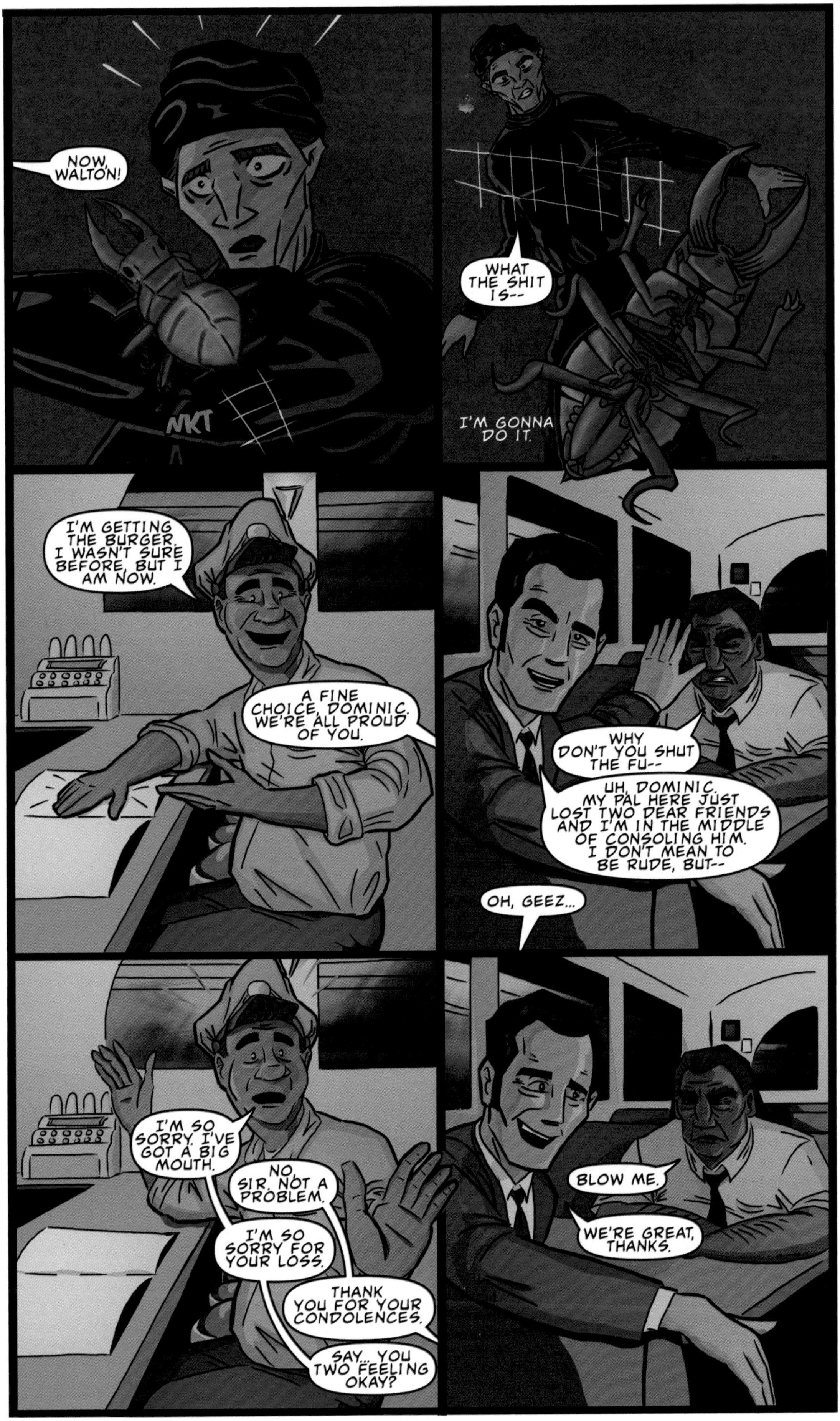
NOW, WALTON!
WHAT THE SHIT IS--
I'M GONNA DO IT.
I'M GETTING THE BURGER. I WASN'T SURE BEFORE, BUT I AM NOW.
A FINE CHOICE, DOMINIC. WE'RE ALL PROUD OF YOU.
WHY DON'T YOU SHUT THE FU--
UH, DOMINIC. MY PAL HERE JUST LOST TWO DEAR FRIENDS AND I'M IN THE MIDDLE OF CONSOLING HIM. I DON'T MEAN TO BE RUDE, BUT--
OH, GEEZ...
I'M SO SORRY. I'VE GOT A BIG MOUTH.
NO, SIR. NOT A PROBLEM.
I'M SO SORRY FOR YOUR LOSS.
THANK YOU FOR YOUR CONDOLENCES.
SAY... YOU TWO FEELING OKAY?
BLOW ME.
WE'RE GREAT, THANKS.

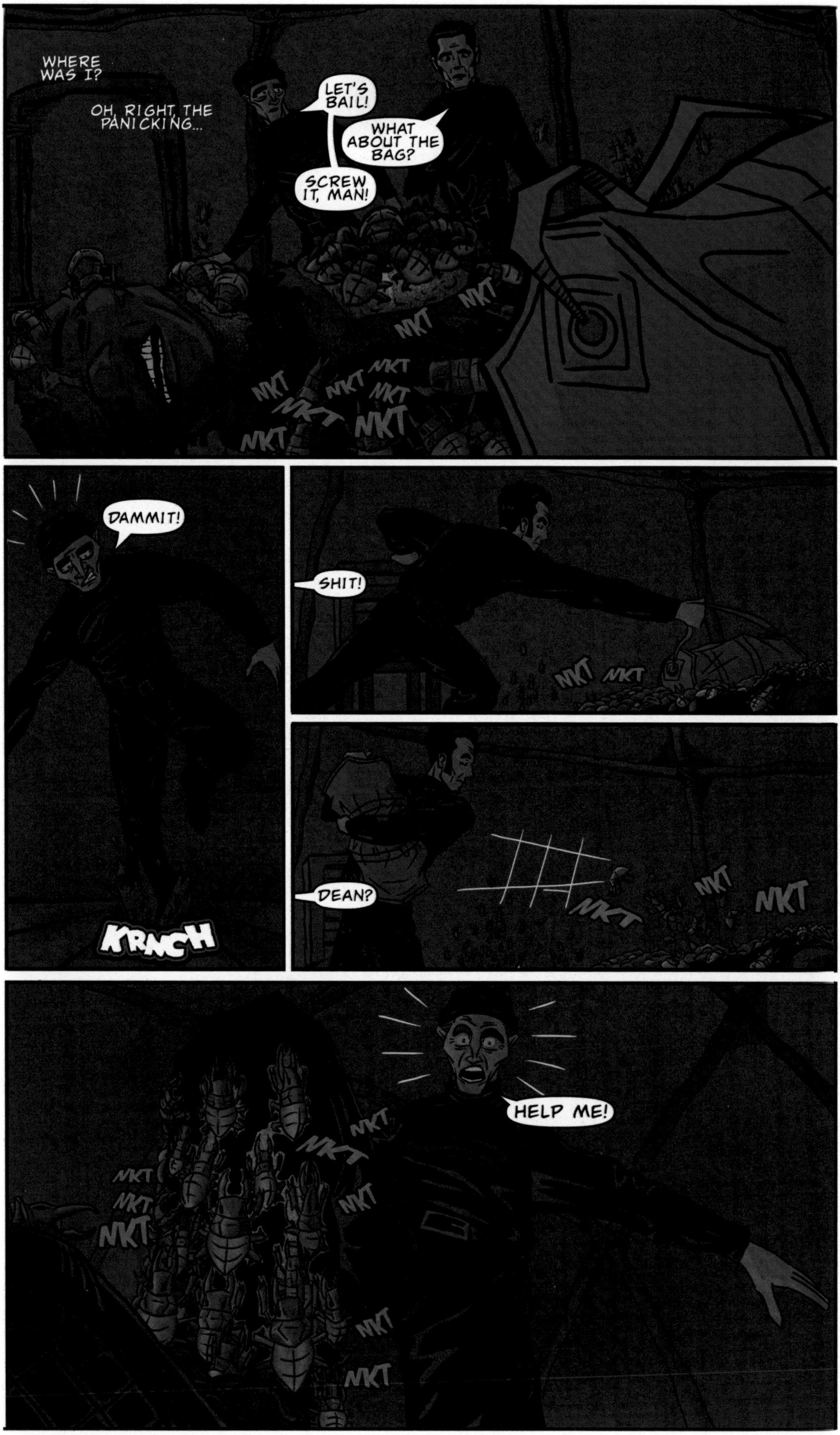
WHERE WAS I?
OH, RIGHT, THE PANICKING...
LET'S BAIL!
WHAT ABOUT THE BAG?
SCREW IT, MAN!
NKT NKT NKT NKT NKT NKT NKT NKT
DAMMIT!
KRNCH
SHIT!
NKT NKT
DEAN?
NKT NKT NKT
HELP ME!
NKT NKT NKT NKT NKT NKT NKT NKT

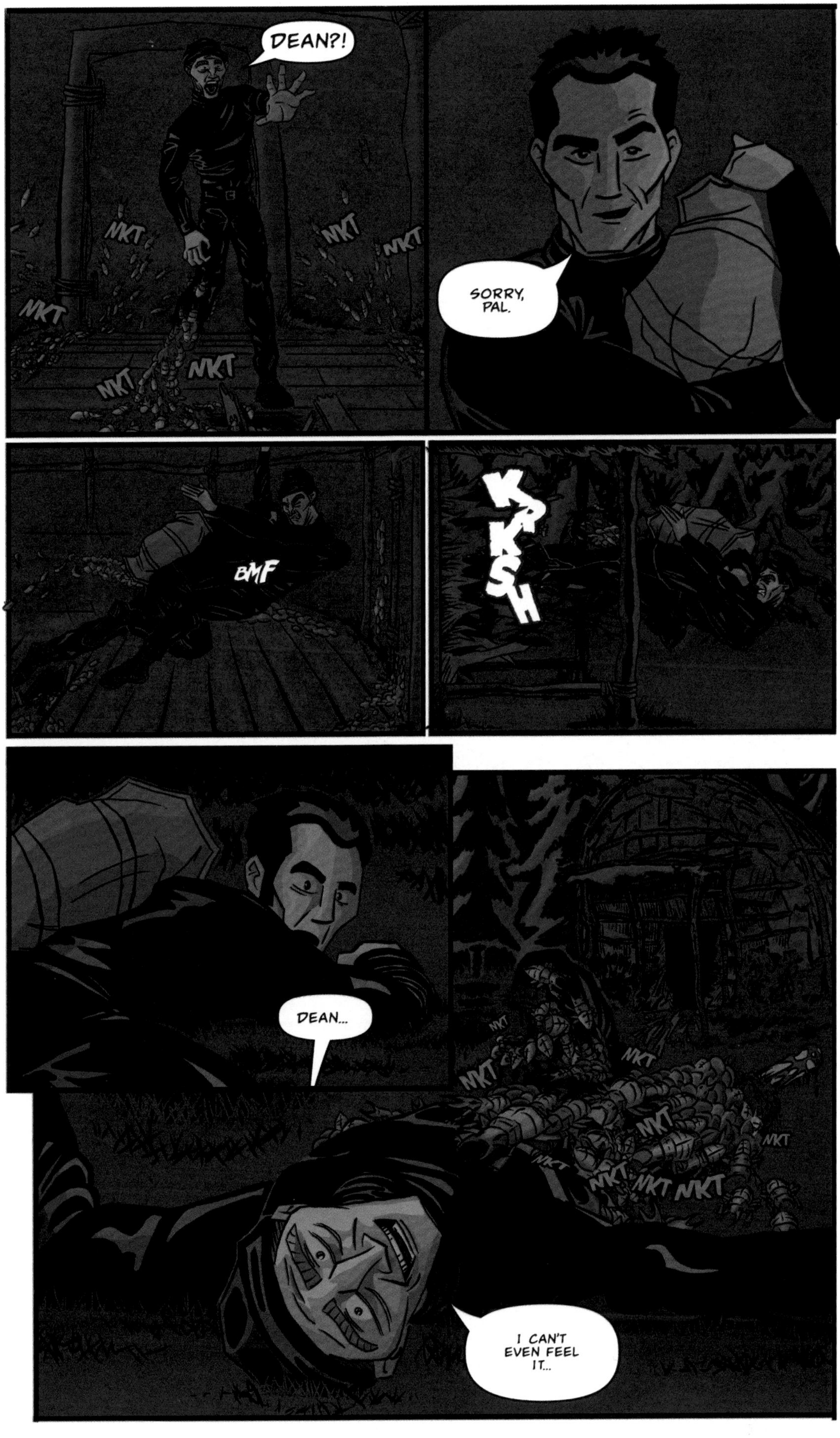
DEAN?!
NKT
NKT
NKT
NKT
NKT
NKT
SORRY, PAL.
BMF
KRKSH
DEAN...
NKT
NKT
NKT
NKT
NKT
NKT NKT
NKT
I CAN'T EVEN FEEL IT...

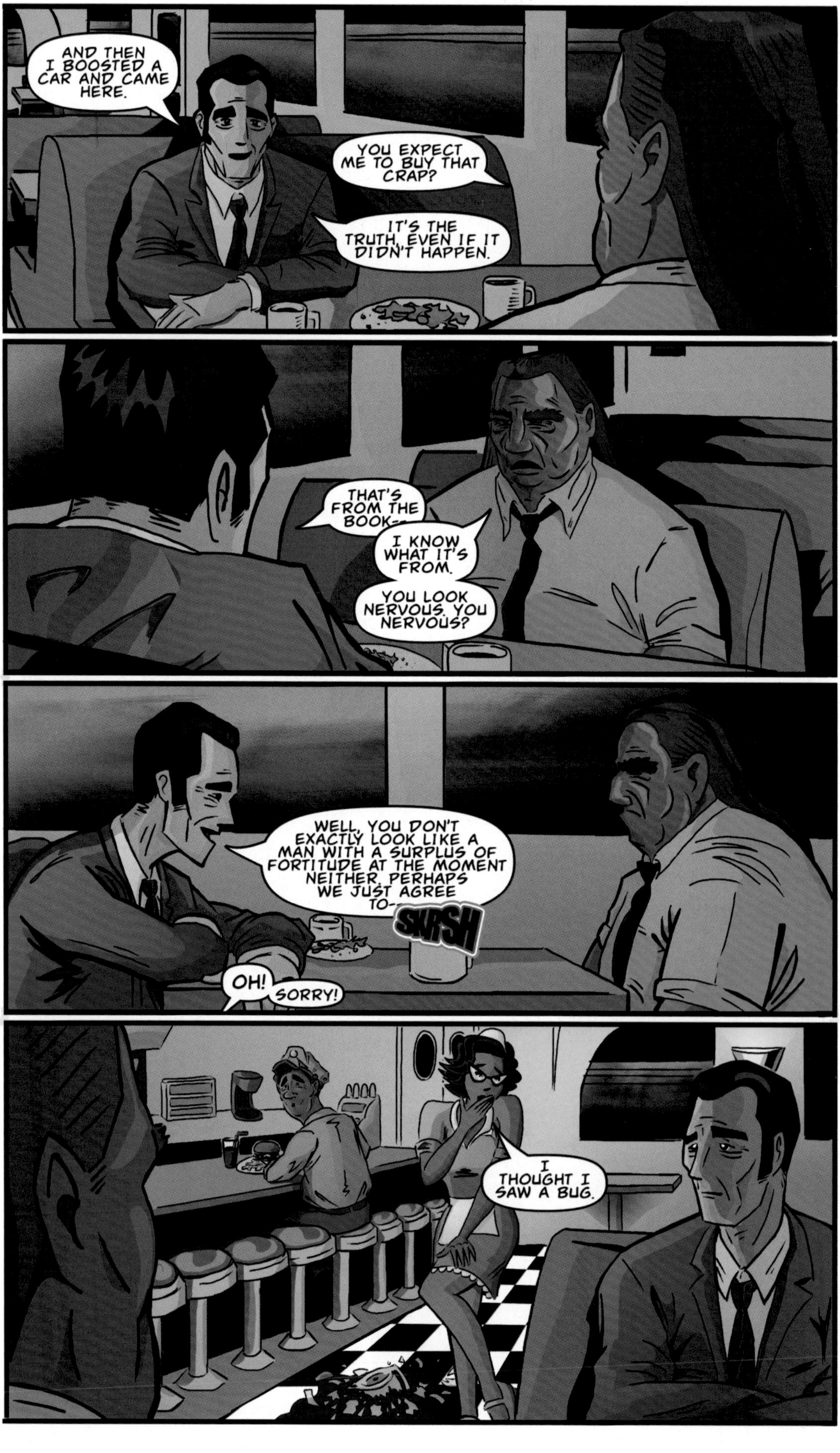
AND THEN I BOOSTED A CAR AND CAME HERE.
YOU EXPECT ME TO BUY THAT CRAP?
IT'S THE TRUTH, EVEN IF IT DIDN'T HAPPEN.
THAT'S FROM THE BOOK--
I KNOW WHAT IT'S FROM.
YOU LOOK NERVOUS. YOU NERVOUS?
WELL, YOU DON'T EXACTLY LOOK LIKE A MAN WITH A SURPLUS OF FORTITUDE AT THE MOMENT NEITHER. PERHAPS WE JUST AGREE TO--
SKRSH
OH!
SORRY!
I THOUGHT I SAW A BUG.

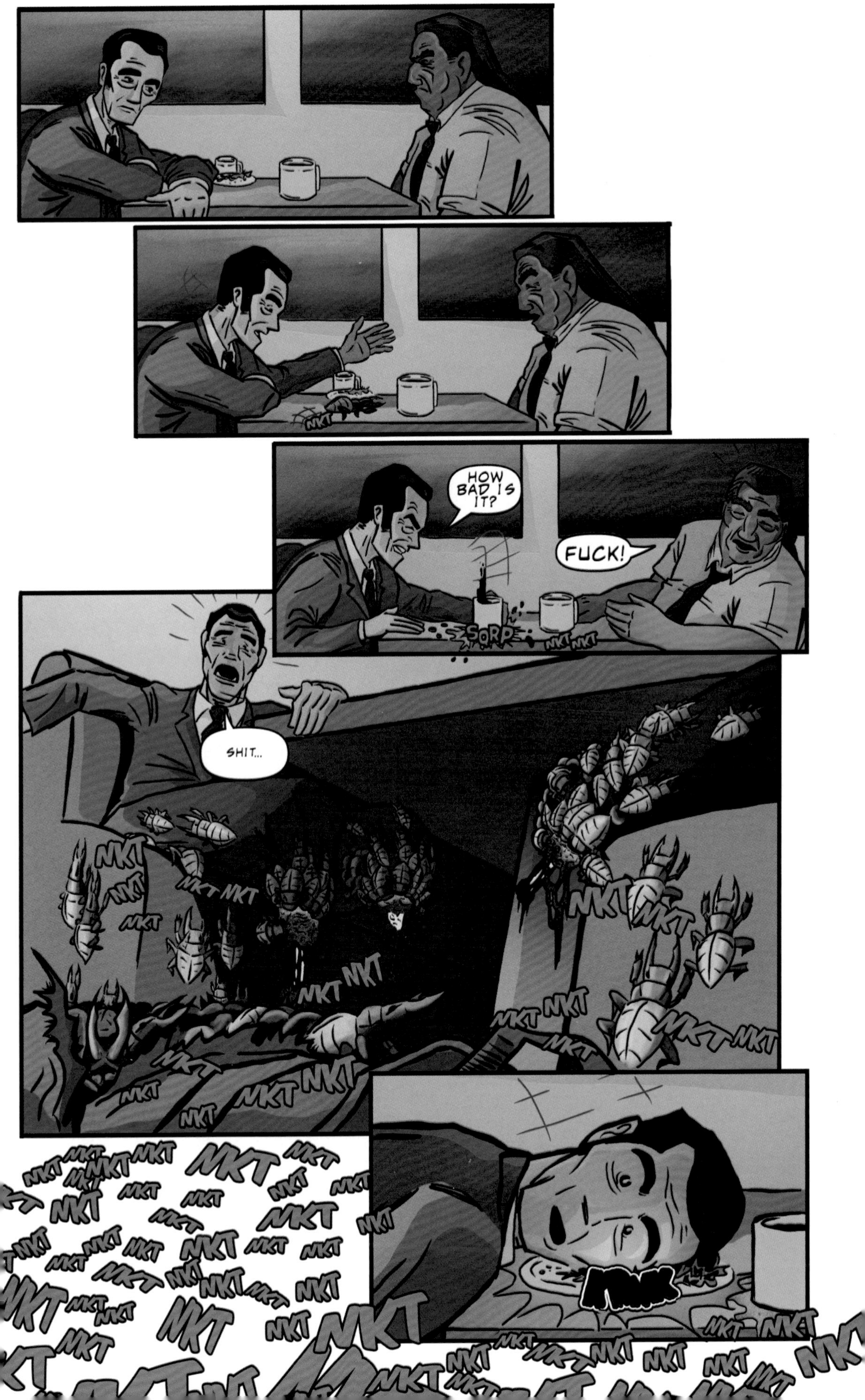
NKT
HOW BAD IS IT?
FUCK!
SORP
NKT NKT
SHIT...
NKT

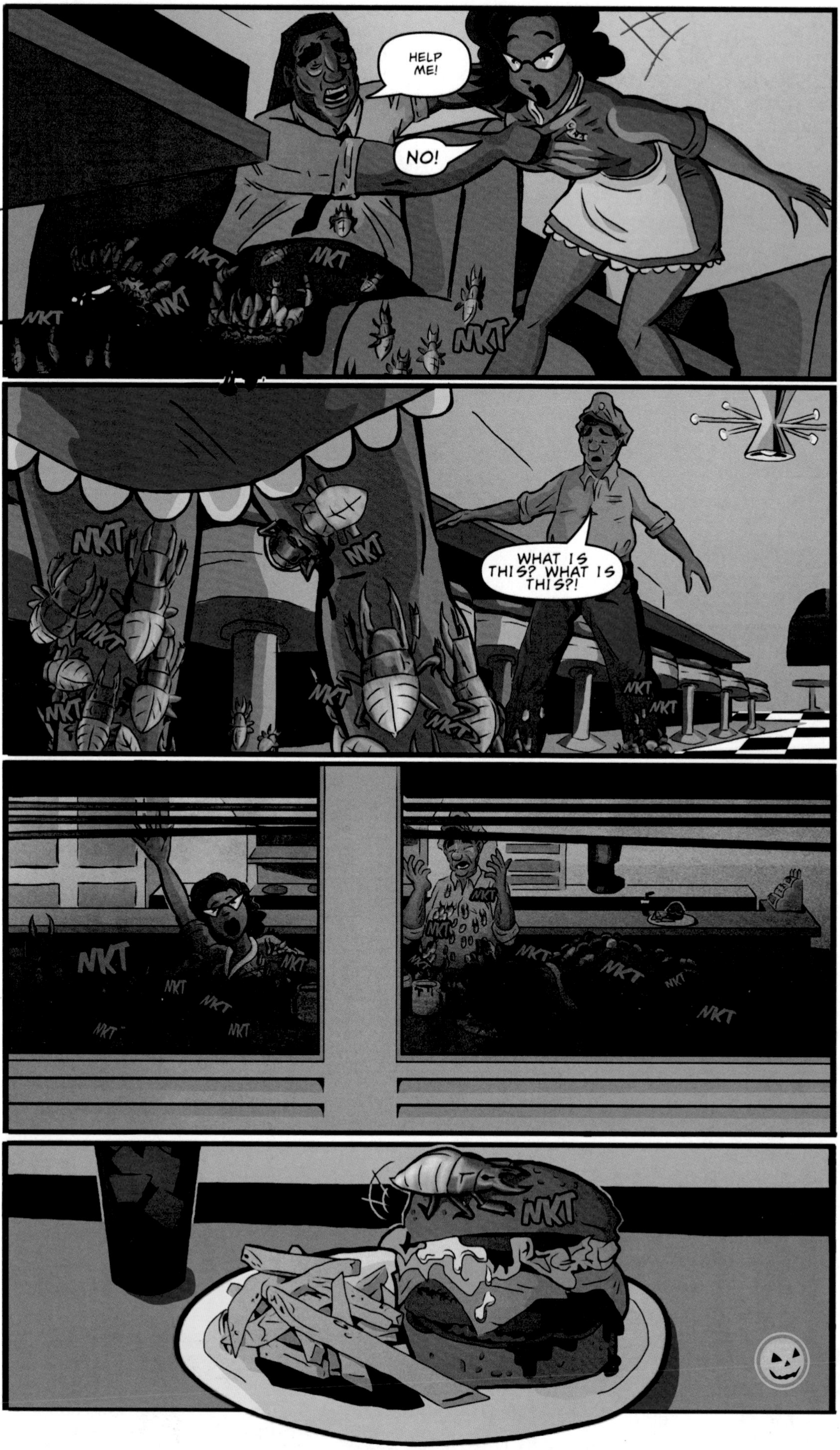
HELP ME!
NO!
NKT
NKT
NKT
NKT
NKT
NKT
NKT
NKT
NKT
WHAT IS THIS? WHAT IS THIS?!
NKT
NKT
NKT
NKT
NKT
NKT
NKT
NKT
NKT
NKT
NKT
NKT
NKT
NKT
NKT
NKT

The keeper dabs the corner of his mouth with a bandana that he produces from somewhere.

Nothin' quite like a good burger, wouldn't you agree? Really hits the spot.

He closes up his lunch pail and returns it to its home in the trailer.

Moving through the older cemetery and back into a more modern area, the ambient light lessens noticeably. The dark fights with the occasional hints of moonlight that break through the trees, but there's something else going on here.

The darkness seems to have more substance here, holding a firmer grasp over visibility and limiting clear, comprehensive vision.

Dagnabbit, it would appear that the lights are on the fritz.

Small amounts of light that make it through the canopy play off the strange contours of his face, forming a mask even more gruesome than his normal visage.

Oh, well. You're not afraid of the dark, are ya?

Continuing on through the dark space, he doesn't appear to have any issues navigating past the stones and trees, relaying a knowledge of many ages of travel in the darkest of places.

Have ya' ever looked in the mirror and not recognized the person lookin' back? Yeah...me neither, but that'd be weird, huh?

Sweeping through the inky space, he arrives at the spot he was searching for. A highly polished marble headstone. It works to reflect what available light exists, bouncing even more off his face, an ever-morphing landscape of high-lighted peaks and abyssal valleys.

Now, take ol' Dennis here.

Dennis had nothing left to live for, or so he thought, until he became acutely aware of what the alternatives might entail. Of course, yer choices narrow somewhat, once you receive yer...

NOTICE TO QUIT

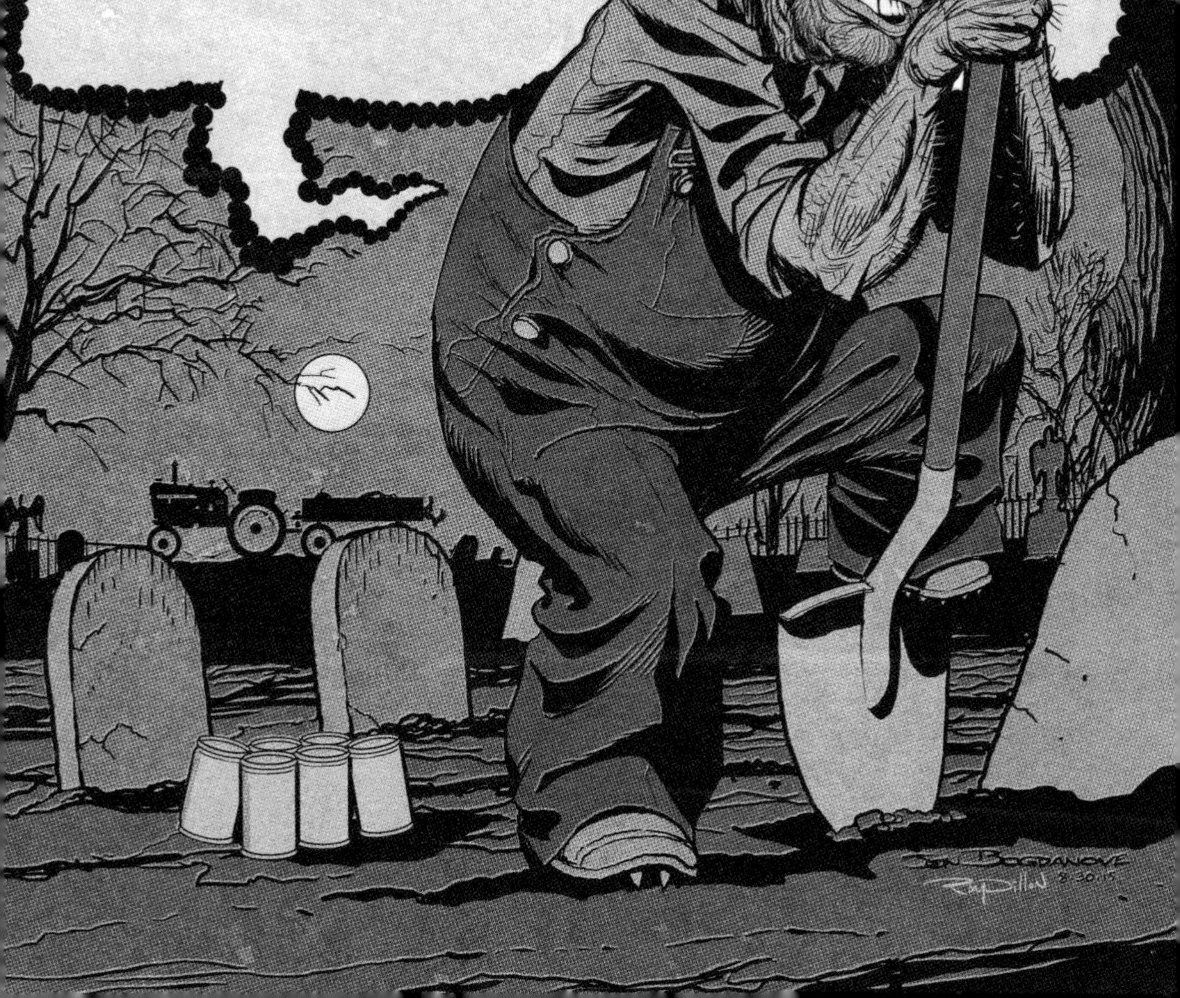
BEN BOGDANOVE
RAY DILLON

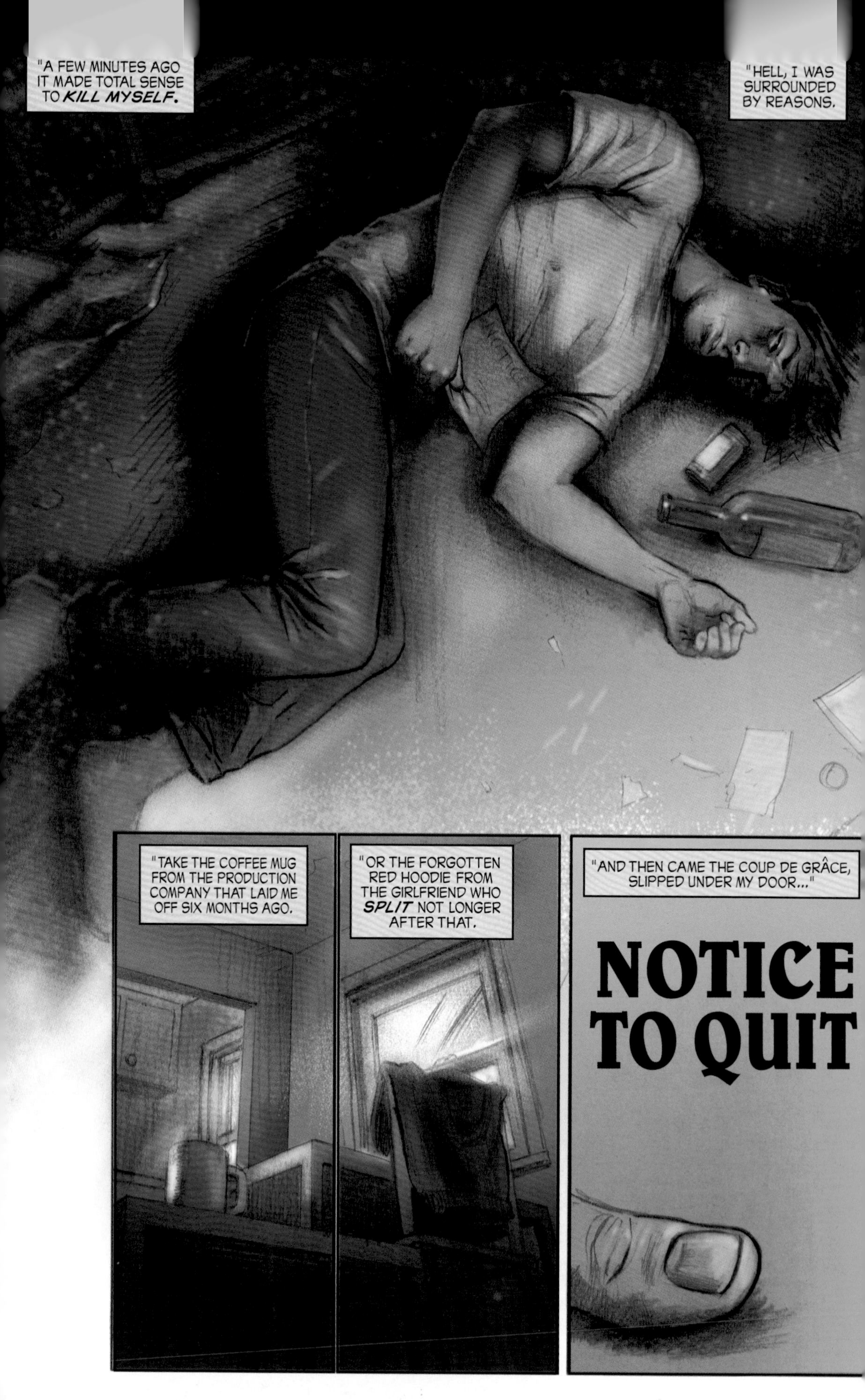
"A FEW MINUTES AGO IT MADE TOTAL SENSE TO KILL MYSELF.
"HELL, I WAS SURROUNDED BY REASONS.
"TAKE THE COFFEE MUG FROM THE PRODUCTION COMPANY THAT LAID ME OFF SIX MONTHS AGO.
"OR THE FORGOTTEN RED HOODIE FROM THE GIRLFRIEND WHO SPLIT NOT LONGER AFTER THAT.
"AND THEN CAME THE COUP DE GRÂCE, SLIPPED UNDER MY DOOR..."
NOTICE TO QUIT

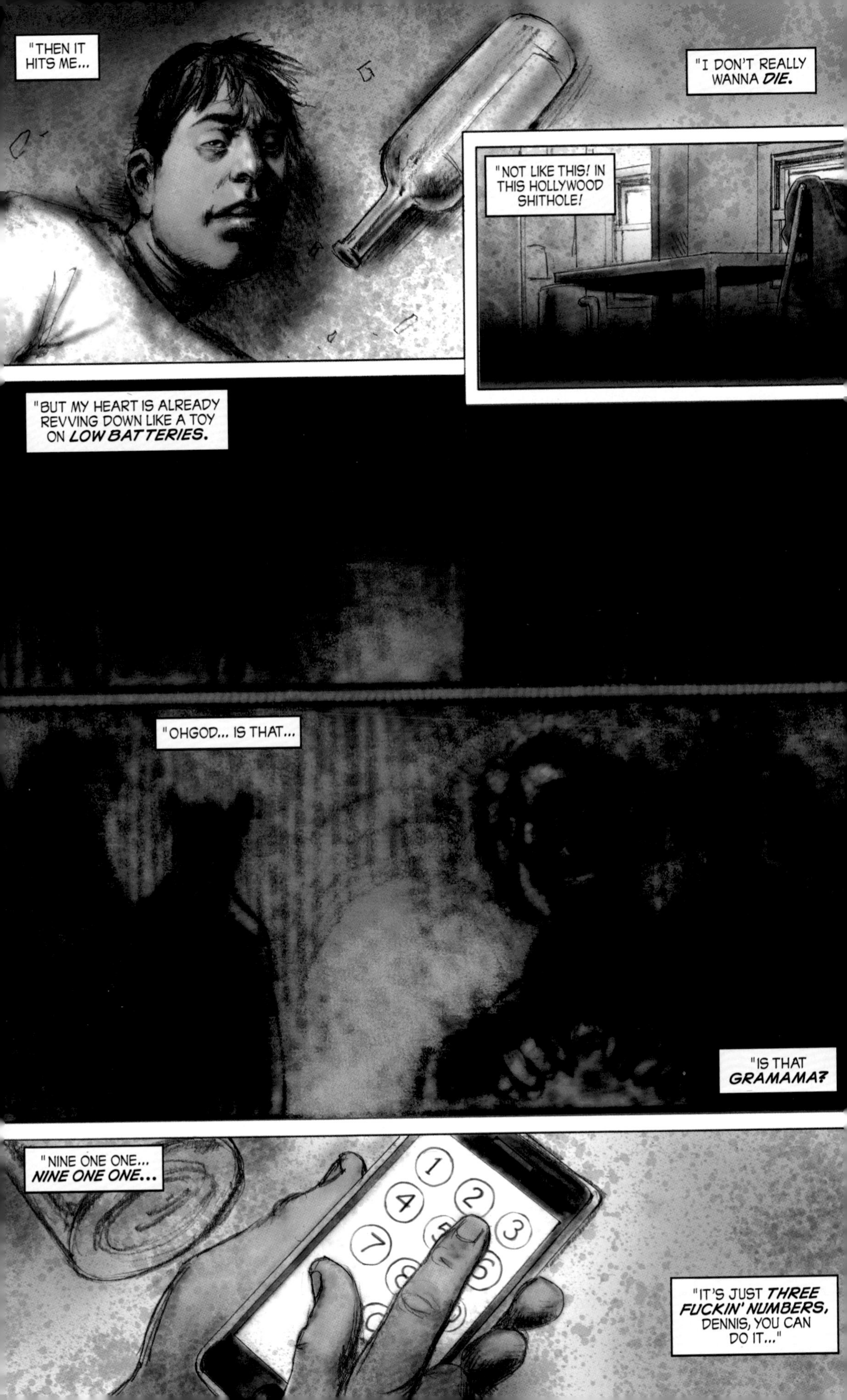
"THEN IT HITS ME...
"I DON'T REALLY WANNA *DIE*.
"NOT LIKE THIS! IN THIS HOLLYWOOD SHITHOLE!
"BUT MY HEART IS ALREADY REVVING DOWN LIKE A TOY ON *LOW BATTERIES*.
"OHGOD... IS THAT...
"IS THAT *GRAMAMA?*
"NINE ONE ONE... *NINE ONE ONE...*
"IT'S JUST *THREE FUCKIN' NUMBERS,* DENNIS, YOU CAN DO IT..."

"OH MAN THAT WAS A *CLOSE ONE*.

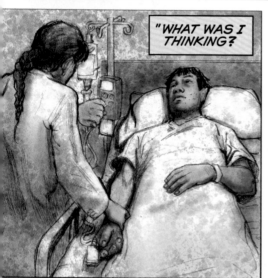

"*WHAT WAS I THINKING?*

"THERE'S SO MUCH TO LIVE FOR.

"I'M ONLY 35, FOR CHRIST'S SAKE.

"PLENTY OF TIME TO *START OVER SOMEPLACE NEW...*"

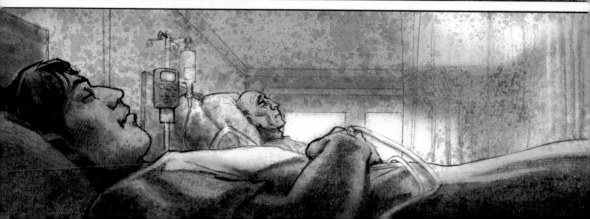

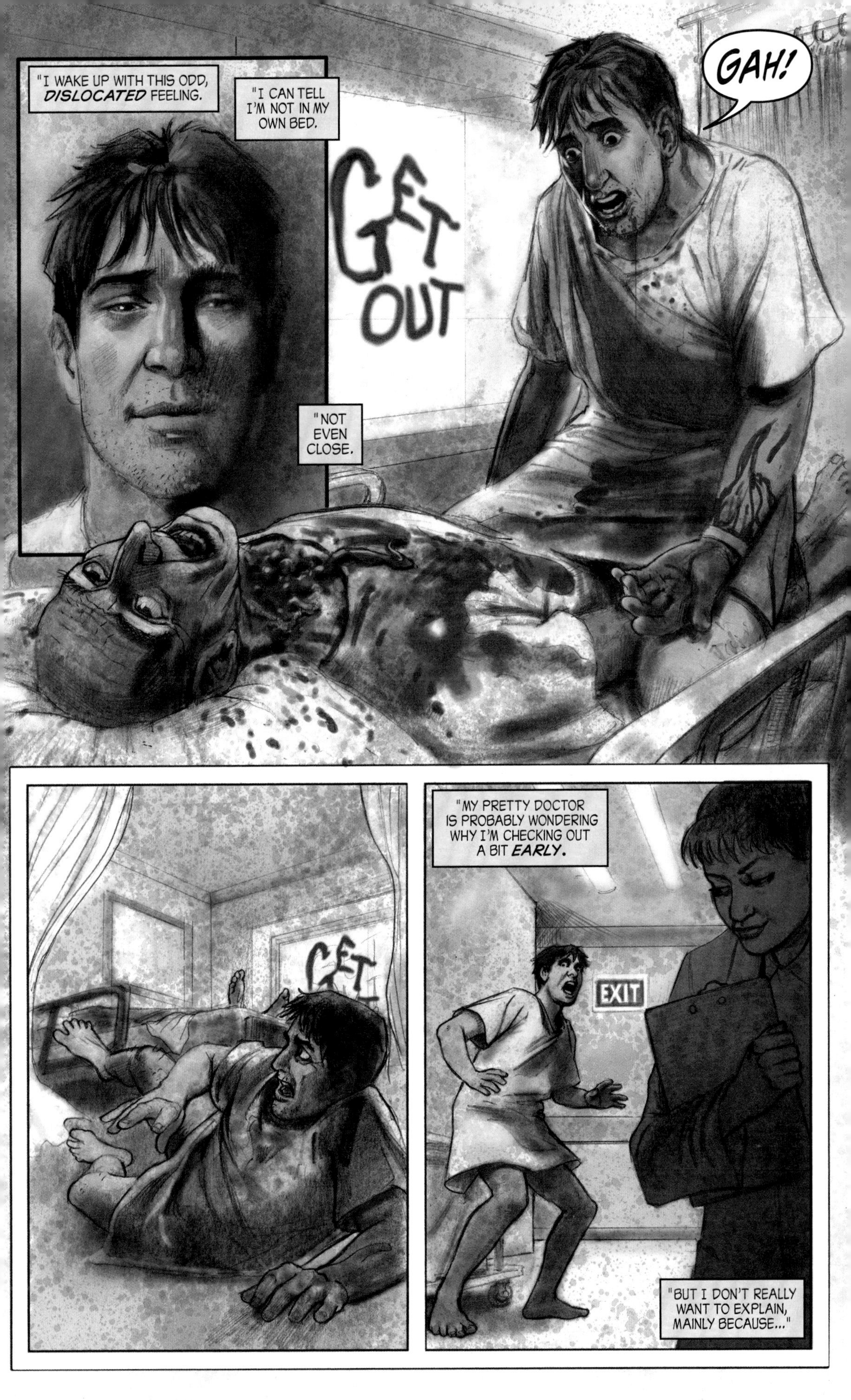
"I WAKE UP WITH THIS ODD, DISLOCATED FEELING.
"I CAN TELL I'M NOT IN MY OWN BED.
GET OUT
"NOT EVEN CLOSE.
GAH!
GET
"MY PRETTY DOCTOR IS PROBABLY WONDERING WHY I'M CHECKING OUT A BIT EARLY.
EXIT
"BUT I DON'T REALLY WANT TO EXPLAIN, MAINLY BECAUSE..."

"I HAVE **NO FUCKING IDEA** WHAT'S GOING ON**!!!**

"WONDERFUL—NOW I'M HAVING A **PANIC ATTACK**... BLOOD RUSHING OUT OF MY HEAD...

÷UGH!÷

WHAT'S THAT SMELL?

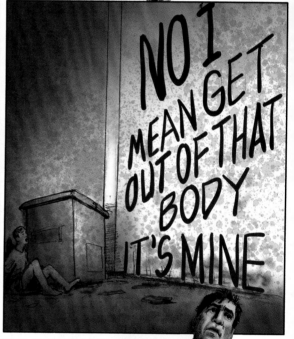

NO I MEAN GET OUT OF THAT BODY IT'S MINE

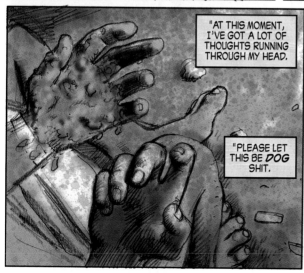

"AT THIS MOMENT, I'VE GOT A LOT OF THOUGHTS RUNNING THROUGH MY HEAD.

"PLEASE LET THIS BE **DOG** SHIT.

"WHAT THE HELL?

"DID MY JACK-AND-PERC COCKTAIL GIVE ME **PERMANENT BRAIN DAMAGE?**"

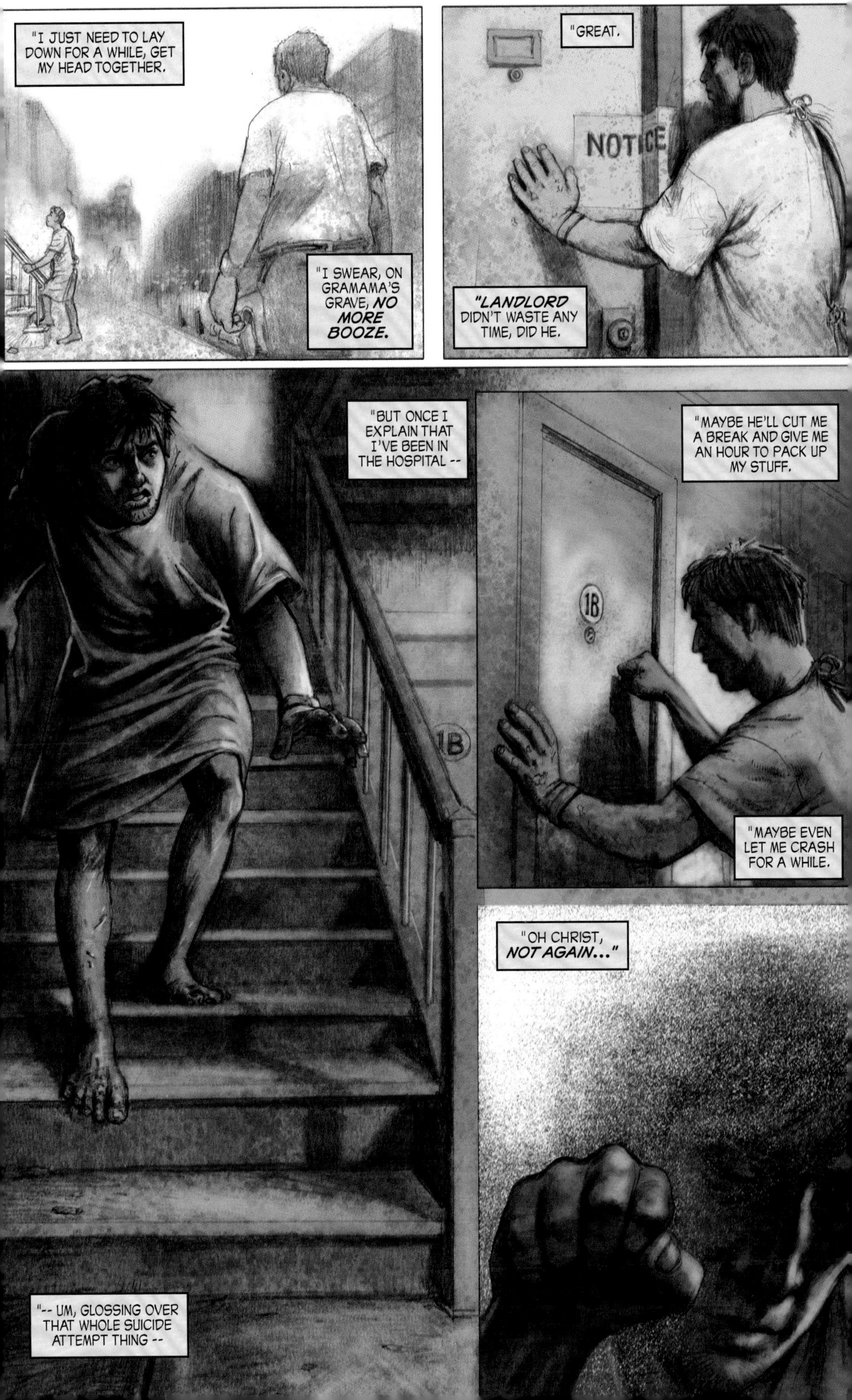
"I JUST NEED TO LAY DOWN FOR A WHILE, GET MY HEAD TOGETHER.
"I SWEAR, ON GRAMAMA'S GRAVE, ***NO MORE BOOZE.***
"GREAT.
NOTICE
"LANDLORD DIDN'T WASTE ANY TIME, DID HE.
"BUT ONCE I EXPLAIN THAT I'VE BEEN IN THE HOSPITAL --
"-- UM, GLOSSING OVER THAT WHOLE SUICIDE ATTEMPT THING --
1B
"MAYBE HE'LL CUT ME A BREAK AND GIVE ME AN HOUR TO PACK UP MY STUFF.
1B
"MAYBE EVEN LET ME CRASH FOR A WHILE.
"OH CHRIST, ***NOT AGAIN...***"

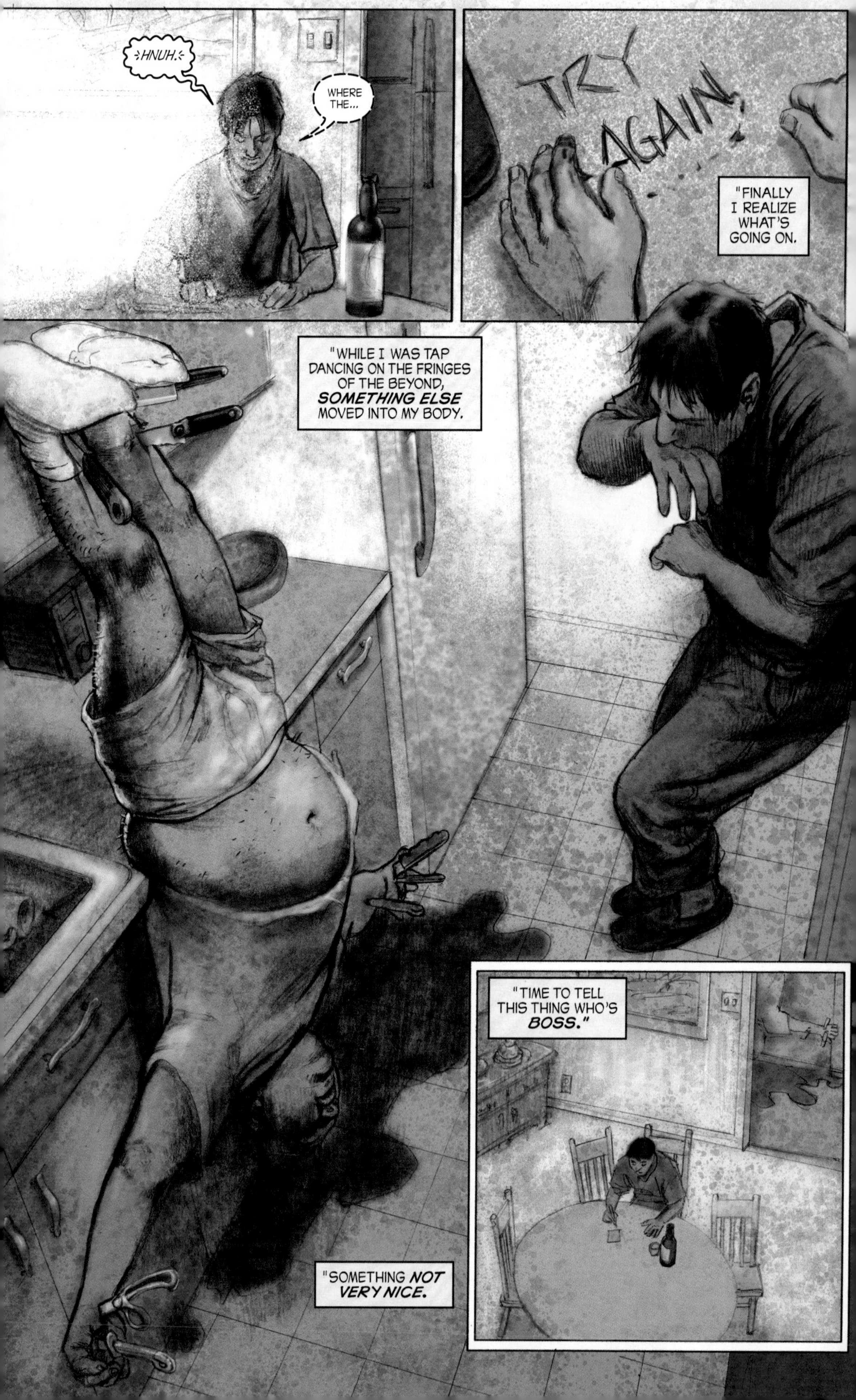
HNUH.
WHERE THE...
TRY AGAIN
"FINALLY I REALIZE WHAT'S GOING ON.
"WHILE I WAS TAP DANCING ON THE FRINGES OF THE BEYOND, SOMETHING ELSE MOVED INTO MY BODY.
"SOMETHING NOT VERY NICE.
"TIME TO TELL THIS THING WHO'S BOSS."

SORRY, STILL USING THIS BODY.

Hey— you threw it away

"AS WE CHAT IN SLOW MOTION --

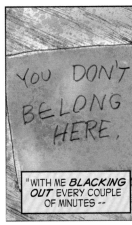

YOU DON'T BELONG HERE.

"WITH ME *BLACKING OUT* EVERY COUPLE OF MINUTES --

"I LEARN A FEW THINGS...

Fingers Keepers Fucko

GO PICK ON SOME OTHER NEAR-SUICIDE!

Idiots like you are rare

"WE CAN'T CONTROL MY BODY AT THE SAME TIME.

YOU DON'T WANT MY BODY. MY LIFE SUCKS.

Better than where I came from Buddy

"SOMEHOW, *THIS THING* IS FORCING ME TO BLACKOUT. BUT HE CAN'T MAINTAIN CONTROL FOR TOO LONG.

"IF I CAN JUST *SEIZE CONTROL* FOR A *LONGER* PERIOD OF TIME..."

FUCK YOU! I'M KEEPING MY BODY!

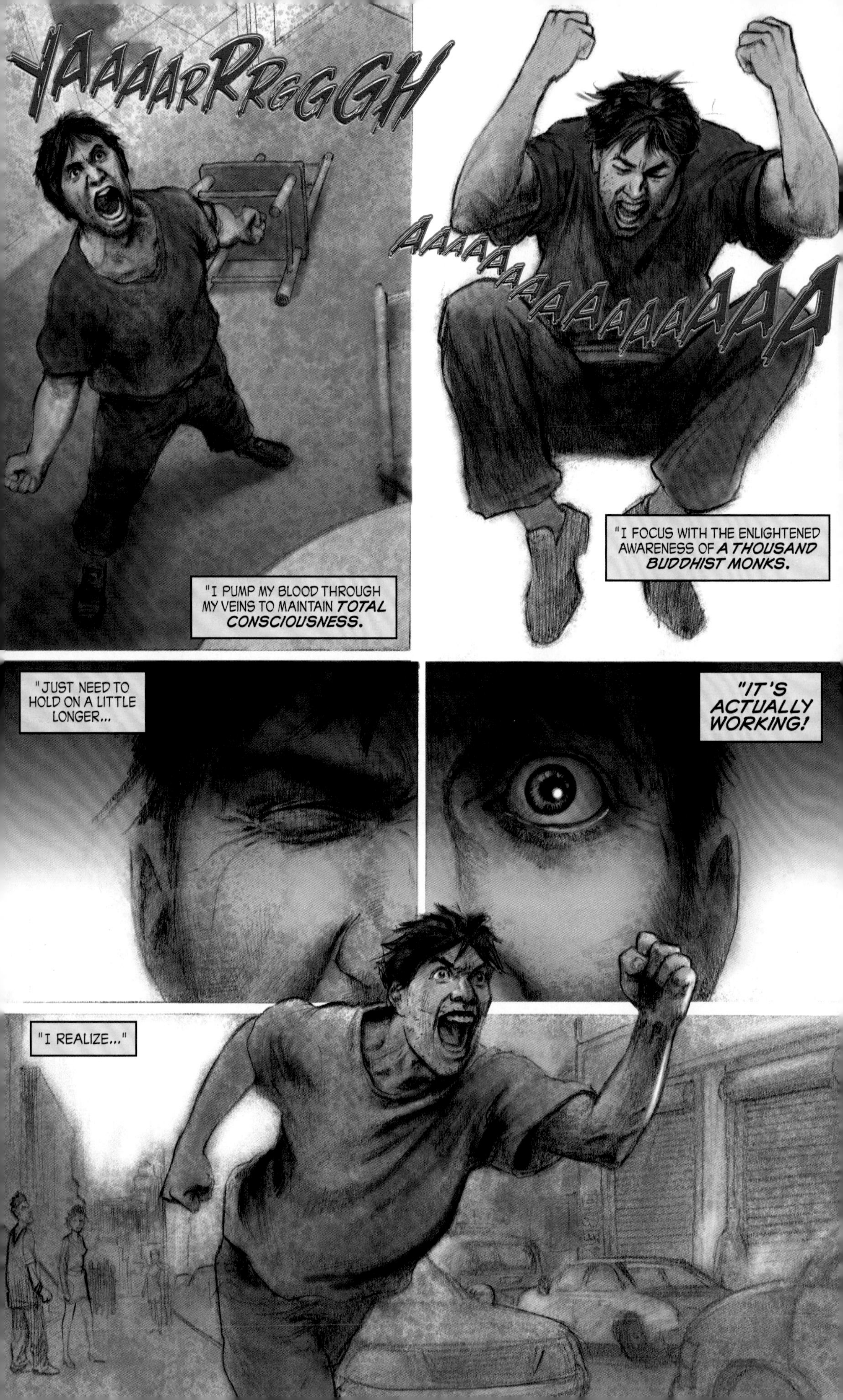
YAAAARRRGGGGH
"I PUMP MY BLOOD THROUGH MY VEINS TO MAINTAIN TOTAL CONSCIOUSNESS.
AAAAAAAAAAAAAAAAAA
"I FOCUS WITH THE ENLIGHTENED AWARENESS OF A THOUSAND BUDDHIST MONKS.
"JUST NEED TO HOLD ON A LITTLE LONGER...
"IT'S ACTUALLY WORKING!
"I REALIZE..."

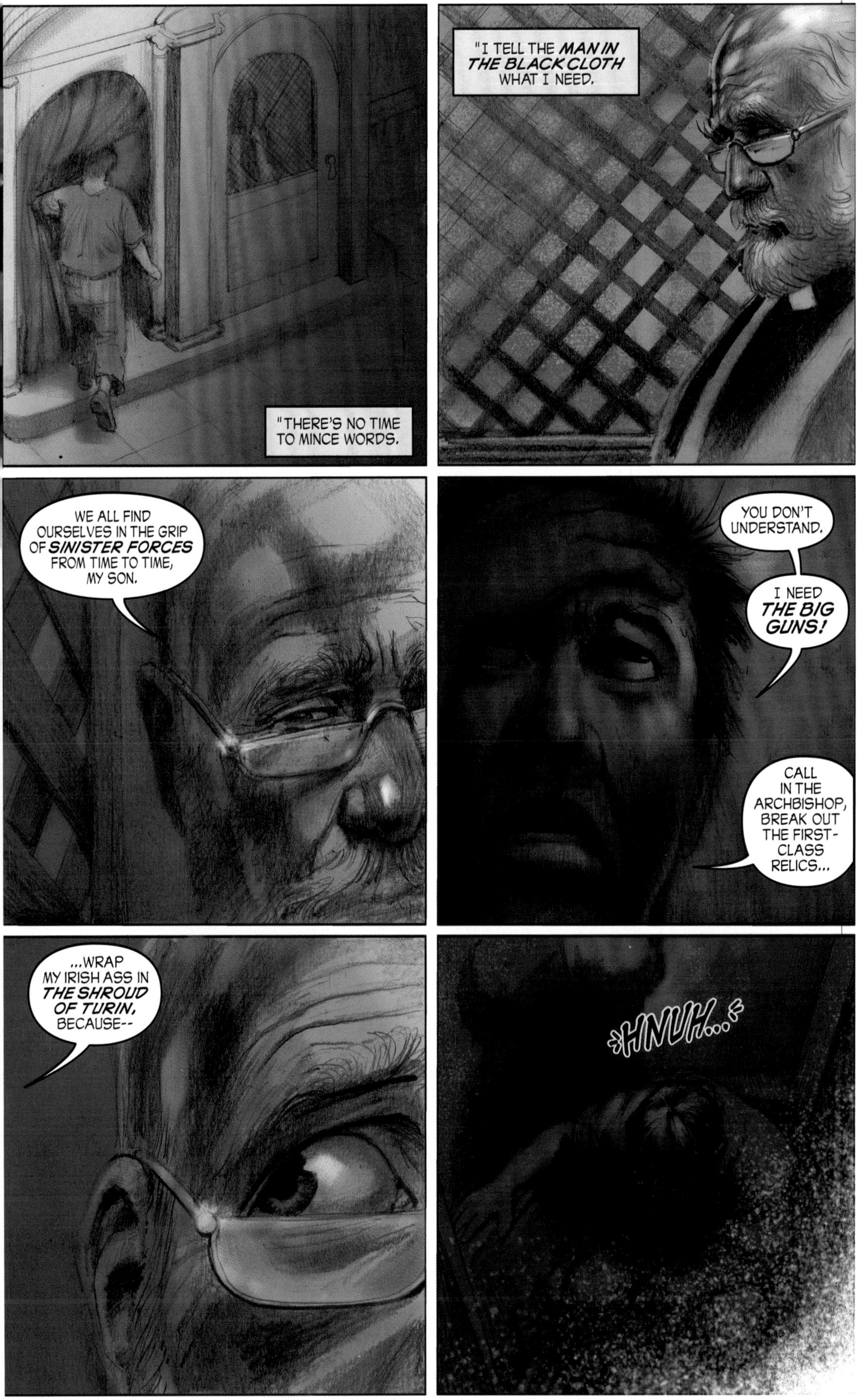

"THERE'S NO TIME TO MINCE WORDS.
"I TELL THE MAN IN THE BLACK CLOTH WHAT I NEED.
WE ALL FIND OURSELVES IN THE GRIP OF SINISTER FORCES FROM TIME TO TIME, MY SON.
YOU DON'T UNDERSTAND.
I NEED THE BIG GUNS!
CALL IN THE ARCHBISHOP, BREAK OUT THE FIRST-CLASS RELICS...
...WRAP MY IRISH ASS IN THE SHROUD OF TURIN, BECAUSE--
HNUH...

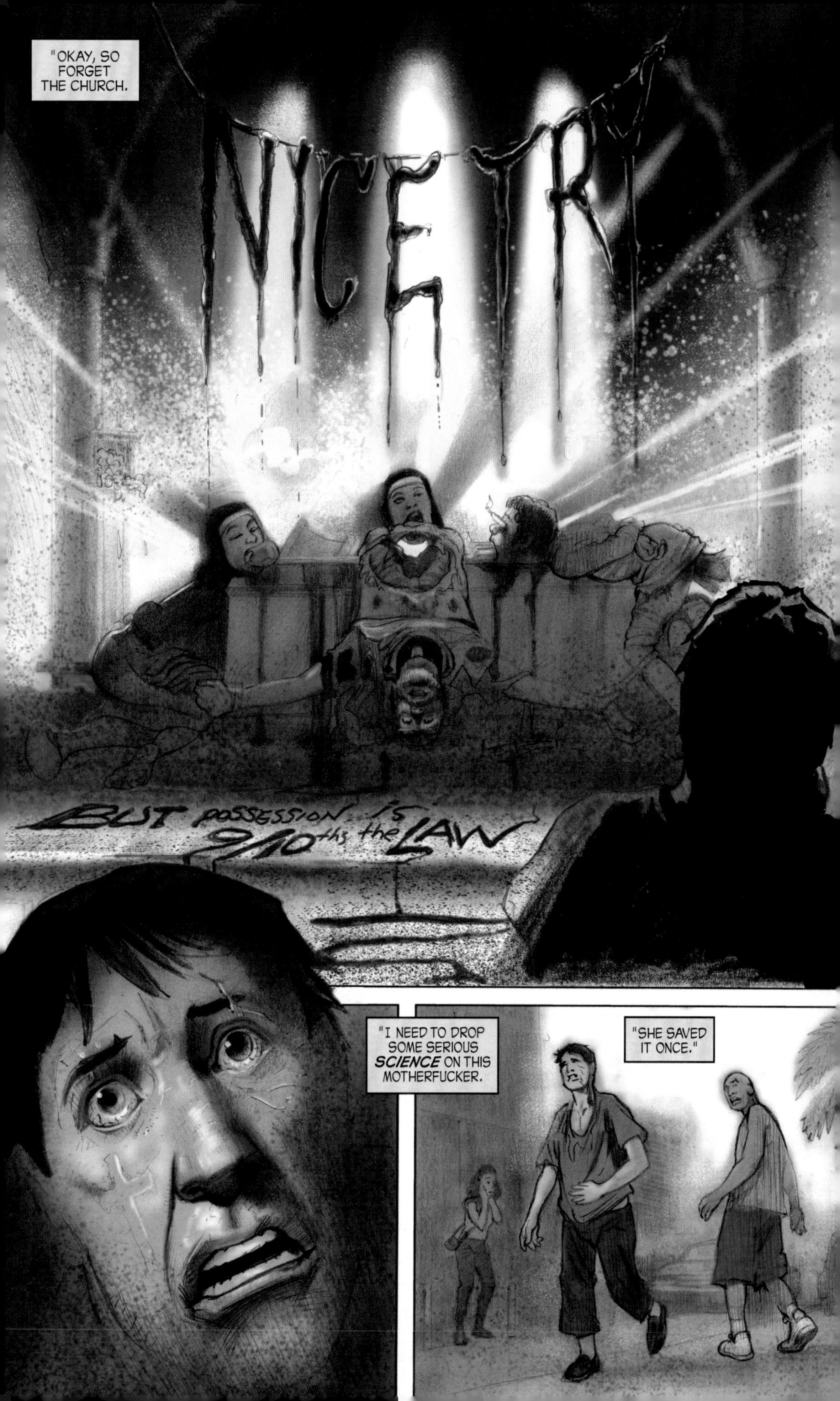
"OKAY, SO FORGET THE CHURCH.
NICE TRY
BUT possession is 9/10ths the LAW
"I NEED TO DROP SOME SERIOUS *SCIENCE* ON THIS MOTHERFUCKER.
"SHE SAVED IT ONCE."

"MAYBE SHE'LL *SAVE MY LIFE* ONE MORE TIME..."

DON'T SCREAM.

I NEED YOU TO *ALMOST KILL* ME.

WHAT?

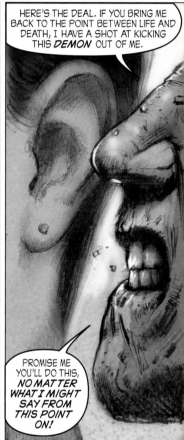

HERE'S THE DEAL. IF YOU BRING ME BACK TO THE POINT BETWEEN LIFE AND DEATH, I HAVE A SHOT AT KICKING THIS *DEMON* OUT OF ME.

PROMISE ME YOU'LL DO THIS, *NO MATTER WHAT I MIGHT SAY FROM THIS POINT ON!*

YOU'RE INSANE.

I'M TRYING TO FIX THAT.

OKAY.

OKAY *WHAT?*

I'LL ALMOST- KILL YOU.

UH...

WHAT HAPPENED TO YOUR WRISTS? THOSE CUTS LOOK KINDA *FRESH.*

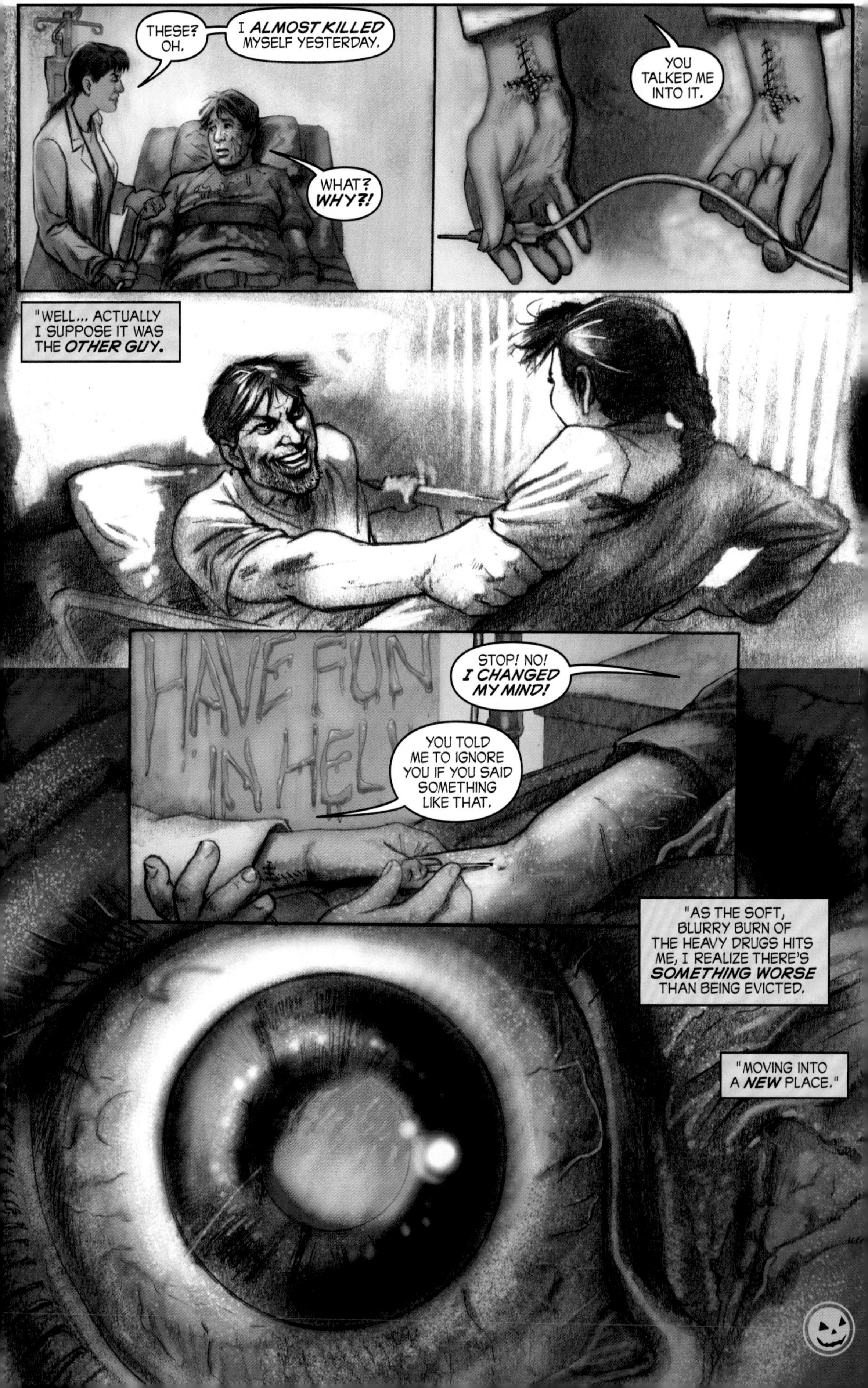

THESE? OH.
I ALMOST KILLED MYSELF YESTERDAY.
WHAT? WHY?!
YOU TALKED ME INTO IT.
"WELL... ACTUALLY I SUPPOSE IT WAS THE OTHER GUY.
HAVE FUN IN HEL
STOP! NO! I CHANGED MY MIND!
YOU TOLD ME TO IGNORE YOU IF YOU SAID SOMETHING LIKE THAT.
"AS THE SOFT, BLURRY BURN OF THE HEAVY DRUGS HITS ME, I REALIZE THERE'S SOMETHING WORSE THAN BEING EVICTED.
"MOVING INTO A NEW PLACE."

The blanket of darkness has begun to dissolve. He sits atop the tractor's hood, one foot up, strumming a guitar and singing.

You don't know what you got, 'til it's go-o-o-one!

He stops cold.

Too much? Probably a little over the top.

Chucking the guitar into the trailer with everything else, he hops back into the driver's seat.

Alrighty then.

Off he goes. Traveling on, he re-enters the part of the old cemetery that looks very similar to where he started, a more modern feel; well-lit, with cleanly organized and kept rows of stones, with the occasional obelisk-shaped memorial. The horizon reveals the fact that the new day is beginning its daily battle against the night.

Must be gettin' late...or early, as the case may be.

He looks to his wrist at the spot where a watch might normally reside, of course, he wears no such device.

Yup. Daylights-a-comin'. Ya' know what, though? I think we got time for just one more story. 'One fer the ditch,' my friend likes to say.

He stops the tractor and walks over to a small, non-descript marker set flush with the earth. He kneels and sweeps the

dead leaves and small branches off, clearing it. Producing a garden trowel out of a pocket, he trims the sod back from where it has encroached past the edges of the stone. He blows the loose dirt off and, using his bandana, wipes the marker clean.

There you go, Dear. He tucks the bandana away once again and returns to his feet.

This one...well, this one is an age-old tale of what can happen when you get exactly what you wish for even if it's not exactly what you really wanted.

So, sit back and take in the story of Amanda and what transpires when she finds her...

FORTUNE BROKEN

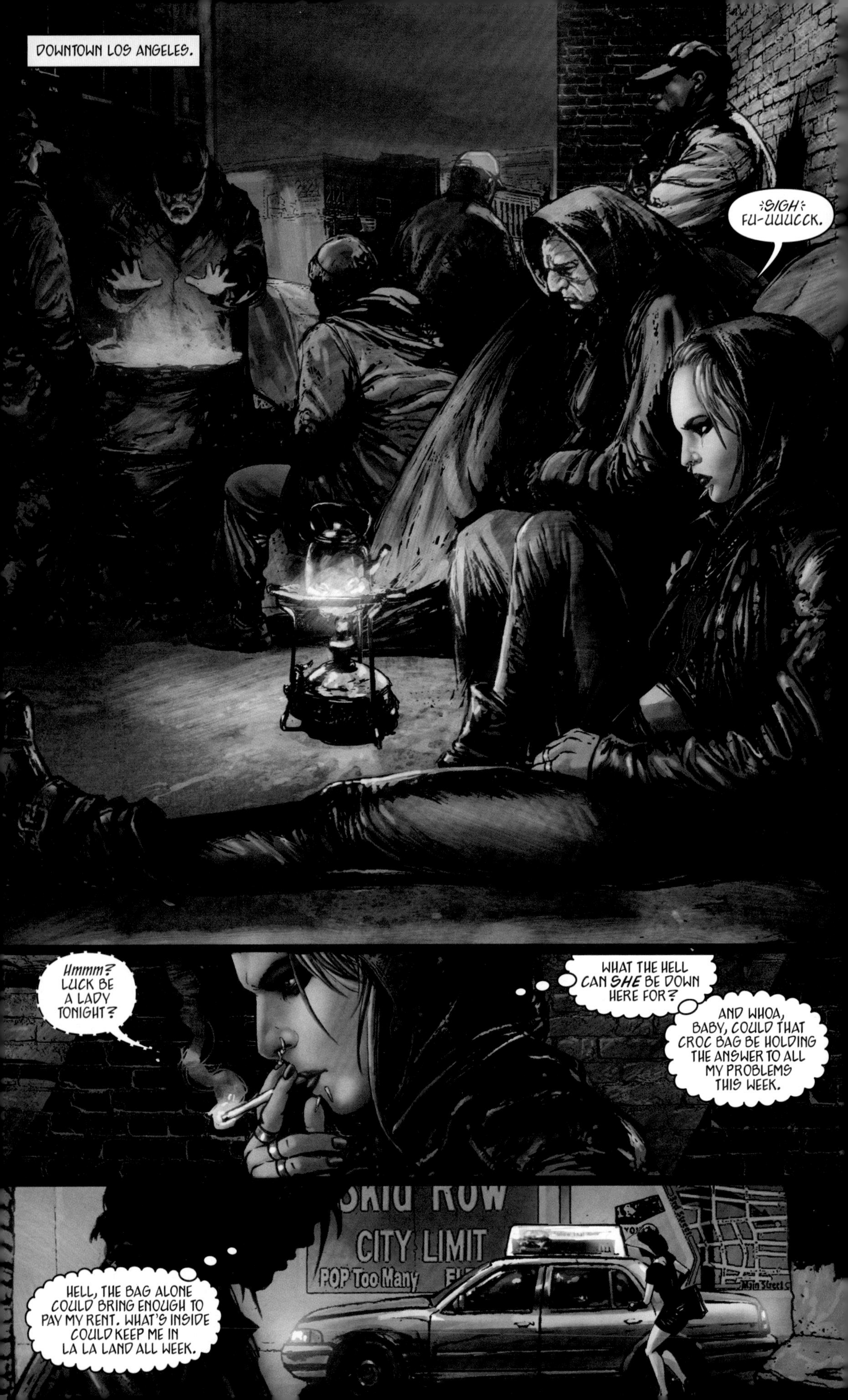
DOWNTOWN LOS ANGELES.
:SIGH: FU-UUUCCK.
Hmmm? LUCK BE A LADY TONIGHT?
WHAT THE HELL CAN SHE BE DOWN HERE FOR?
AND WHOA, BABY, COULD THAT CROC BAG BE HOLDING THE ANSWER TO ALL MY PROBLEMS THIS WEEK.
SKID ROW
CITY LIMIT
POP Too Many
HELL, THE BAG ALONE COULD BRING ENOUGH TO PAY MY RENT. WHAT'S INSIDE COULD KEEP ME IN LA LA LAND ALL WEEK.

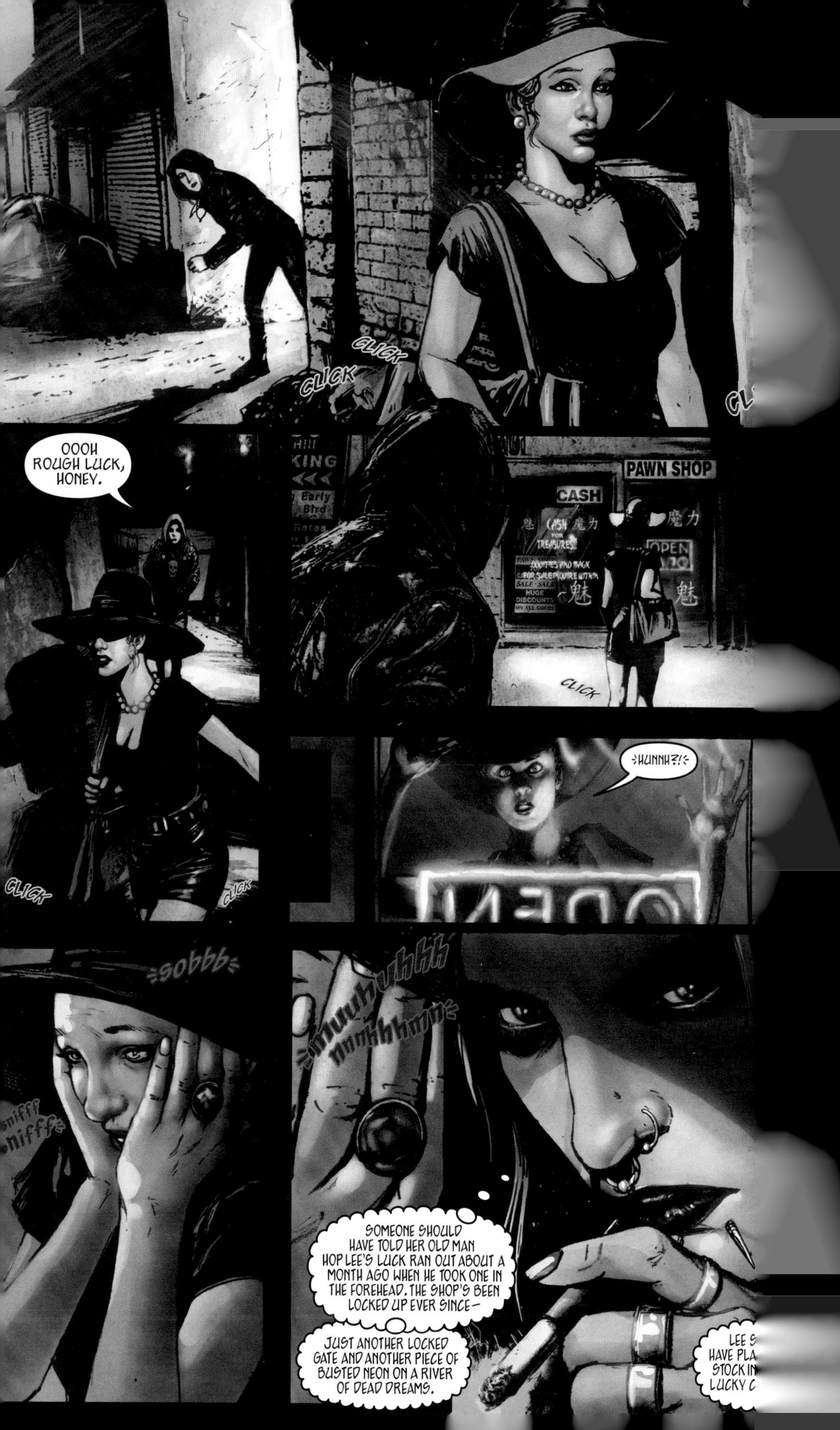
CLICK
CLICK
OOOH ROUGH LUCK, HONEY.
PAWN SHOP
CASH
OPEN
CLICK
CLICK
CLICK
HUNNH?!
OPEN
sobbb
SOMEONE SHOULD HAVE TOLD HER OLD MAN HOP LEE'S LUCK RAN OUT ABOUT A MONTH AGO WHEN HE TOOK ONE IN THE FOREHEAD. THE SHOP'S BEEN LOCKED UP EVER SINCE—
JUST ANOTHER LOCKED GATE AND ANOTHER PIECE OF BUSTED NEON ON A RIVER OF DEAD DREAMS.

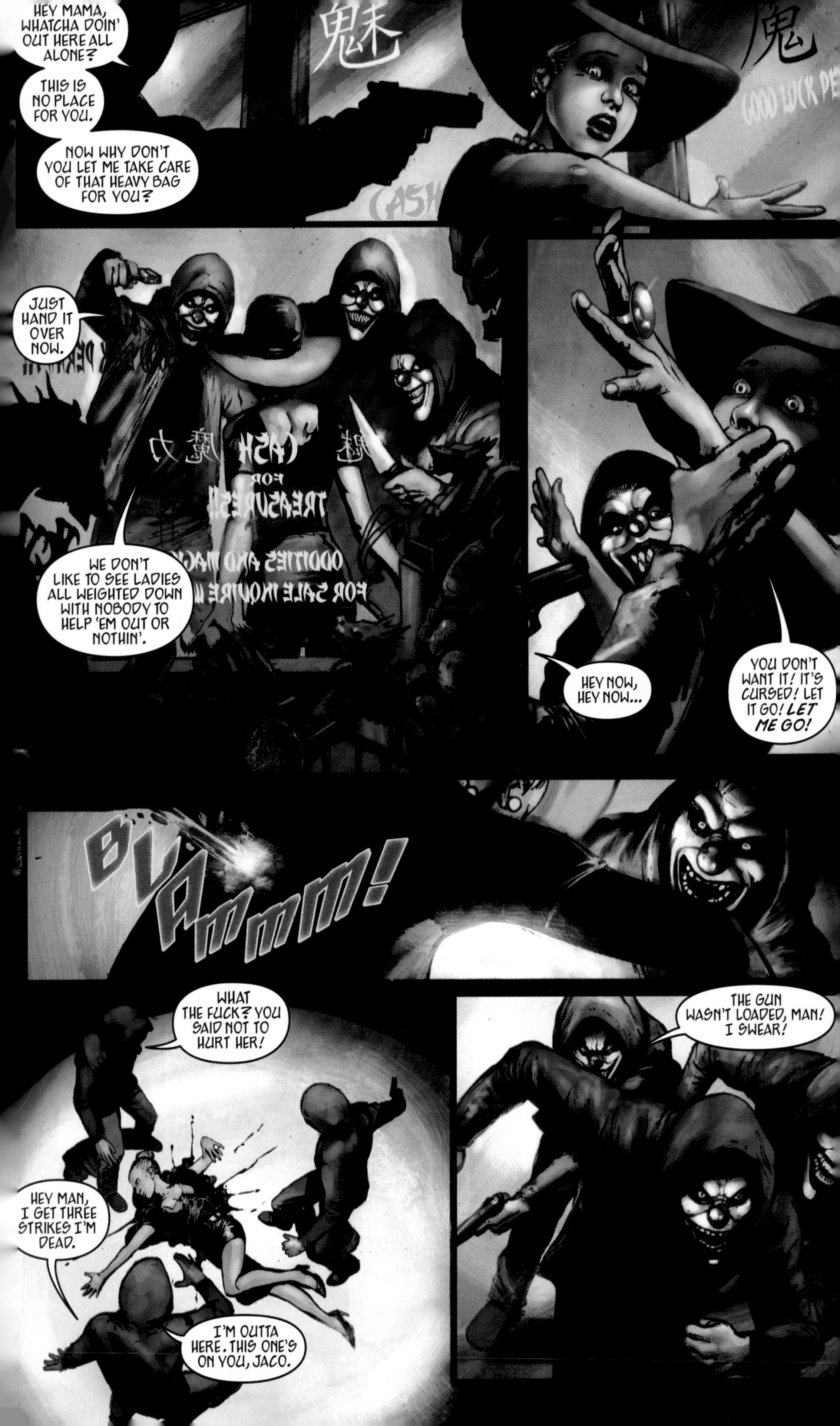
HEY MAMA, WHATCHA DOIN' OUT HERE ALL ALONE?
THIS IS NO PLACE FOR YOU.
NOW WHY DON'T YOU LET ME TAKE CARE OF THAT HEAVY BAG FOR YOU?
GOOD LUCK PE
CASH
JUST HAND IT OVER NOW.
CASH FOR TREASURES!!
ODDITIES AND MAG
FOR SALE INQUIRE W
WE DON'T LIKE TO SEE LADIES ALL WEIGHTED DOWN WITH NOBODY TO HELP 'EM OUT OR NOTHIN'.
HEY NOW, HEY NOW...
YOU DON'T WANT IT! IT'S CURSED! LET IT GO! LET ME GO!
BLAMMMM!
WHAT THE FUCK? YOU SAID NOT TO HURT HER!
HEY MAN, I GET THREE STRIKES I'M DEAD.
I'M OUTTA HERE. THIS ONE'S ON YOU, JACO.
THE GUN WASN'T LOADED, MAN! I SWEAR!

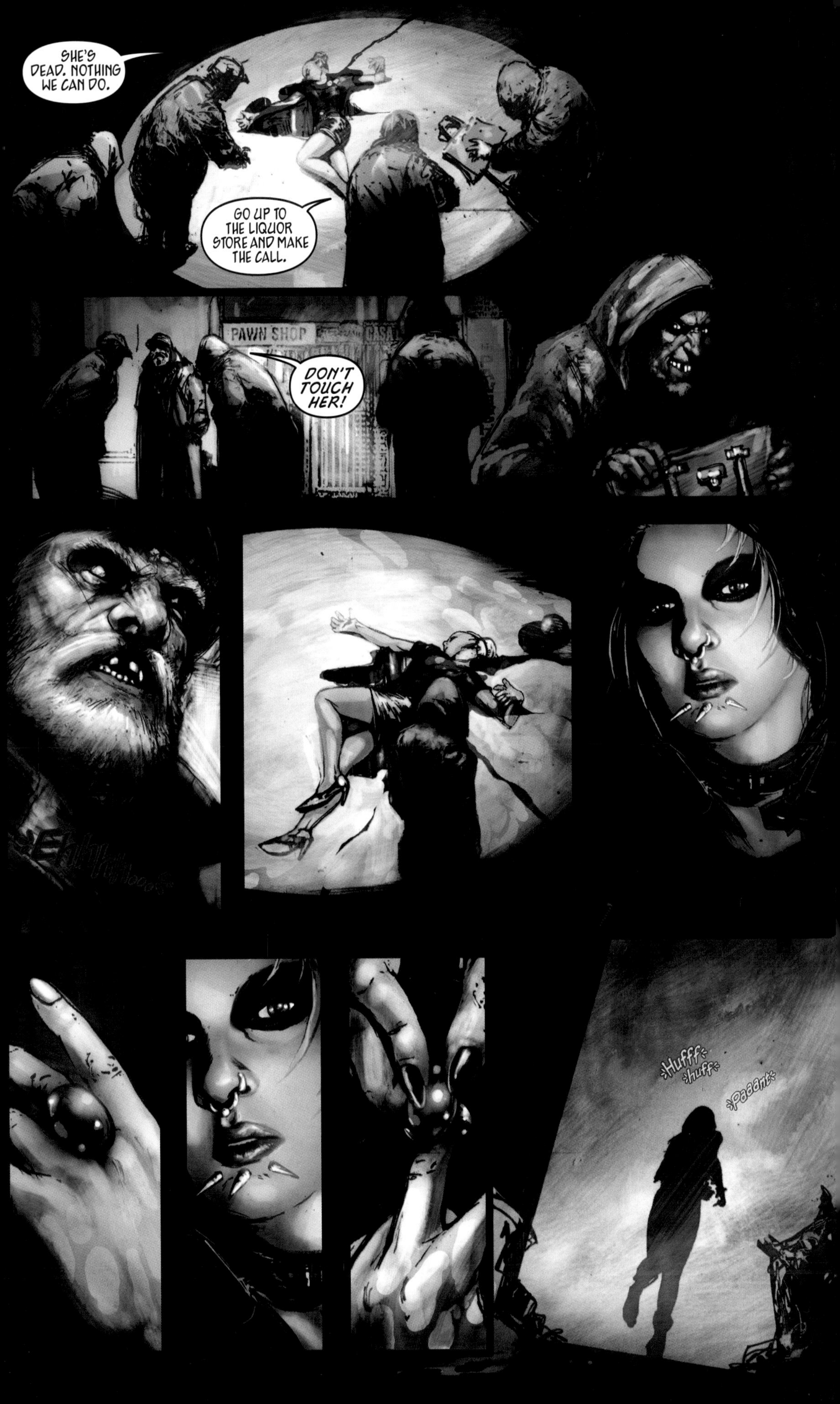
SHE'S DEAD. NOTHING WE CAN DO.
GO UP TO THE LIQUOR STORE AND MAKE THE CALL.
PAWN SHOP
DON'T TOUCH HER!
Hufff huff
Paaant

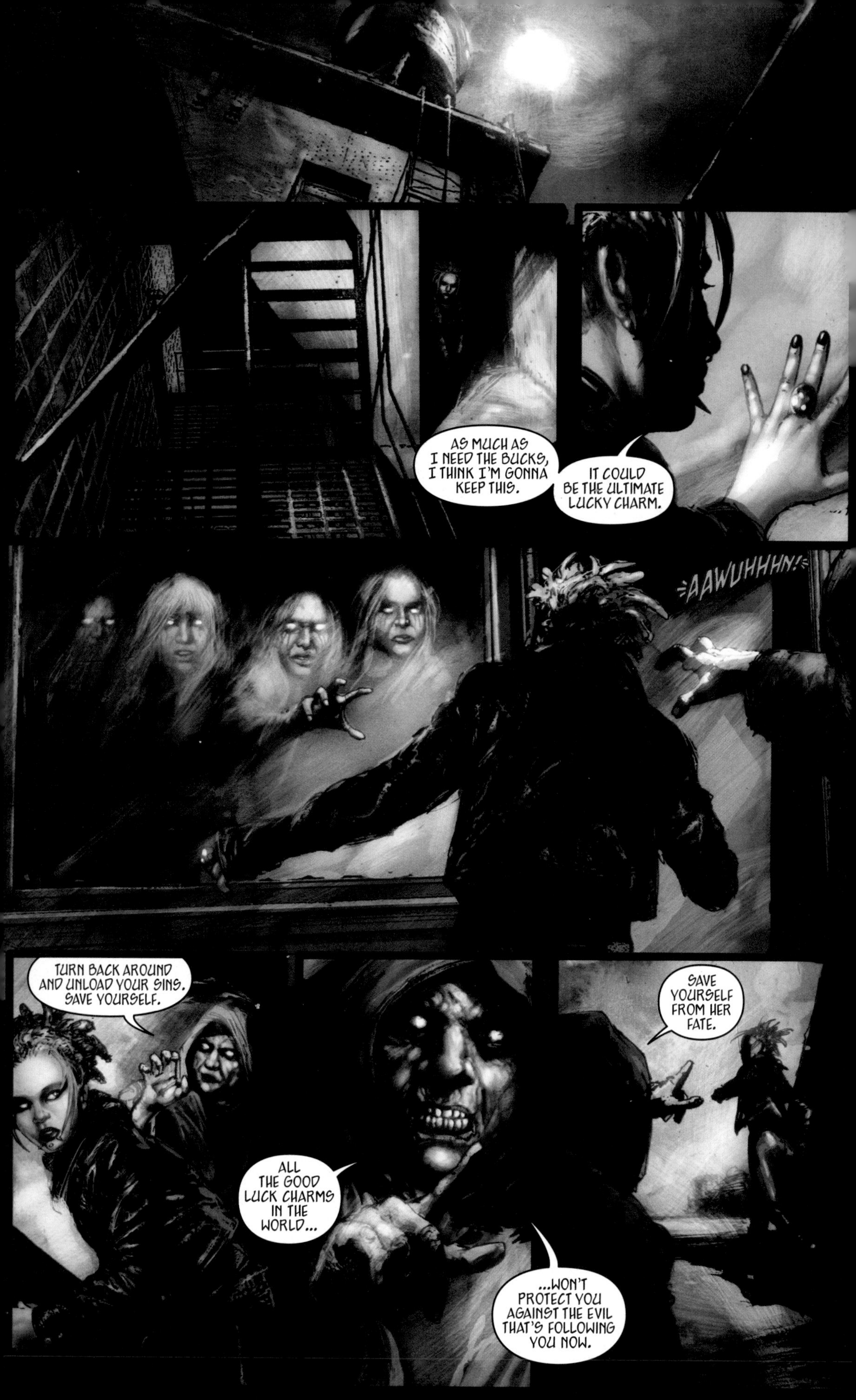

AS MUCH AS I NEED THE BUCKS, I THINK I'M GONNA KEEP THIS.
IT COULD BE THE ULTIMATE LUCKY CHARM.
AAWUHHHN!
TURN BACK AROUND AND UNLOAD YOUR SINS. SAVE YOURSELF.
SAVE YOURSELF FROM HER FATE.
ALL THE GOOD LUCK CHARMS IN THE WORLD...
...WON'T PROTECT YOU AGAINST THE EVIL THAT'S FOLLOWING YOU NOW.

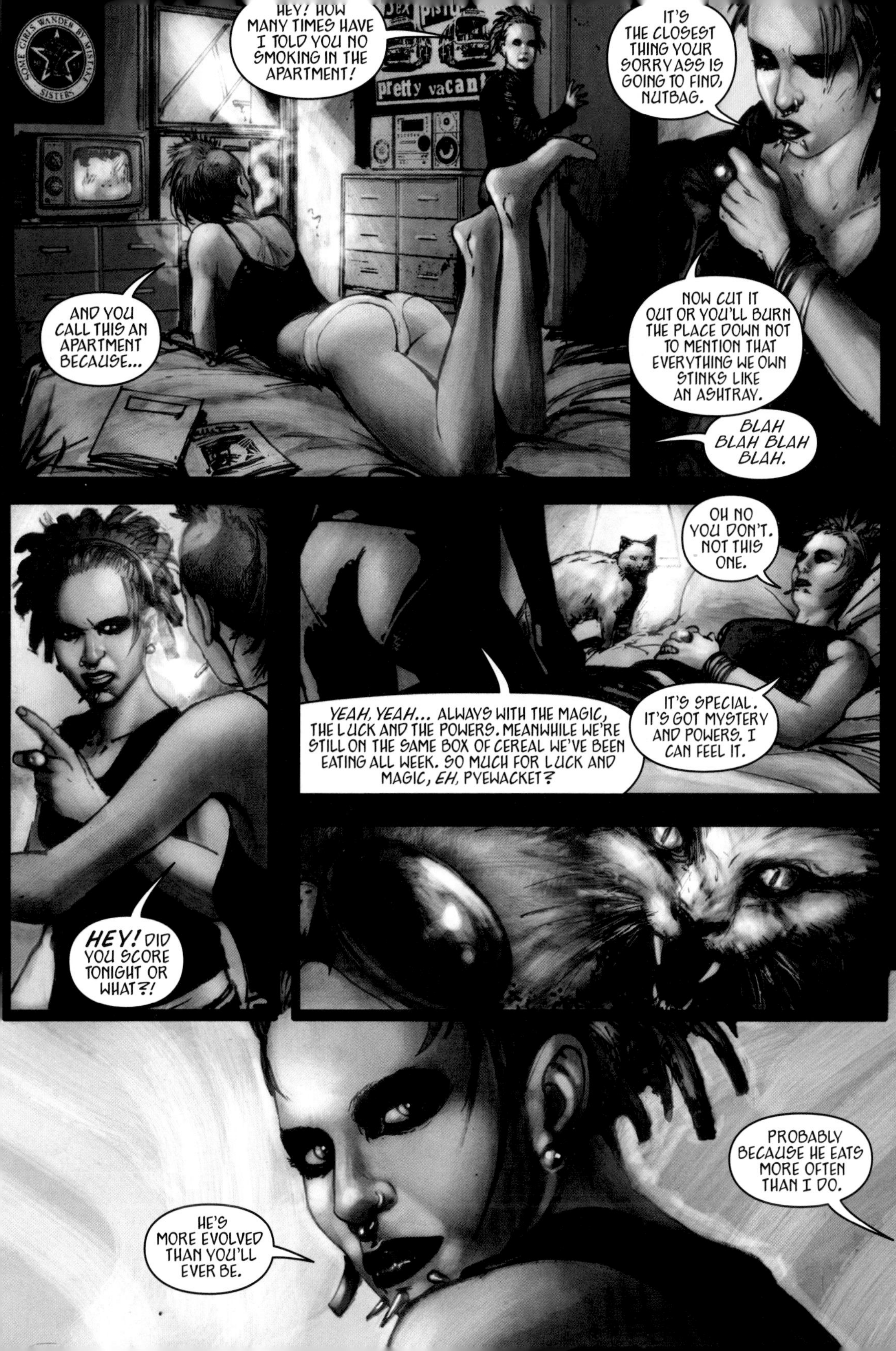
SOME GIRLS WANDER BY MISTAKE
SISTERS
pretty vacant
HEY! HOW MANY TIMES HAVE I TOLD YOU NO SMOKING IN THE APARTMENT!
AND YOU CALL THIS AN APARTMENT BECAUSE...
IT'S THE CLOSEST THING YOUR SORRY ASS IS GOING TO FIND, NUTBAG.
NOW CUT IT OUT OR YOU'LL BURN THE PLACE DOWN NOT TO MENTION THAT EVERYTHING WE OWN STINKS LIKE AN ASHTRAY.
BLAH BLAH BLAH BLAH.
HEY! DID YOU SCORE TONIGHT OR WHAT?!
OH NO YOU DON'T. NOT THIS ONE.
IT'S SPECIAL. IT'S GOT MYSTERY AND POWERS. I CAN FEEL IT.
YEAH, YEAH... ALWAYS WITH THE MAGIC, THE LUCK AND THE POWERS. MEANWHILE WE'RE STILL ON THE SAME BOX OF CEREAL WE'VE BEEN EATING ALL WEEK. SO MUCH FOR LUCK AND MAGIC, EH, PYEWACKET?
HE'S MORE EVOLVED THAN YOU'LL EVER BE.
PROBABLY BECAUSE HE EATS MORE OFTEN THAN I DO.

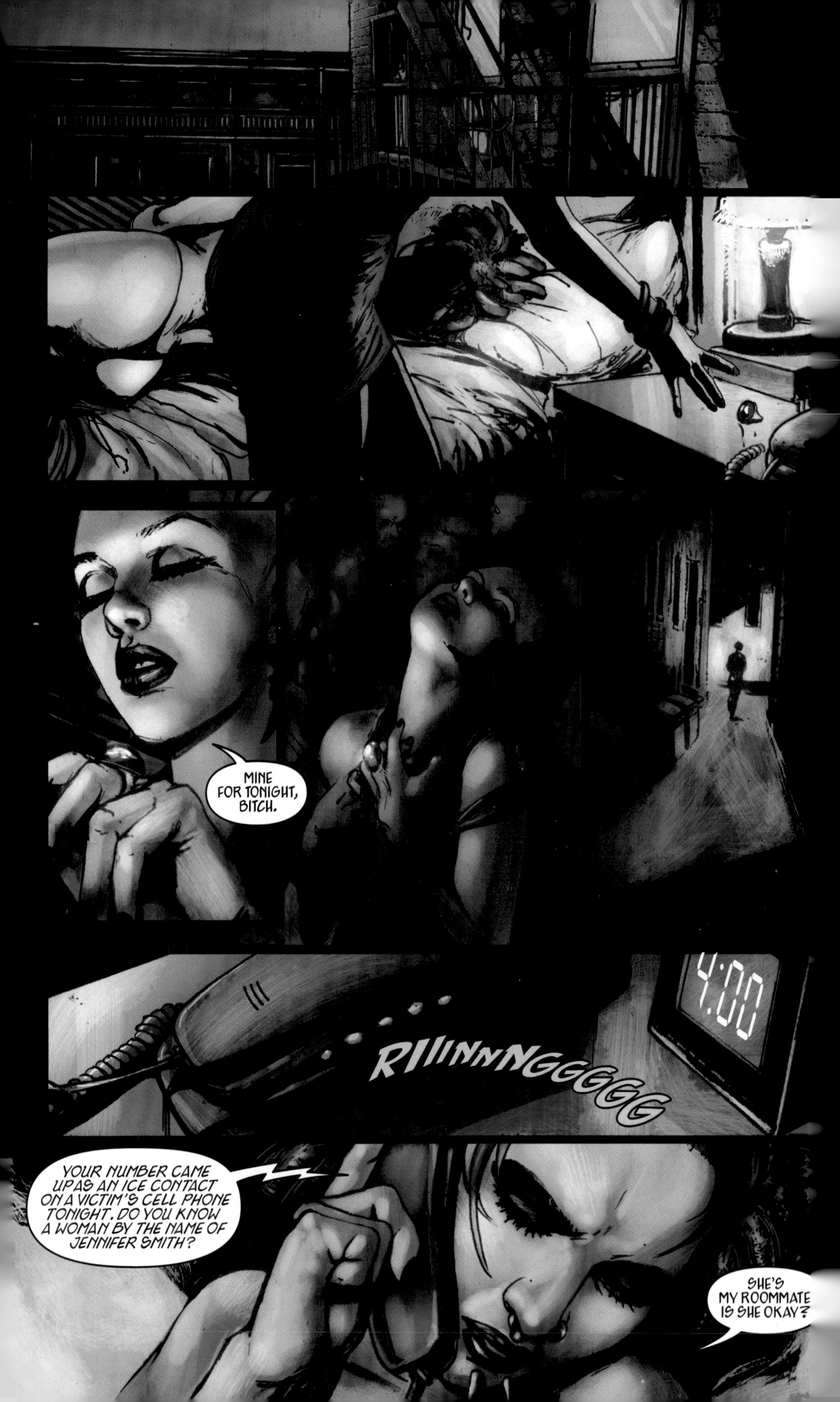
MINE FOR TONIGHT, BITCH.
4:00
RIIINNNGGGGGG
YOUR NUMBER CAME UPAS AN ICE CONTACT ON A VICTIM'S CELL PHONE TONIGHT. DO YOU KNOW A WOMAN BY THE NAME OF JENNIFER SMITH?
SHE'S MY ROOMMATE IS SHE OKAY?

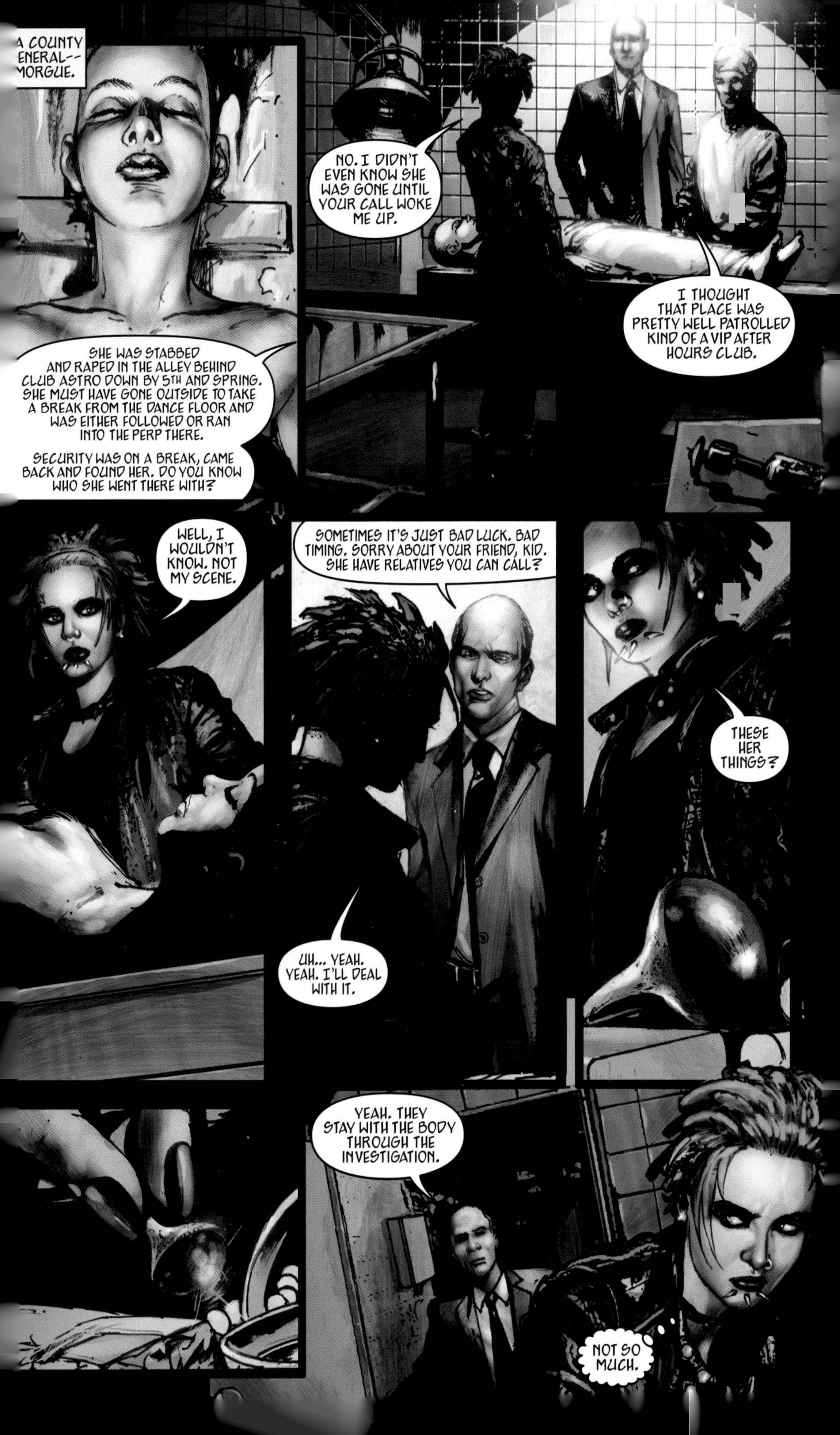
A COUNTY
ENERAL--
MORGUE.
SHE WAS STABBED AND RAPED IN THE ALLEY BEHIND CLUB ASTRO DOWN BY 5TH AND SPRING. SHE MUST HAVE GONE OUTSIDE TO TAKE A BREAK FROM THE DANCE FLOOR AND WAS EITHER FOLLOWED OR RAN INTO THE PERP THERE.
SECURITY WAS ON A BREAK, CAME BACK AND FOUND HER. DO YOU KNOW WHO SHE WENT THERE WITH?
NO. I DIDN'T EVEN KNOW SHE WAS GONE UNTIL YOUR CALL WOKE ME UP.
I THOUGHT THAT PLACE WAS PRETTY WELL PATROLLED KIND OF A VIP AFTER HOURS CLUB.
WELL, I WOULDN'T KNOW. NOT MY SCENE.
SOMETIMES IT'S JUST BAD LUCK. BAD TIMING. SORRY ABOUT YOUR FRIEND, KID. SHE HAVE RELATIVES YOU CAN CALL?
UH... YEAH. YEAH. I'LL DEAL WITH IT.
THESE HER THINGS?
YEAH. THEY STAY WITH THE BODY THROUGH THE INVESTIGATION.
NOT SO MUCH.

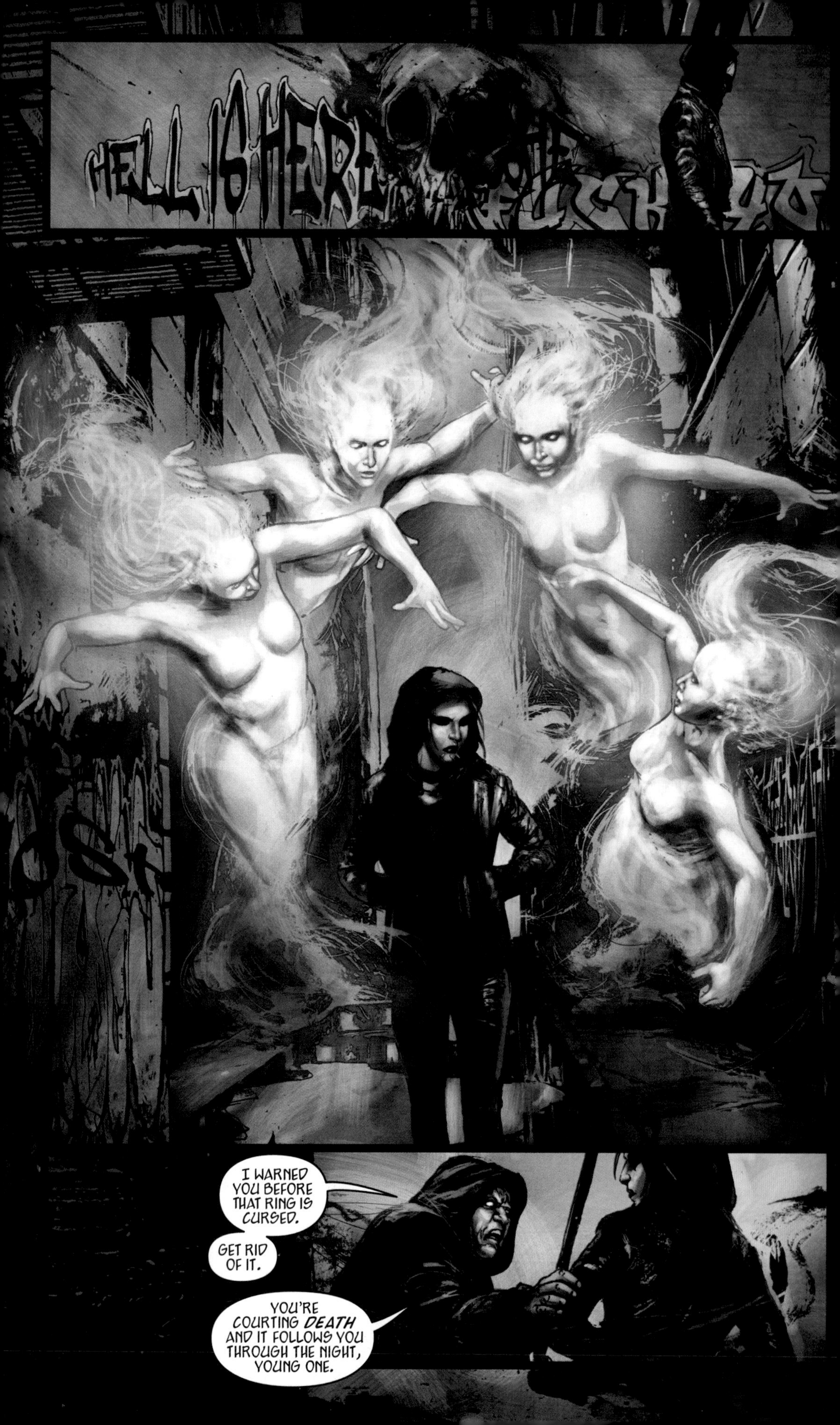
HELL IS HERE
I WARNED YOU BEFORE THAT RING IS CURSED.
GET RID OF IT.
YOU'RE COURTING *DEATH* AND IT FOLLOWS YOU THROUGH THE NIGHT, YOUNG ONE.

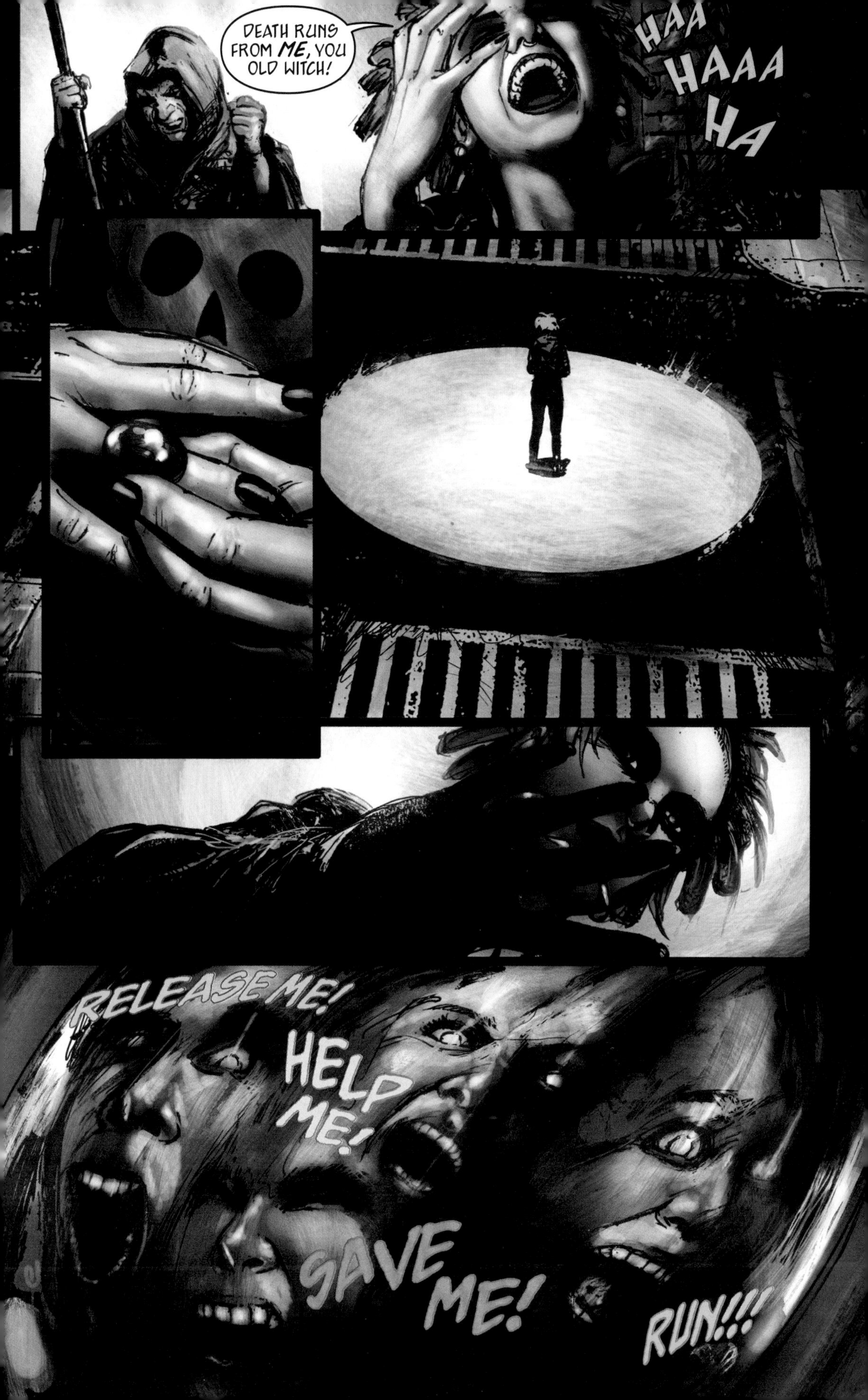
DEATH RUNS FROM ME, YOU OLD WITCH!
HAA HAAA HA
RELEASE ME!
HELP ME!
SAVE ME!
RUN!!!

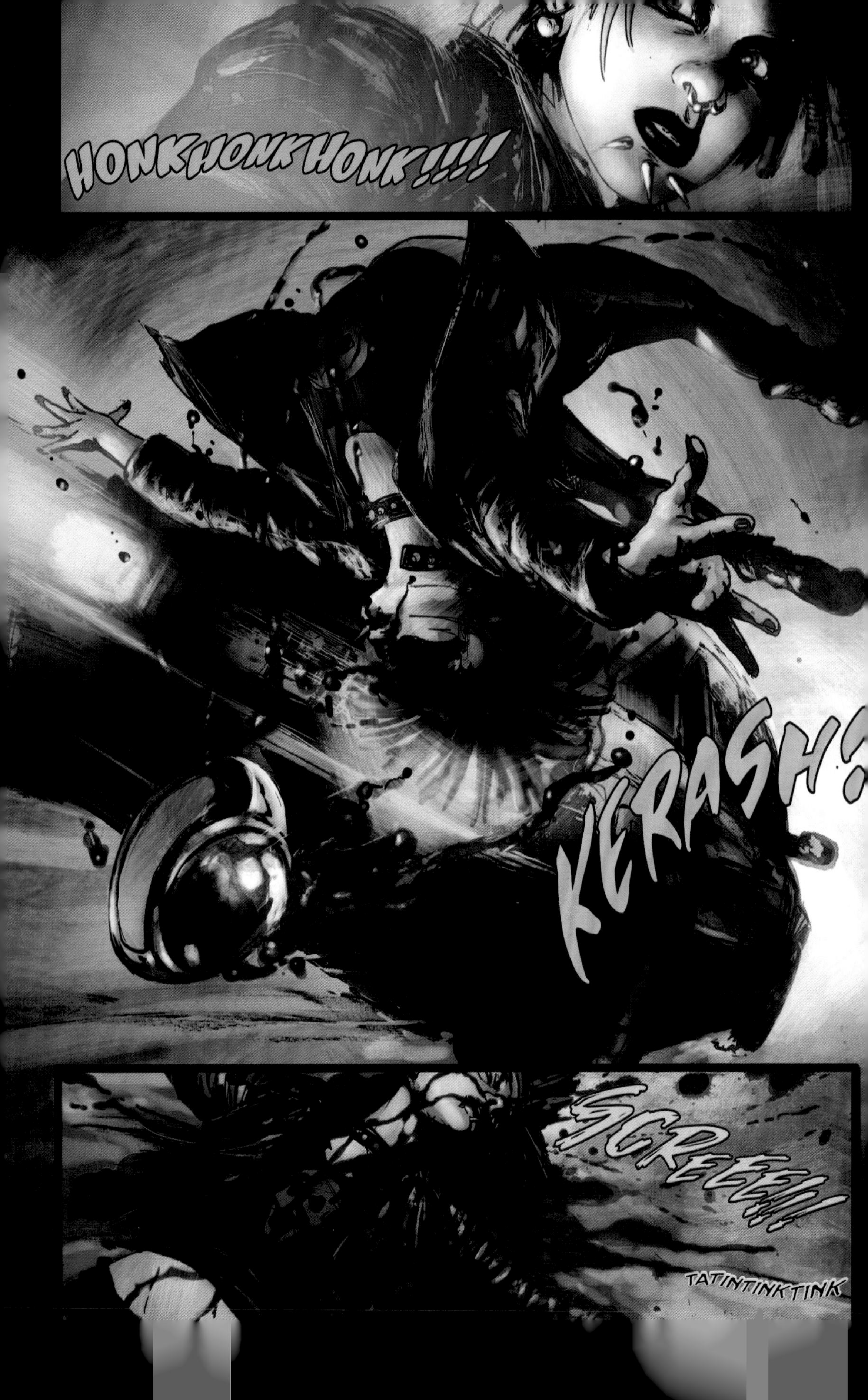
HONKHONKHONK!!!!
KERASH!
SCREEEE!!!
TATINTINKTINK

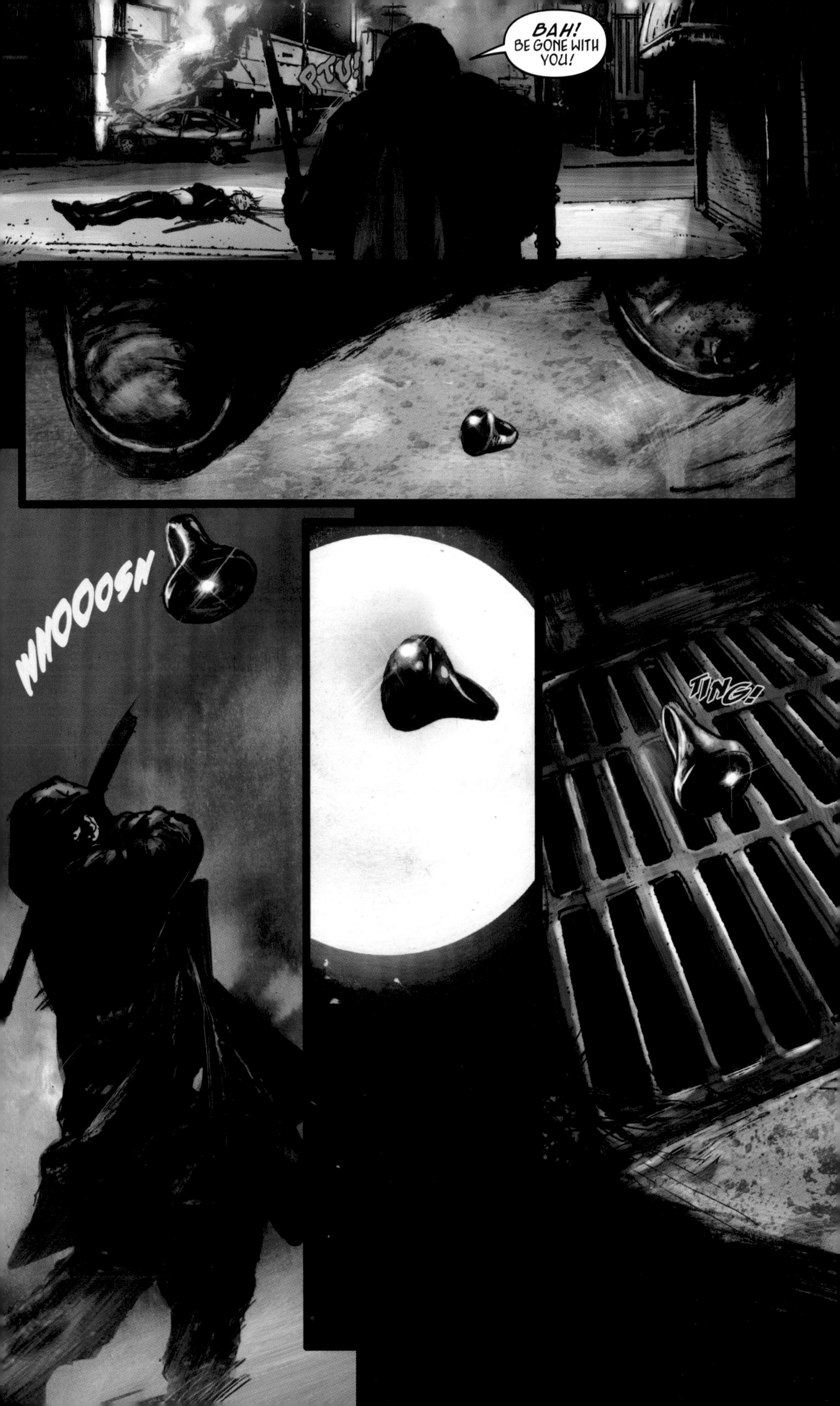
BAH!
BE GONE WITH YOU!
PTU!
WHOOOSH
TING!

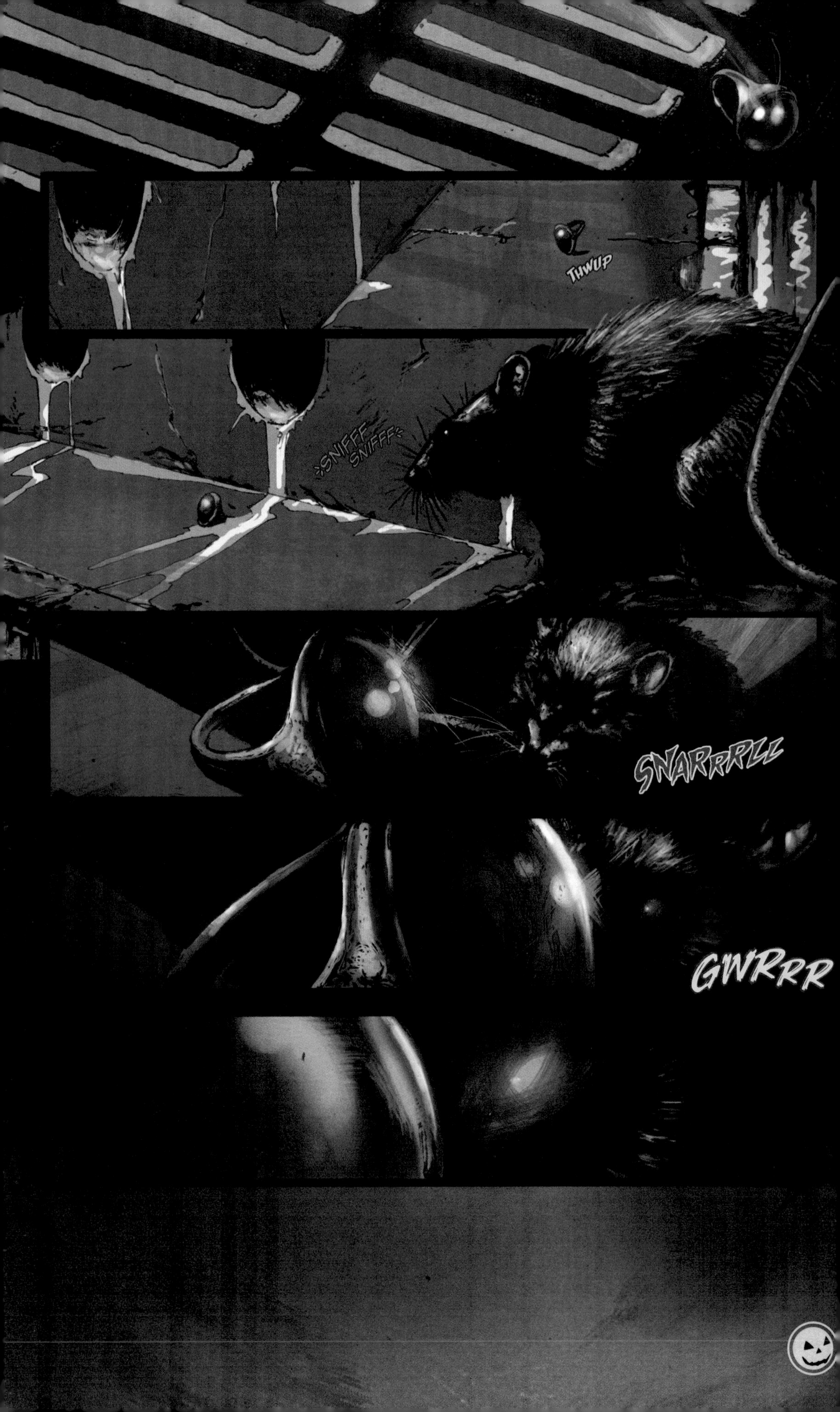
THWUP
SNIFFF SNIFFF
SNARRRLL
GWRRR

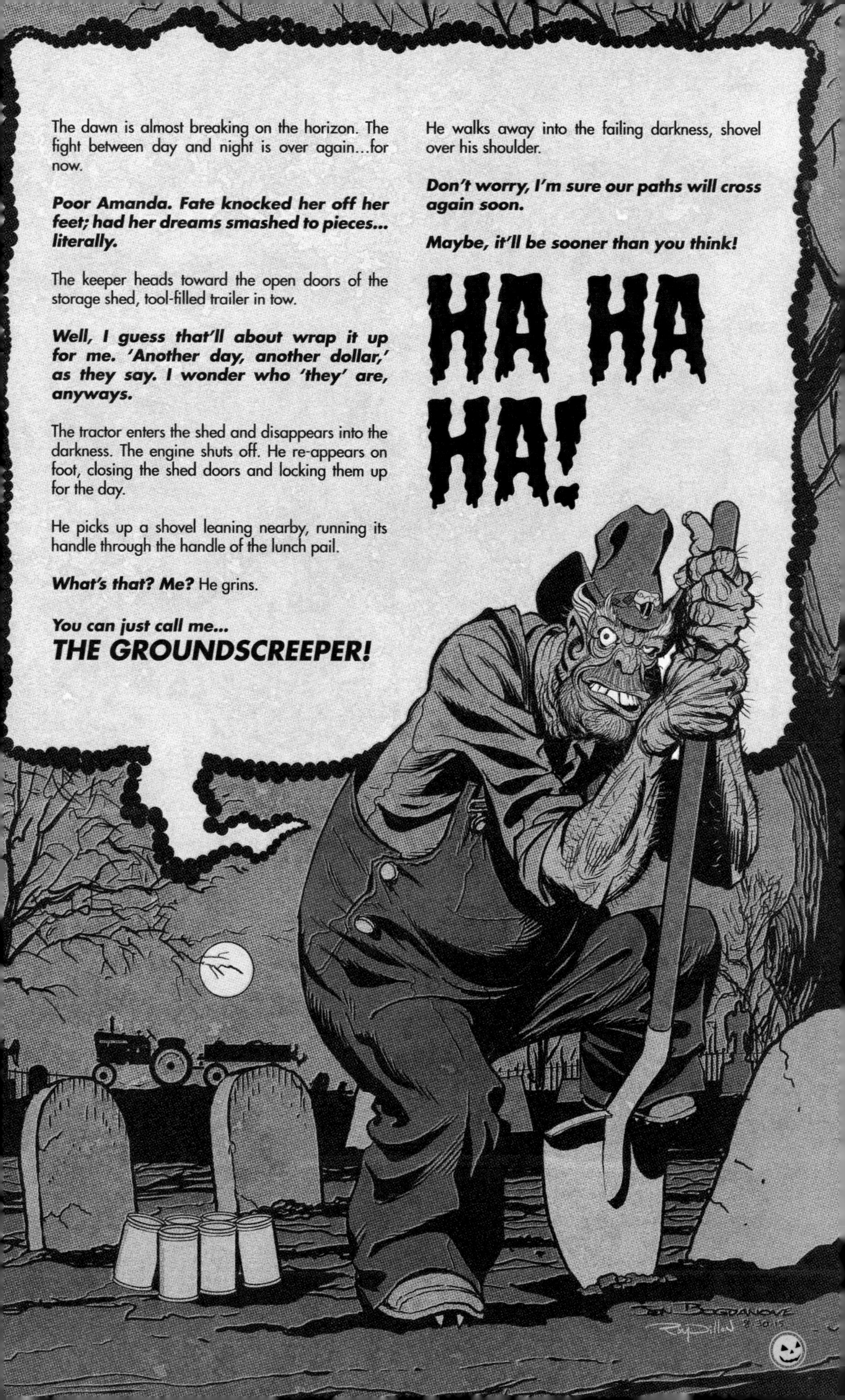
The dawn is almost breaking on the horizon. The fight between day and night is over again…for now.
Poor Amanda. Fate knocked her off her feet; had her dreams smashed to pieces... literally.
The keeper heads toward the open doors of the storage shed, tool-filled trailer in tow.
Well, I guess that'll about wrap it up for me. 'Another day, another dollar,' as they say. I wonder who 'they' are, anyways.
The tractor enters the shed and disappears into the darkness. The engine shuts off. He re-appears on foot, closing the shed doors and locking them up for the day.
He picks up a shovel leaning nearby, running its handle through the handle of the lunch pail.
What's that? Me? He grins.
You can just call me...
THE GROUNDSCREEPER!
He walks away into the failing darkness, shovel over his shoulder.
Don't worry, I'm sure our paths will cross again soon.
Maybe, it'll be sooner than you think!
HA HA HA HA!

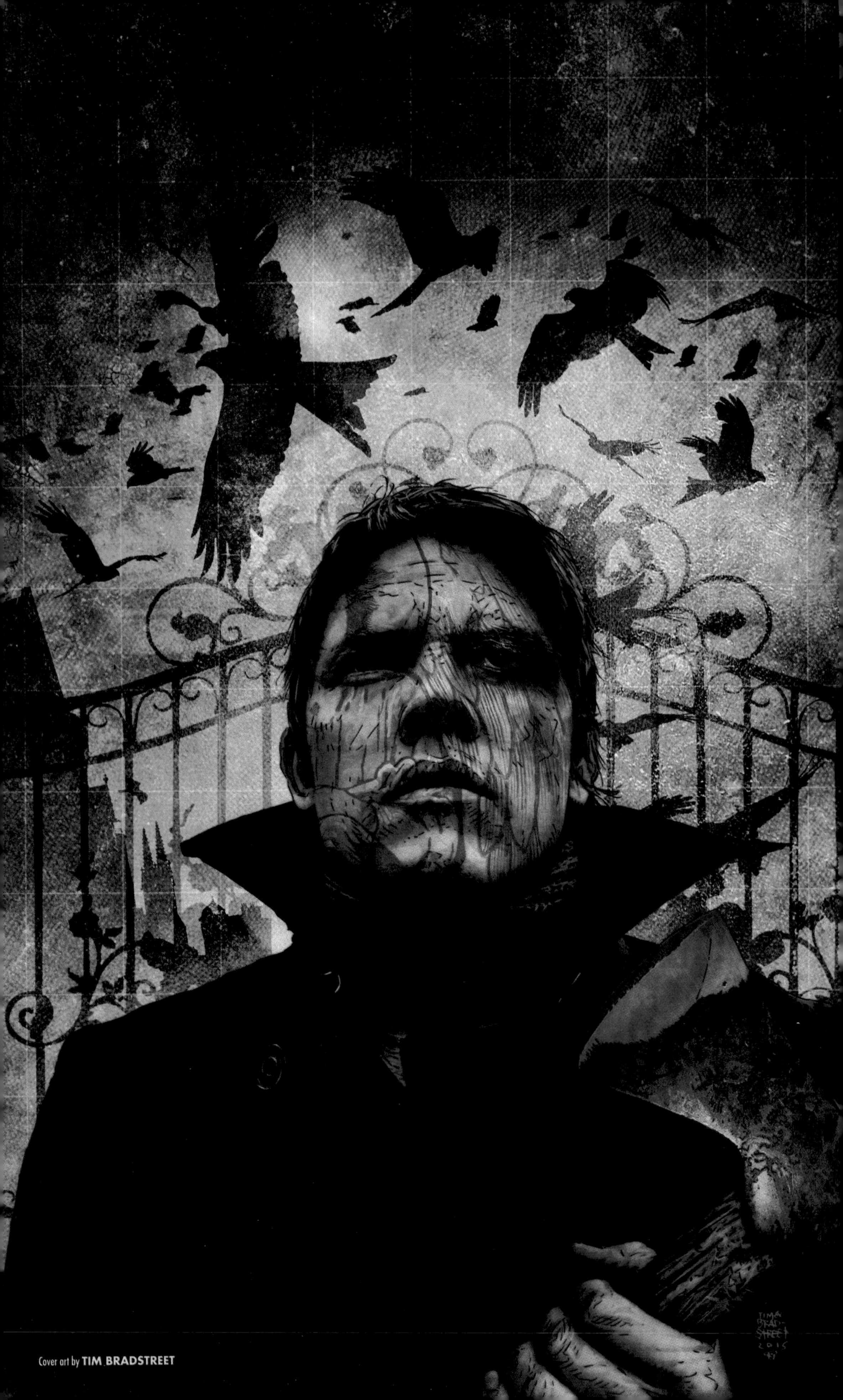

Cover art by **TIM BRADSTREET**

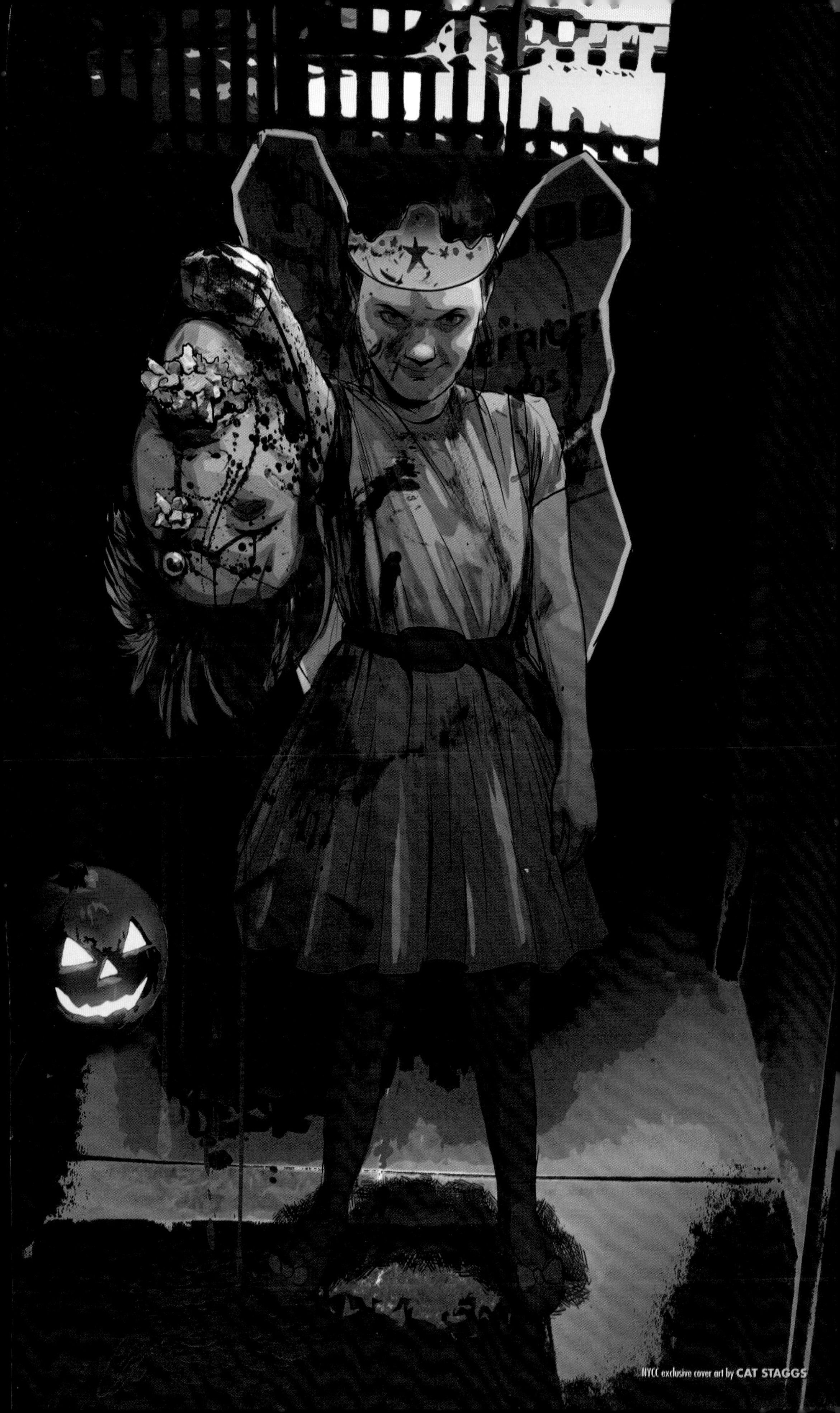

NYCC exclusive cover art by **CAT STAGGS**

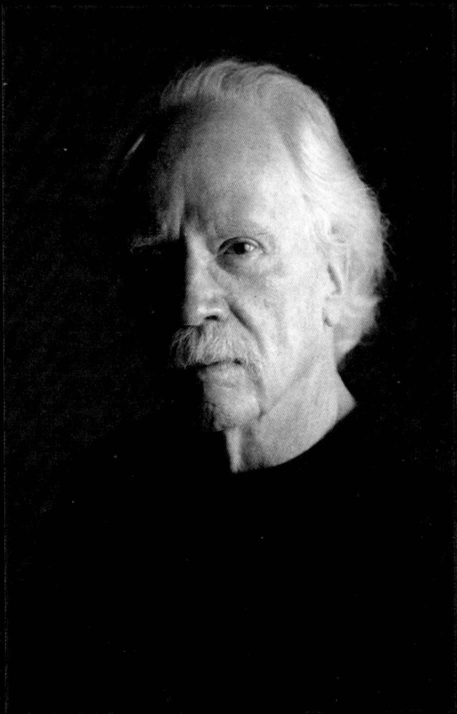

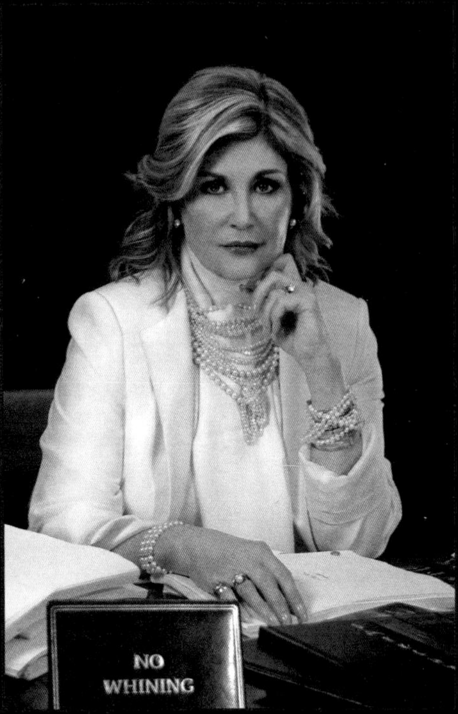
NO
WHINING

Halloween nights are made for scary stories. Monsters roam, witches fly, the dead rise and human beings sit around fires telling each other tales of evil and darkness.

It's in our DNA to scare each other on October the thirty-first. On the pages within, we bring you stories of ghoulies and ghosties and all things that go bump in the night.

Relax, enjoy…and hold close that lantern to find your way home in the dark.

John Carpenter and Sandy King